W9-AFN-199

BERNARD SHAW
A Psychological Study

BERNARD SHAW
A Psychological Study

Daniel Dervin

LEWISBURG
BUCKNELL UNIVERSITY PRESS
LONDON: ASSOCIATED UNIVERSITY PRESSES

© 1975 by Associated University Presses, Inc.

Associated University Presses, Inc.
Cranbury, New Jersey 08512

Associated University Presses
108 New Bond Street
London W1Y OQX, England

Library of Congress Cataloging in Publication Data
Dervin, Daniel, 1935–
  Bernard Shaw: a psychological study.
  Bibliography: p.
  Includes Index.
  1. Shaw, George Bernard, 1856–1950.
PR5366.D48   822'.9'12   73–8301
ISBN 0–8387–1418–8

*For permission to quote from the works of
Bernard Shaw, the author makes grateful
acknowledgment to The Society of Authors,
London, on behalf of the Bernard Shaw
Estate.*

PRINTED IN THE UNITED STATES OF AMERICA

You see things; and you say "Why?"
But I dream things that never were;
and I say "Why not?"

These lines from *Back to Methuselah* were often spoken in the Spring of 1968 by Robert F. Kennedy (1924–1968), to whom this book is dedicated.

61168

CONTENTS

Key to Titles   9

Acknowledgments   11

Introduction   13
    Drama and the Question of Energy   13
    Enter Shaw   15
    Enter Freud   17
    The Author's Apology   21

1 The Superfluous Child   29
    Not of this World   29
    Domestic Anarchy   39
    Family Romance   53
    Natural History   58
    Collective Alternates   63
    Narcissus, or the Birth of Ego   65
    In the Grip of His Gift   86
    The Secret of Gravitation   91
    The Heavenly Country   96
    The Force behind the Life Force   103

2 Impecunious Son   111
    Dancing Skeleton   111
    Intruding Lover   124
    Opposing Sprite   128
    Formidable Man   154

3 Fatherlandless Fellow   155
    Immaturity   155

Fabian Fellowship 160
I Am a Politician 166
The Identity of Genius 172
"An Original Didactic Realistic" Playwright 175

4 Ibsenite 180
Innovators 180
A Description of Humanity 186
Well-Made Geniuses 190
Ibsen's Classic : An Excursus 194
Three in One 202

5 Unpleasant Plays and Melodramas 206
Unshavian Phase 207
Authorial Eclipse 217
Disciple of Vitalism 220
The Structure of Vitalism 227
Allegorical Dreamer 234

6 Man and Superman 237
Shaw Reshavianized 237
Strindberg Improved 244
Master of Reality 254
To Steer or To Drift 259

7 Discussion Plays 267
The Miracle Worker 267
Shavian Eros 274

8 Heartbreak House and After 279
The Great Curve 280
And the Psychic Curve 283
Shaw's Middle Phase 285
The Third Manner 288
The Fate of Narcissism 290

9 Conclusion 293
Shaw and Freud 293
Comedy and Energy 303
Shaw's Genius and His Creativity 313
Shaw's Corner 333

Bibliography 338

Index 347

Key to Titles

I–V refers to the five volumes of Freud's *Collected Papers*; I–VI to the *Complete Plays with Prefaces*, Dodd Mead Edition, 1963.

AB   *The Adventures of the Black Girl in Her Search for God*

AH   *George Bernard Shaw: Man of the Century*, Archibald Henderson

BB   *Buoyant Billions*, I

BM   *Back to Methuselah*, II

BR   *Shaw of Dublin: The Formative Years*, B. C. Rosset

BX   *Preface to Three Plays by Brieux*

CB   *Captain Brassbound's Conversion*, I

CD   *Civilization and Its Discontents*, Freud

CR   "George Bernard Shaw," an interview in 1896 by Clarence Rook

DD   *The Devil's Disciple*, III

EB   *Bernard Shaw*, Eric Bentley

EM   "George Bernard Shaw as a Boy," Edward McNulty

EP   *Everybody's Political What's What?*

ET   *Ellen Terry and Bernard Shaw: A Correspondence*

FF   *Farfetched Fables*, VI

FH   *Bernard Shaw*, Frank Harris

GM   *Getting Married*, IV

HH   *Heartbreak House*, I

HP   *G. B. S.: A Full Length Portrait*, Hesketh Pearson

IK   *Preface to the Irrational Knot*

IM   *Preface to Immaturity*

IW   *The Intelligent Woman's Guide to Socialism and Capitalism*

JB   *John Bull's Other Island*, II

JD   *Mrs. G. B. S.: A Portrait*, Janet Dunbar

JE   *George Bernard Shaw: His Life, Work and Friends*, St. John Ervine

JS   "Shaw's *Man & Superman*: His Struggle for Sublimation," Julian Stamm

LA   *Love among the Artists*

LM   *Preface to London Music*

LS   *Collected Letters* (1874–1897), Dan H. Lawrence, ed.

MB   *Major Barbara*, I

MD   "The Making of a Dramatist (1892–1903)," Eric Bentley

MI   *Misalliance*, IV

MM   *Shaw and the Nineteenth Century Theatre*, Martin Meisel

MO   *Moses and Monotheism*, Sigmund Freud

MS   *Man and Superman*, IV

9

MY   *The Myth of the Birth of the Hero,* Otto Rank
OB   Letters to T. D. O'Bolger (unpublished; quoted by permission of the Harvard College Library)
OC   "A special type of Object Choice Made by Men," Freud, IV
OT   *Our Theatres in the Nineties* (3 vols.)
P   P before a play title refers to the Preface
PC   *Bernard Shaw and Mrs. Pat Campbell: Their Correspondence*
PA   "The Childhood of the Artist," Phyllis Greenacre
PB   "The Family Romance of the Artist," Phyllis Greenacre
PH   *The Philanderer,* VI
PL   *Preface to Pleasant Plays*
PM   *Platform and Pulpit*
PP   *Bernard Shaw: Playboy and Prophet,* Archibald Henderson
PU   *Preface to Three Plays for Puritans*
RM   *Recollections of George Bernard Shaw,* R. J. Minney
RR   *The Rationalization of Russia*
RS   *The Religious Speeches of George Bernard Shaw,* Warren Smith, ed.
SB   *The Shewing-up of Blanco Posnet,* V
SS   *Sixteen Self Sketches*
SU   *The Simpleton of the Unexpected Isles,* VI
SW   *Shaw: An Autobiography* in 2 vols., ed. Stanley Weintraub
TT   *Table Talk,* Archibald Henderson
WA   "Shaw's Childhood and *Pygmalion,*" Philip Weissman
WH   *Widowers Houses,* IV
WP   *Mrs. Warren's Profession,* IV

ACKNOWLEDGMENTS

Through the early stages of this study, I have been most fortunately assisted by Steven Marcus, who stayed with me every step—at times it seemed every line—of the way, directing me into appropriately new areas, suggesting needed revisions, challenging points, but without intruding his own views. As a consequence the project during its most crucial period remained my own, and yet I doubt if I could ever have completed it alone. This is as it should be, and I trust that Mr. Marcus will agree. Working with him has been a pleasure.

Dr. Arnold Cooper has been most kind and cooperative in keeping the clinical material in sharp focus. Several of his leads I have followed, and many of his views I have belatedly and independently corroborated for myself. In the main, where uncertainty arises, I have tended as far as possible to let the reader come to his own conclusions—as indeed he will anyway. Donald M. Kaplan has also gone over certain sections in later revisions with me, and I am happy to have had his sympathetic interest along with a much-needed coaching in psychoanalytic theory.

To the Department of English and Comparative Literature at Columbia University I remain profoundly grateful. One believes himself to be working alone while all the time the

11

work is a collaboration of many diverse minds. Those who stand out as ideals of excellence and for whom I have the warmest regard are William Appleton, Robert Brustein, Tom Driver, Evert Sprinchorn, John Unterrecker, and Maurice Valency. In addition, Professors Martin Meisel, Quentin Anderson, and John Scott Bratton have provided judicious readings with valuable comments.

Dr. Arthur Nethercot, one of the best Shavians to be found anywhere, gave the manuscript, nearing its final stage, an all-important critical going-over, a gratuitous and extremely generous act of devotion to Shavian scholarship.

Dr. Grellet Simpson, President of Mary Washington College, has aided me throughout by his loyal interest and generous support. Among colleagues, Nathaniel Brown, Susan Hanna, Glen Thomas, and Sidney Mitchell have sustained my work by their sympathetic interest.

Last of all, my wife, to whom it never occurred that I might not finish, at times even helped convince me it was possible.

For one man to undertake the study of another man's life is vain, presumptuous, and audacious. It may also be hopeless; the undertaking reduced to an embalming and funeral rites. Yet it can be invigorating, with all sorts of unforeseen side effects (along the way I have grown a beard, and given up smoking and going to church). Perhaps this book is my initiation rite as a Shavian. Leaving such a project after several years is rather like getting out of the military: one only hopes the discharge is honorable.

INTRODUCTION

Now I have had no heroic adventures. Things have not happened to me : on the contrary it is I who have happened to them; and all my happenings have taken the form of books and plays. Read them or spectate them, and you have my whole story : the rest is only breakfast, lunch, dinner, sleeping, wakening, and washing, my routine being just the same as everybody's routine. . . . Perhaps our psychoanalysts may find in such dull stuff clues that have escaped me. (SS, 18, 21)

DRAMA AND THE QUESTION OF ENERGY

We go to the theater to be moved. And if we are, regardless of how much or in what direction, we will in all likelihood exit satisfied. Afterwards, in trying to formulate our moving experience, we may express our feelings as having been pleasurable, painful, enriching, on the one hand, or attribute to the play properties of being exciting, boring, disturbing, on the other. To move or to be moved requires energy, and it occurred to me that just as one kind of energy is required to produce motion, so is another kind of energy required to arouse and allay emotion. I began to wonder if what we experience in the theater first of all might not be a transference of energy.

Drama has been studied with attention to character and

motive, theme and idea, form and convention, imagery and symbol, audience and taste, theatrical and political conditions; and although a play may be regarded today as a source of energy capable of producing various and wide-ranging effects on audiences and readers, the problem of energy itself in drama has seldom if ever been confronted. A play provides us with the manner in which creative energy has been fixed in its final state. We speak about this as form, and whatever we separate from form, what the play is about, we call content. Energy and structure would perhaps be better terms. At the outset this kind of energy may be thought of as the driving creative force that animates that fixed thing we call form and produces a structure individual to each play.

The spectator, upon entering the theater, suspends not only his disbelief but temporarily disengages his energies and emotions from their customary posts and operations, allowing the magnetism of the dramatic action to refocus and reengage them. By this shifting of affective pressure points and resetting of his reticulating psychic antennae, he disposes himself to be moved. In seeing a play, or, as we say, in being drawn into it he is in effect re-creating its structure and allowing its energies to be reproduced with him. He is moved by an experience that he tries to, but cannot quite, put into words.

Thus, while drama must have energy if it is to engage us, in discussing plays we tend to fall back on descriptive verbs and participles, approximating nouns and adjectives. Perhaps it is as impossible to find verbal equivalents for art as it is for any other lived experience, and if we are always to be "wrong" about the work, as T. S. Eliot claimed we would always be about *Hamlet*, we should, as he recommended, try to be wrong in constructive and up-to-date ways. But if we can only inarticulately encounter energy after it enlivens structure, just as water in a rapids becomes vividly realized, we should at least acknowledge the crucial if less visible presence of energy in drama. For I have found in researching the present study that, practically speaking, energy is basic primarily as a starting point, and before progressing very far, I have had to table questions of energy in order to contend with other questions of developmental processes, fantasy, creativity, and the peculiar circumstances under which my subject came into the world.

ENTER SHAW

Shaw's plays have been examined from the point of view of political and philosophical ideas, types of character, dialectical structure, and the popular theater. Biographies relating his works to his life abound, positively bulging with vital data, myriad details, and colorful anecdotes. It is only when everything is assimilated that real difficulties arise. He was present on our planet for nearly a century, certainly long enough for many to get to know him, and for almost everyone to get a look at him. They by no means agreed on what they saw. Beatrice Webb knew him as well as anyone. She and Sidney Webb were his fellow Fabians and among his closest friends for nearly half of his century. Her diaries record the evolution of their friendship and her attempts to understand him. Beginning as an "enigma," he soon becomes a "brilliant sprite" and a "perverse and stimulating genius." At worst he is a "union of the fanatic and the manipulator," at best a "magnificent critic of life," although "absolutely futile as a constructive thinker," and throughout a "marvel of kindness" as well as a "faithful friend."[1] Chesterton, in the first published book on Shaw, sections him into Puritan, Irishman, and Progressive. In addition he was a

[1] Margaret Cole, ed., *Beatrice Webb's Diaries* (London, 1965); Beatrice and Sidney Webb, *Our Partnership* (New York, 1948).

school drop-out, a rent collector and cashier, a novelist, a critic of the arts, a playwright and essayist, a Socialist reformer and a religious mystic, a Nietzschean Life Worshipper and a staunch Stalinist, a vestryman and a globe-trotter, a philandering vegetarian and a celibate husband; in his own terms an artist-philosopher and a poet-playwright. The words used most often to describe him, "clever" and "brilliant," he most detested. And before we forget, he was a genius, too, though in his mother's mind a "dreadful procrastinator" (PP, p. 182). The list is legion. And when we try to arrange them all somehow behind the mask of GBS, the enterprise collapses into a clamorous rabble. Seeking a single identity in such a crowd becomes maddening. Defeated, we can only conclude with Eric Bentley that while he may not have been an original thinker, he was an original person.

In a ground-clearing sort of way that rather negative adjective is helpful. When all-of-the-above leads to none-of-the-above, we have begun to face the first real problem. How *does* one go about speaking of a bona fide, authentically original person, who also happens to be a human dynamo? With commonplace nouns, with provocative paradoxes, metaphysical conceits? Considering his five novels, his fifty-seven plays and playlets, his numerous pamphlets, prefaces, essays, and articles, his speaking career spanning seventy years and averaging several speeches a fortnight for twenty of them, and his quarter of a million letters, we have a pretty good idea of where his energy went. The question is, how did it become available to him and what conditions governed its deployment?

If all the things he was and did in life, and all the roles he played, overwhelm us, what about those simple and basic relationships we are all born into? It is irrefutably true that Shaw was once a son to his parents, a brother to his two sisters, a nephew to assorted aunts and uncles. Having taken these steps, we appear to have backed into the Department of Psychology, and may as well pause there to see what it can offer.

ENTER FREUD

Few psychological sketches have been made of Shaw. One by Philip Weissman (WA, pp. 146–70), interpreting *Pygmalion*, concludes that Shaw had an Oedipus complex like the rest of us, which may be reassuring if less helpful than the statement that he had a "creative romance with the world" instead of with idividuals. The other, by Erik Erikson, examining Shaw's "Identity,"[2] is pertinent only in a limited way since Erikson is primarily concerned with establishing his own hypotheses and not with exploring all the aspects of Shaw's personality—for which he will not be faulted. If we then turn back to the works of Freud for clues to the composition of this original person, we come across the following discussion of three types of personality in terms of libido. In one:

> There is no tension between ego and super-ego—indeed, starting from this type one would hardly have arrived at the notion of the super-ego; there is no preponderance of erotic needs; the main interest is focused on self-preservation; the type is independent and not easily overawed. The ego has a considerable amount of aggression available, one manifestation of this being a proneness to activity; where love is in question, loving is preferred to being loved. People of this type impress others as being "personalities"; it is on them that their fellowmen are specially likely to lean; they readily assume the role of leader, give a fresh stimulus to cultural development or break down existing conditions. (V, pp. 248–49)

[2] Erik H. Erikson, *Identity: Youth and Crisis* (New York 1968), pp. 142-150. Another psychoanalytic critic has raised the question of whether Shaw was a "hypomanic character" (JS, p. 254).

This is the narcissistic type in its pure state. There is also the narcissistic-obsessional subtype, which is

> the variation most valuable from a cultural standpoint, for it combines independence of external factors and regard for the requirements of conscience with the capacity for energetic action.

Freud could hardly have had Shaw in mind; yet he seems to be sketched in as though he had sat for the drawing. Promising as this appears, the fact is, that we have only a classification of personality, which does not carry us very far into actual life. But before dismissing it entirely, we should recall that Freud is discussing personality from the viewpoint of libido. Libido is a certain kind of psychic energy, and we are interested in energy (which in the above types is concentrated largely in the ego), especially when it goes into creative work.

However, we must take account of whatever we find. *Energy* is a simple word, but its meanings are various. There is the physical energy that goes into labor and exercise, and the kind of energy that everyone depends on to get through the day. There is the sense of energy purely as capacity for performing work, and with it goes the consideration that energy *per se* is a word coined by Aristotle and only recently borrowed from the physical sciences to describe mental processes. In this respect, energy is a metaphor. Indeed it is a metaphor many psychoanalysts would prefer Freud had avoided, but for the present we too are stuck with it.

Psychic energy arises from the two sets of instincts. The death instincts are manifested as destructive or aggressive impulses; the libidinal instincts may be self-preservative or sexual, and are combined in the term *Eros*. Among other things, the instincts "drive or impel the mind to activity."[3] Mental

[3] Jacob Arlow and Charles Brenner, *Psychoanalytic Concepts and the Structural Theory* (New York, 1964), p. 7. This work, along with the

processes, which may be conscious or unconscious, are distinguished as primary and secondary, depending on how energy is distributed.[4] Generally speaking, primary process aims at pleasure through immediate instinctual discharge, is highly mobile in its capacity to invest objects with libidinal significance, is undifferentiated, and until recently has been associated with the timeless, infantile, irrational, primitive, and pre-verbal in mental life. Secondary process, owing to its interaction with the environment, tends to bind up or tone down pleasure by "inhibiting, postponing, or modifying the instinctual gratification." Since artistic creation draws on both processes in varying degrees and combinations, both are pertinent to questions of Shavian energy. And at the outset they may be useful in pointing to an apparent trend in Shaw's work, which, in its relative disavowal of wish-fulfilment and neglect of condensation and symbolization on the one hand, as well as its reliance of civilized modes of discourse, logic, and rationality as means of control on the other, points toward a prevalence of secondary process and the preeminent role of his ego's capacities for neutralizing instinctual processes and for synthesizing diverse

Encyclopedia of Psychoanalysis, forms the basis for the remarks that immediately follow.

[4] Ernst Kris's classic study, *Psychoanalytic Explorations in Art* (London, 1953), is based on the above distinction, while Arlow and Brenner extend primary process beyond its location in the id and assign adaptive functions to it.

From another quarter Kris's concept of "regression in the service of the ego" as a prerequisite of creativity has been called into question. Philip Weissman emphasizes the dissociative and synthetic functions of the ego in "Theoretical Considerations of Ego Regression and Ego Functions in Creativity," *Psychoanalytic Quarterly* (1967), pp. 37f.

Along with these two ego functions, the concept of the artist as deflecting instinctual drives from the mother to the large sphere of reality to carry on a "creative romance with the world," using his art as a "love gift," which has been tentatively described by Phyllis Greenacre (PA, PB) and quoted by Weissman, probably applies in a useful sense to Shaw's creative life. But all of these ideas are still in a provisional stage, and much more elaboration and illustration of them is necessary before they can be used confidently.

systems of thought.[5] In a roughly analogous sense to primary and secondary process, creativity has been divided by Kris into the components of inspiration and elaboration, of receiving and of working out the new idea or image. In this respect also Shaw gives the impression of greater attention to the elaborating and intellectualizing aspect of creativity. On the other hand we will encounter sufficient biographical material and fantasy structures to give credence to Shaw's paradoxical boast that "all of my plays are about myself . . . and my friends." Just as his jests are frequently earnest, so his boasts are often confessions. His drawing of attention to his narcissistic ego is certainly justified, though hardly the last word on the subject, for the Shavian ego has struck its roots deep in the unconscious as well as having let itself be nourished by interaction with its social environment.

Like *energy,* the term *adaptation* has various uses. At a popular level we speak of persons being adaptable to others or to new situations. There are social-science connotations, and in biology the principle of adaptation has been related to survival. In psychology, the area from which I will be borrowing it, the reference is to the kind of functioning, whether through defenses, or in the "conflict-free ego sphere," related to "reality mastery."[6] For example, Shaw's greatest strength may well have been in his conflict-free mastery of language,[7] while his exercise of language is conditioned by instinctual conflicts and serves defensive needs along with adaptive goals.

[5] In one of the first psychological points scored against Shaw, John M. Thornburn in *Art and the Unconscious* (1925), singled out Shaw's excessive control over his materials in the creation of his plays. For an opposing and more recent view, see JS.

[6] Heinz Hartmann, *Ego Psychology and the Problem of Adaptation* (New York, 1958).

[7] ". . . to me the whole vocabulary of English literature, from Shakespear to the latest edition of the Encyclopaedia Britannica, is so completely and instantaneously at my call that I have never had to consult even a thesaurus except once or twice when for some reason I wanted a third or fourth synonym" (PBM, p. xxvii). The reader may object to this as Shavian exaggeration, but he will be doing so at his own peril.

We should not be surprised to find him singling out the adaptability of his own mind in such a way that includes several aspects of the term, or to find him attacking the adaptations of his fellowmen as "the almost boundless docility and submission to social convention which is characteristic of the human race" (BX, p. 199). His own adaptation to society as its opponent compelled him to save it from those same complacent citizens who were by standards of "social compliance" better adapted than he. Nor would we want to overlook the preeminence he ascribes to the "masters of reality" in *Man and Superman*. But particularly we want to examine his own reality mastery and to balance the limits and strengths of his adaptive strategies.

These considerations loom as distant signs far up the road. At the moment we are aware of the ambiguities of energy, the paradoxes of adaptation, and the general frame of reference in which they will be used. In speaking of Shaw's energies, I mean mental or psychic energies; in referring to his adaptations, I mean primarily psychological ones. And among them, creativity will ultimately be examined as one of the most complex.

THE AUTHOR'S APOLOGY

"Freud and the 'Libido' school" of psychology that Shaw once found a "bit tiresome" (TT, p. 96) will be frequently consulted; and perhaps before we have finished, the reader may feel that not only has Shaw been invited to spend some time on the analytic couch but that his wife, father, mother, and her alleged lover have all been crowded aboard as well. If this reclining posture seems uncharacteristic of the man who has been so eloquent not to say indomitable on platform, street-corner, stage, parlor, and study, who has been so assertive in every stance, he will for all that not be likely to disappoint in his new setting. In any case, the couch as far as possible will be an orthodox Freudian one and not a revisionist Castro-Convertible model. But the danger is not so much in strapping a vital genius ludicrously and posthumously onto a procrustean couch as in getting him to recline comfortably and associate freely instead of having him leap about manically and score points polemically; and, in brief, less in analyzing Shaw than in being Shavianized by him. To resist being shouted down or talked into submission while we willingly remain open in our responses to the most unlikely material will not be easy.

The result, however, will not be a psychoanalysis of Shaw, with all the haggling over fees and hours that attends such affairs, not because the patient is no longer with us, hardly a deterrent for so many of the artist class, but because the author is not a psychoanalyst. In fact, he is somewhere between a devoted lay brother and a brash interloper. What is worse, in his innocence and folly he believes himself to be in possession of a secret shared by many yet acknowledged by few. It is simply this, that the most fitting and most challenging subject of psychoanalysis is not the Victorian hysteric or the male neurotic, not the sadist or the sociopath, the criminal, the psychotic, or today's man in the street with his dreams of Hawaii and retirement plans, who cannot afford analysis anyway, but the artist. Yes, the artist. Throughout history he has been the figure of awe and envy, the one who above all his fellows holds in his creativity the sources and secrets of our human identity. On the rock of Sophocles the Church of Freud still stands. No living patient has ever inspired in his analyst a fifteen-hundred-page study as the ghost of Goethe has inspired in K. R. Eissler. The number of artists who have been psycho-analyzed is wildly disproportionate to any other group, profession, or class. There is a growing body of literature on this subject along with journals wholly devoted to its preservation, for the analytic sessions occur not on the private couch but on the printed page. The only other group who have been so widely analyzed are the analysts themselves, and accounts of their sessions, being less newsworthy, seldom or never reach print. Nor is there any artist studied under the psychoanalytic lens who has been so unusual as to call into question the governing theory—though at times it may be stretched. But more likely on the contrary, the artist functions to support the truth of the doctrine, not to mention the expertise of the analyst. This is not to complain—there is a superb discipline in psychoanalysis—nor to deny that the artist may not be flattered and grateful for all the free therapy, but simply to underscore the phenomenon itself. It would have interested Shaw, and must muse his ghost even now.

This fascination with the creative personality, moreover, is not limited to the specialist, for it is at bottom human curiosity. And although the specialized tools of investigation are at the analyst's command, they are not always applied with great dexterity or grace. What is clinically significant may not be humanly central, and the analysis may succeed while the essential artist is lost. The revelation of Conrad's fetishism tells us little about *Heart of Darkness,* and Bernard C. Meyer's "Psychoanalytic Biography" will more readily send the reader off to the works of Freud than to the fiction of Conrad. When applied psychoanalysis vindicates itself by turning the artist into a patient, one does not rejoice in the triumph, for the genius who becomes a case ceases to be. Yet the task is far from simple, and great progress has been made over the years as more attention has been given to normal development and ego functions.

It is at this point that the lay brother becomes the interloper. He would like to apply psychoanalytic concepts, neither to conform nor to advance them, but solely as a mode of understanding and insight. He cannot deny—it is the lay brother speaking—that the trained analyst has access to regions of the mind and corridors of the psyche boarded up to the many. He would indeed have been grateful for some all-explaining "vulture fantasy" such as Freud believed he had found for Leonardo, or for some general concept, comparable to the "production of great art is due to the deflection of a psychosis," that Eissler devised for Goethe. But in their absence the author has had to reconstruct and describe what appear to be the subject's more significant psychological processes, and from them to draw certain inferences or make wild guesses. Worse still, he recognizes that he has not always been consistent in his procedure—now pursuing a fantasy, now dealing with energy, now shifting to psychic structure. He realizes that he is open to the charge of being at times more clinical and somehow less precise than the clinician. Finally, the reader may detect a shift in emphasis and orientation that occurs between chapters 3 and 4. Up to that point literary values have been subordinated to clinical observations, more precisely to pointing out systems of defense and impulse. The ensuing chapters reverse this balance, and literary interpretation dominates, with clinical material perhaps too generally stated. The Conclusion attempts to bring these two lines of procedure together under the topic of creativity, but still the method leaves much to be desired.

The lay brother, surveying these leaps and lapses, quietly prays that further conclusions by better minds may be drawn from the assembled materials, that in good time the ideal analyst on a white charger will arrive bearing the ideal interpretation, and all will be forgiven. The interloper declares that it will be valuable to view Shaw more consistently from the inside, but adds, defiantly folding his arms, that to do so exclusively would be most regrettable.

For the present we may as well begin at the beginning and make the best of what we encounter along the way. If we can

lay out the forces of personality that contributed to the formation of the playwright, perhaps we will have drawn closer both
to his life and to the accomplishments of his creative energies.

In the beginning there was energy.

BERNARD SHAW
A Psychological Study

1

THE SUPERFLUOUS CHILD

The relation between the young and the old should be an innocent relation. It should be something they could talk about. Well, the relation between parent and child may be an affectionate one. It may be a useful relation. It may be a necessary relation. But it can never be an innocent relation. You'd die rather than allude to it. Depend on it, in a thousand years it'll be considered bad form to know who your mother and father are.

—Misalliance

NOT OF THIS WORLD

Shaw was born of woman. Of that much we can be certain. But after his momentous concession to human flesh, resemblances between himself and the rest of mankind appear to diminish sharply. Instead of passing through the usual developmental phases, Shaw asserts, "I never climbed any ladder : I have achieved eminence by sheer gravitation" (IK, p. 685). Newton's gravity deftly supersedes Freud's psychosexual stages. And what Shaw seems to have risen to, like any other physical body seeking its element, is revealed in Yeats's nightmare, induced by a performance of *Arms and the Man,* of a "sewing machine, that clicked and shone" and "smiled perpetually."[1] "A writing and talking machine," Shaw corrected (PC, p. 54). Now a writing machine, even when it is a genius and christened George Bernard Shaw, is a mechanical apparatus invented by man to do his work for him. It is functional or nothing. One does not inquire after its soul any more than one expects it to have an unconscious or any other intangible parts. "Yet I stood aghast before its energy," Yeats is moved to conclude.

A writing machine, one must insist, is not born of woman; Shaw was, and the difference is considerable. Just as Rosencrantz and Guildenstern in a recent play[2] are thrust into a drama that is already under way and must make sense of their lives by depending in large part on the major characters of the drama, so Shaw was born into a drama well begun before him by his parents and by their parents, back to infinity, or, as we used to say, to Adam. Arriving *in medias res* and being none too bright, Rosencrantz and Guildenstern must comprehend the meaning of Hamlet's highly ambiguous drama in order to discover what their own lives are all about. To a certain extent it is every child's dilemma to be born to parents with complex personalities and unresolved conflicts, just as Hamlet himself was. Rosencrantz and Guildenstern seek the answers to their existence from Hamlet; Hamlet turns to his parents, and we also, arriving late for the play, may do well to turn to Shaw's parents.

Let us begin with Elizabeth Gurly, Shaw's mother.[3] She was

---

[1] *The Autobiography of William Butler Yeats* (New York, 1965), p. 188.
[2] Tom Stoppard, *Rosencrantz & Guildenstern Are Dead* (New York, 1968).
[3] Although autobiographical material is scattered through Shaw's writings, the three most useful sources are *Sixteen Self-Sketches* (1949), the prefaces to *London Music* (1890), *Immaturity* (1921), and his unpublished correspondence with a would-be American biographer, T. D. O'Bolger (1913–[quoted by permission of the Harvard College Library]). Allowing for minor variations and occasional lapses, the reader will find that the same events and personages are treated quite similarly and at times identically in all three sources. A common difficulty is the great stretch

born in 1830, the daughter of an "improvident country gentleman" (JE, p. 10) in Shaw's words, an "entirely indifferent and
selfish parent" (OB). Her mother died when Elizabeth was nine,
and she was turned over to her great aunt, a "humpbacked old
lady with a pretty face" and a "will of iron," who brought her
up with "ruthless strictness to be a paragon of all ladylike virtues
and accomplishments." As a consequence, she had a "Spartan
childhood and carried the straight backed stamp of it to her
grave."

Not surprisingly, she "detested her great aunt and regarded
all that had been taught her as religion and discipline as
tyranny and slavery." At nineteen her feelings toward her father
were vividly manifested following the coincidence of her being
"floated in Dublin society to get married" with her fifty-two-
year-old father's marrying the "penniless daughter of an old
friend of his whose bills he had backed with ruinous consequences." Elizabeth "innocently let out the secret" of her
father's debts to another relative, with the upshot being his
arrest for debt en route to the wedding ceremony. The
daughter's motives may be pondered. Had her father earlier
withheld his affection by abandoning her to the great aunt?
And when she came of age did he not reject her a second time
by choosing another woman? A stepmother was no doubt
what Elizabeth needed least from the man, and her vindictive
behavior spoke for the resentment she must have felt. She may
well have carried her revenge into marriage and perhaps in so
doing managed to fit her own punishment to her crime. At least

of time between the experiences and the record of them: Shaw in his
dotage writing of his nonage. I have avoided loading the text with references
to these sources; most of them will be found in *Sixteen Self-Sketches*.
    My account, like those by Shaw, slights his two older sisters. *Bernard
Shaw's Sister and Her Friends* by Henry George Farmer (1959) redresses
this wrong somewhat by giving an account of Lucy (1853-1920). Agnes
(1855-1876), presumed to be the mother's favorite, died of tuberculosis on
the Isle of Wight (AH, p. 63).

a case can be made for such a view. For having gotten back at her rejecting father, she seems in effect to have punished both him and herself in the same act by choosing to marry a failure —her avowed innocence of this notwithstanding. Moreover, her rebellion replicated her father's action and, rather than disengaging her from him, only served to reveal the extent of her identification with him. If not a drunkard, her father was a bit of a bounder, being more adept at spending money than at making it, and the "only means of living he knew was marriage." Not so complete a failure as his son-in-law, he was nonetheless on a downard social spiral; and in his daughter's eyes, he had certainly failed as a father. Freud has said that girls marry their fathers in the hope of finding their mother, which, insofar as this may apply to Elizabeth, augured doubly ill, for she would find neither.

George Carr Shaw (1814–1885) came from a family beneath his wife's in social standing. He had a very modest annual pension, prided himself on being related to a baron, and was rumored to be a drunkard. The Gurly family held him to be unacceptable; yet when he proposed, Elizabeth accepted. Out of this unpromising cluster of motives, ranging from revenge and defiance to envy and identification, with a compound of self-punishment thrown in for good measure, she married George Carṛ Shaw in 1852, barely three weeks after her father's second marriage. So slightly was she interested in this man that when he reassured her that he was a "lifelong teetotaler" she readily took him at his word; and it was only on their honeymoon, when she conceived her first daughter, that she found his wardrobe full of empty bottles and realized she had wed a confirmed alcoholic and that she had gotten more as well as less than she had bargained for. It was a situation enacted countless times throughout the century, both banal enough to be reflected in stage melodramas and serious enough to be treated in Dickens's

novels, but it was certainly real enough in its consequences for
Shaw, who arrived on the scene in 1856 and gradually came to
realize that he had been born into a "loveless" marriage.

That negation, however, scarcely does justice to the complex array of feelings engaged. And granted that there is nothing
like marriage to bring out the irrational in man and woman,
Elizabeth Gurly appeared to be even more blindly driven than
most when she went about punishing her father and herself
through her marriage. Mr. Shaw's contribution to the *mélange*
will be examined later. At the moment let us note that this
humane and harmless, "least formidable of men," was well
suited for his assigned part and may have been selected for that
reason. The prospect of competing with thirteen other siblings
for emotional supplies in his own family, which had lost its
male parent while he was growing up, may have predisposed
him to withdraw from the field of battle and settle for passive
pleasures. Without doubt his alcoholism rendered him ineffectual
as a husband. And when Mrs. Shaw became interested in
studying music under a popular Dublin instructor, the stage
was set for her to bring her "lover"[4] into the Shavian household
to parade before her children and flaunt before her inebriated
husband, propped, it seems, in some corner staring out through
glazed eyes at the spectacle before him.

> When we made a joint household with George John Vandeleur
> Lee, my mother's musical colleague, his mesmeric energy and
> enterprise reduced my father to nullity in the house. (SS, p. 147)

[4] It is clear that their love of music carried them beyond the concert
hall and into the parlour, but whether their love for each other was
sufficient to carry them into the bedroom is a question that Shaw's
biographers have pondered indecisively; and Shaw is either so elusive or
inconsistent on this score as to raise doubts over whether even he knew
for certain (cf. SS, pp. 140f). Either a plainly sexual motive or a professional one would greatly simplify things. But since neither appears sufficient, one is all the more disposed to discover the working-out of earlier
needs.

By 1896, when Shaw was ten and the "blameless *ménage à trois*," as he later called it, was firmly established, the family moved into more comfortable quarters set up by Lee. And finally when Lee left to settle in London in 1873, Mrs. Shaw followed soon after, leaving her now sobered husband permanently and her adolescent son temporarily behind. That departure on their twenty-first wedding anniversary so relieved Mr. Shaw as to make it the happiest day in his life, but it made his son feel like a piece of abandoned furniture (OB).

At some point in their account of Mrs. Shaw's adventures, Shaw's biographers customarily pause to moralize over her conduct. Was it defensible under the circumstances? Was she a good or an immoral woman? A heartless, cruel, and unloving mother; or one capable of warmth and maternal feeling? What we want to ask is, what does it all mean? Since speculation of some order is inevitable, our effort may be better applied to answering the question: when did things first go wrong for Elizabeth? Unfortunately, in view of the few shreds of fact, only partial answers are possible. From a developmental perspective we may imagine an only child who for the first year of life enjoys the benefits of a capable mother and nurse. In the second year, the course of events changes drastically. Her mother gives birth to a boy, and Elizabeth comes to recognize that she must share the family's favored position with a younger sibling as well as with the mother's spouse and bedmate. Is it farfetched to suppose that at some point in her early years Elizabeth attributed this double fall from infantile majesty to the presence and imagined importance of an appendage on the two usurpers that she found herself lacking? I don't know. I believe psychoanalysts would once have quite readily invoked Freud's concept of the castration complex, based on the inevitable discovery little girls make of "organic inferiority" (V, p. 259). Perhaps they would now rather ask whether the penis might not be a substitute for the all-important breast of which she was deprived by the precipitate arrival of a younger brother and the untimely loss of her mother; but regardless, Freud's patriarchal bias and his tendency to overemphasize or misread biology are not easily overlooked at a time when to mention "penis envy" is tantamount to praising bourbon at a W.C.T.U. Convention; yet the concept when fitted into a developmental context and biological base appears indigenous to patriarchal culture. The one presupposes the other, and so on a psychosocial level, discounting male chauvinist conspiracies, the term may retain a degree of validity, especially for the period in question. To say more would stretch an interesting digression to the breaking point, and for our purposes would overestimate a link—albeit a vital one—in the pattern to be described. Granting the qualified thrust of Freud's phallocentric assumption then, we hypothesize with him that the girl who encounters castration may either : 1) become so frightened as to turn away from sexuality altogether; 2) choose defiantly to overemphasize her masculinity; or 3) take the first steps toward "definitive femininity" by accepting her "father as love-object." What did Elizabeth Gurly do? Her marriage and motherhood rule out the first. The third was probably attempted but disrupted by her father's disappointing behavior. And therefore the second, in which the girl "clings in obstinate self-assertion to her threatened masculinity," and "the hope of getting a penis sometime is cherished to an incredibly late age and becomes the aim of her life," seems most nearly the option to which many aspects of her behavior lend credence.

Her photographs reveal a strong-looking woman with steady eyes and a mouth fixed in a hard, humorless expression; but Shaw's verbal portrait is more revealing :

Everybody had disappointed her, or betrayed her, or tyrannized over her.

She was not at all soured by all this. She never made scenes, never complained, never nagged, never punished nor retaliated nor lost her self-control nor her superiority to spites and tantrums and tempers. She was neither weak nor submissive; but as she never revenged, so also she never forgave. There were no quarrels and consequently no reconciliations. You did a wrong; and you were classed by her as a person who did such wrongs, and tolerated indulgently up to a point. But if at last you drove her to break with you, the breach was permanent: you did not get back again. (SS, pp. 28–29)

This is a description of a wounded woman, outwardly spiteful and inwardly angry, mistrustful, ambivalent, something of a grievance-collector, and one who has felt such pain in her object-relations that only extreme measures can be relied on to preserve self-esteem.

Whatever one may conclude about her early development, later events would not make things easier. Bereft of her mother at nine, rejected by her father, and dispatched to the iron-willed aunt—these are severe enough deprivations to have fostered a heightened defensive posture, technically denoted as identification with the aggressor. That is, not only did she cope with her father's second marriage by undertaking her own (as if to say, learn by my example of how you're throwing yourself away), but her libido becomes active, and she lives as a self-assertive, "masculinized" woman, adopting a role in her own marriage that could readily be idealized as liberated, indeed one that was not without psychological assets, which along with her singing career and lessons provided release from unconscious conflicts through sublimations, but one that apparently could not undo the deeper damage. For in due time she effects a reenactment of her father's abandonment of her by deserting her own husband and children, and her features harden into the rigid lines of Shaw's sketch—except that the girl he depicts in revolt against the iron-willed aunt becomes iron-willed herself, and the rejected child grows into the rejecting mother.

The extent of her hostile identification with her father bespeaks not only the force of underlying instinctual conflicts but also impairments in securing other satisfying emotional relationships. Toward her two daughters she appeared to have been at least protective and capable of concern (she traveled to the Isle of Wight when Agnes was dying of tuberculosis), but toward her son she tended to deny the love she apparently never received from her father or found in her husband. It may be inferred that Elizabeth directed some of the blame for the unfortunate events in her early years onto herself. The inward turning of anger leads to depression and withdrawal from object-relations—a disposition to be kept in mind when her children are growing.

What really happened during her marriage may only be guessed at in light of this emerging pattern and by attempting to verbalize certain meanings implied in her behavior : "Since father has deprived me of his penis, I will castrate him (in having him arrested). Moreover, if I am this powerful, maybe it is I who possess the penis. Although it is a stolen, forbidden object, I must retain it. Accordingly, I will marry an emasculated man. However, as a male he becomes a surrogate for my father and revives early conflicts, which I will now attempt to master by attaching myself to the nurturing penis of my music teacher, Mr. Lee." Proceeding thus, she may have attempted to reinstate the original mother-child bond, which, by constituting her a completed individual, could be flaunted before her discredited husband.

Which she may have done, or at least something roughly like it. She was in a sense angrily exhibiting Lee when she brought him into the Shaw family, and he apparently enjoyed being exhibited. A lifelong bachelor who taught music and conducted music programs, he was seen through Shaw's young eyes as a "man of mesmeric vitality and force," a "magnetic conductor." He evidently engaged in numerous affairs, most of which were merely flirtations and all of which were transitory. A childhood fall had left him "permanently and seriously lame," a condition that Shaw believed thwarted his chances of marriage (OB). It is possible that the accident also affected his psychic growth and led to the compensatory pleasures of conducting, a way of exhibiting himself and swaying his audience by waving his baton, symbol of his power. He did not do well after he cut himself loose from Mrs. Shaw and tried to make his way in London. After a time he was no longer welcome at the Shaw residence, and he drifted into obscurity. He died in 1886 at the age of 56, his funeral unattended by any Shaws.

Ultimately one cannot establish the above propositions. They can only be proposed and placed in a hopefully intelligible pattern. The paucity of facts is more conducive to conjecture than to interpretation, and the reader must himself decide as to the usefulness of the most unlikely assertions no less than of the most strongly documented argument. It is being advanced at the moment that Mrs. Shaw's wish to connect herself with Lee and exhibit him before her husband was reciprocated by a wish on the part of Lee to be exhibited. This helps account for what others perceive as the sexual ambiguity and what I take as the asexuality of the arrangement. The *ménage à trois,* being built on a *folie à deux,* thrived as long as Mr. Shaw was on hand to hold up his corner, and the whole business ultimately proceeded from Elizabeth Gurly Shaw's feelings of resentment and depression, arising from the confounding of maternal loss with paternal rejection.

At any rate, so appears the tragi-comic stage of the Shavian household—with the elder Shaw waving his bottle about, Lee waving his baton, and Mrs. Shaw waving Lee—on which young George Bernard grew up. It was a world made up more of symbols, magical gestures, and impostures than of substantial realities. Its unreality left as much room for despair as for hope. For if such an unimposing world fails to gratify, it can at least be altered. Shaw was born of woman, but he never celebrated his birthday. And he was once delighted to trace his genealogy back to the revenging MacDuff, of no woman born (IM, p. 650). In his most humanly revealing reflection he muses:

> Whether it be that I was born mad or a little too sane, my kingdom was not of this world; I was at home only in the realm of my imagination, and at ease only with the mighty dead. (IM, p. 670)

And yet Ellen Terry moved him to write, "from our birth to our death we are women's babies, always wanting something from them." (LS, p. 622)

DOMESTIC ANARCHY

As far as Shaw was concerned, his mother had discharged her responsibilities in giving birth to her three children. "She abandoned her own children to the most complete anarchy," leaving them

> wholly to the promptings of our blood's blueness, with results which may be imagined. (IM, p. 622)

> She did not hate her children. She did not hate anybody, nor love anybody. (SS, p. 29)

But the powerful drives behind her behavior were as undeniable as they were often obscure and inexpressible, and what seems to have happened is that she never succeeded in finding an appropriate object for either her hate or her love, a consequence that would follow from the deep conflicts described. Moreover, her apparent refusal to be a parent to her children may well be a reproduction of her father's parental neglect of her. In her last years she turned to ouija boards and the occult, seeking perhaps in the spirit world what the real world had denied her. But she never turned to her son. It may have been Shaw's unacknowledged good fortune that in her frustration she did not merely seek him out for compensation and make him a substitute love-object. In that case he might easily have turned homosexual. But she did not, and he did not. At least there is no reason to believe that he did. He had his difficulties with women, but he never adopted a homosexual position, nor exhibited partiality for his own sex.

What was it then that he did become? What was the psychic structure that supported his genius, and through which he expressed it? Are there correspondences between early experiences that went into the formation of a personality and the later formation of the plays?

"She did not concern herself much about us," Shaw continues, "for she had never been taught that mothering is a science, nor that it matters in the least what children eat or drink: she left all that to servants," who, we are told, were incompetent, illiterate, and unloving (SS, p. 29). Only a "Nurse Williams" is positively referred to as a "good and honest woman." The rest were "utterly unfit to be trusted with the charge of three cats, much less three children" (AH, p. 11). In light of all this alleged neglect and mistreatment, why was it not Shaw who left home instead of his mother, whom he indeed followed after and joined in London?

It is not easy to grasp what it meant to a child to grow up in the presence of a woman who by nature, by law, by need, and by necessity was in every way his mother except in actual practice. It is not easy to grasp how he might gain basic satisfactions and have dependency wishes met, given a mother who will not grant them and a father who has not gotten beyond them, especially when their deprivation could lead to serious disturbances in later life. This is the crucial phase for the formation of the Shavian personality. And yet so remote is it from the scope of what passes for normal experience and so difficult to reconstruct that one is tempted to defer to an expert with technical knowledge of child development and thereby paradoxically remove it from the central human sphere where it properly belongs.

On the other hand, the new developmental psychology is also old : Shakespeare saw that when we are born "we come crying hither," even as Lear in his despair had cried for his daughters. What we first cry for is milk and mother love, which, supplied, result in a sense of well-being and further growth. And we keep crying until we are filled. Ordinarily a child interacting with his parents gains these gratifications, and deriving strength thereby, institutes repression and learns control. He introjects the "good breast," works up defensive maneuvers of denial and projection against the "bad breast" of his frustrations until he can unify them into a libidinal object and then set about regulating and redirecting his needs. Shaw would have us believe, and with reason, that such was not the case for him.

I never knew love as child. My mother was so disappointed in my father that she centered all her care on my younger sister, and she left me to fend for myself. (AH, pp. 63–4)

What was done to me in childhood was nothing at all of an intentional kind. I wasn't spoiled, and I wasn't helped. (PC, p.52)

I cannot remember having ever heard a single sentence uttered by my mother in the nature of moral or religious instruction. My father made an effort or two. (SW, p. 25)

I was not treated as a child. I was let to do as I liked; and I

knew everything that was going on and was present on all
occasions as if I were an adult member of the family.
(AH, p. 37)

Just as there seems to have been precious little love bestowed
on him, there were apparently few limits or controls placed on
his behavior, with the implication that he went his way with
all the prerogatives of an adult and missed along the way the
opportunities to be lovingly treated like a child to have done
with it once and for all. And yet the account of what was done
to him is only half the story.

Shaw's self-styled gravitational rise can be taken to mean
that he did not climb the developmental ladder, or it can illustrate what Freud held that every child in his own way eventually does. For regardless of the latitude of behavior permitted
him or the restrictions of reality imposed on him, it is finally
the child himself who internalizes what he must have, represses
himself, organizes his energies, and grows—or rises—up. All of
this Shaw did, but in an extraordinary, or Shavian, manner.

Growing up, he often must have had to estimate across a
great emotional distance and surmise what was expected of him.
Since his mother would not nourish him (leaving it up to a
servant to feed him "stewed beef" and "badly cooked potatoes"
in the kitchen), then perhaps food, he may have concluded, was
not "good" for him—not to be desired; perhaps by forsaking it
he would measure up to her expectations and gain his mother's
love. Once two maids implored him to eat his dinner, while he,
refusing politely, demonstrated to a boyhood friend that he had
taught himself notation well enough to play the piano. At that
time his mother was the "foremost amateur singer in Dublin,
and her house the centre round which musical Dublin revolved"
(EM, p. 9). Just to show that he could be on the fringe of this
magic circle meant more to him than eating in the kitchen with
the maids.

Nor could he have missed the loss of love incurred by his father's excessive appetite for liquor. And despite his mother's presumed indifference, she was not above drawing a link between the children's misbehavior and their father''s weakness. To be sure, the imagined demands and deficient responses of his mother may have been exaggerated by Shaw; and although they were not disproportionate to the still-primitive level on which they were being experienced, they would likely have been reinforcements of earlier events. And so there must be more to be told.

Insofar as he had a depriving mother, who was at least waging a battle against her predicament, and an alcoholic father, who was pretty much resigned to being an all-around failure, Shaw clearly banked more fervently on the one than on the other. And for this to occur he must have been able to derive some strength from his mother somehow, for genius cannot spring wholly from the desert of deprivation. And since even a desert has sunlight, where was the sun in Shaw's early years? The picture he draws—and it is about all we have—is an arid one: "rich only in dreams, frightful and loveless in realities" (LS, p. 773). It is also tantalizingly incomplete. By whom and for how long was he nursed? His mother, Nurse Williams, or someone else? And if it was his mother, did she fondle him and sing to him, or did she proceed with the "almost complete neglect" that generally characterized her as a parent? There is very little to go on. She taught him a "half dozen childish rhymes," and these are unhappily associated with a "stock of unprintable limericks that constituted almost an education in geography," which his Rabelaisian uncle taught him (SS, p. 32). And yet he can maintain in the following passage:

> I hated the servants and liked my mother because, on the one or two rare and delightful occasions when she buttered my

bread for me, she buttered it thickly instead of merely wiping a knife on it. (LM, pp. 856–857)

Even an intended tribute veils an accusation. And it relates at best obliquely to the very early and hence very primitive stage of life when the pure consumer of the oral phase perceives his mother as the object of his consumption. We might say the tiny infant has a consuming interest in his mother. He believes he is literally devouring her and fears the same fate for himself. His nourishment is indeed her depletion, and her depletion is also his loss. And if we can grant that children act like savages, we might as well consider that infants carry on like cannibals, though all that remains of this jungle of orality may be the bridges built in escaping it. Among what remains for Shaw are his dietary restrictions along with his opposition to vaccination and vivisection, in other words, ordinances against using teeth and teethlike instruments (knives, needles) on human or animal flesh.[5]

[5] It would be foolhardy to expect to demonstrate a direct connection between Shaw's most infantile, cannibalistic urges and fears and his later dietary prohibitions. The two, however, seemed to have been associated in his mind when he said, "I was a cannibal for twenty years (SS, p. 85), and that his wife was "beginning to doubt the necessity of cannibalism" (ET, p. 280), although she apparently continued as a carnivore. And he once defined carnivority as "cannibalism with its heroic dish omitted" (CR, p. 536). The breast, food, and the taboo are associated in a letter to Mrs. Pat Campbell after he had apparently suffered a momentary rebuff from her. "You turned a cold cheek to me, and with a most wonderful pursing of your lips and eyes and wrinkling of your neck and pouting of your bosom like a pigeon, made yourself exactly like a pork chop." But if she aroused Shaw's devouring impulses, he is quick to add, "I am a saint and a vegetarian : and I won't have porkchops, I will have my own Stella and nobody else" (PC, pp. 1-4). He also once used his vegetarianism as a disclaimer of interest in his wife's fortunes, which is something of a *non sequitur*, unless he attributed a forbidden emotional significance to her financial wealth (JD, p. 151). "Love is a devouring thing," says his black girl (AB, p. 29). "I come with the love of a lioness and eat you up and make you a part of me." There is a hint that Androcles is not devoured by the lion because as a zealous Christian he abstains from meat and not just on Fridays. *Man and Superman* is a feast of predatory imagery. The artist in his relations with women is described as "half vivisector, half vampire." In the "struggle between the artist man and

We can also assume so far that these early transactions, of which the only specific remnants are a baby cap cherished by his mother and a later, possible screen memory[6] of thickly buttered bread, were of vital importance for him, that they bespeak a degree of pleasurable transactions, and that he derived benefits from them that were to extend throughout his life (he was not autistic and never became psychotic). But we cannot be as certain as we would like, for they seem at this stage of our inquiry to be so deeply repressed as to be forever beyond recall.[7] This is after all the purpose of repression, and when it is effective, it has the same effect on everyone. When his baby cap turned up among his mother's belongings after her death, he remarked: "Had anyone suggested such a possibility, I should have laughed at him (or her) in scorn. We never know anything about our parents" (PC, p. 21).[8] And so just as Shaw may have mistaken or exaggerated early demands, he may also have overestimated his mother's early indifference or confounded it with her later neglect. He must have had something of her at the start of life. We can be sure that one must be loved to feel lovable, and Shaw was not utterly lacking in that feeling, although he seems at times to have overplayed and underplayed it more than most of us.

But our inquiry reaches an impasse if we rely only on the text of Shaw's words and refrain from drawing more explicitly

the mother woman," the question is, "Which shall use up the other?" (p. 538) When Shaw complains that love is not enough, it might be countered that love is also too much.

[6] That is, a cover for an earlier associated, but repressed, memory.

[7] Stephen Spender remarks on a "very deep repression of feeling and also a reliance on the force of one's own separate life which arises from a lack of confidence in affection." "The Riddle of Shaw," a review of *Sixteen Self Sketches*, reprinted in *George Bernard Shaw: A Critical Survey*, ed. Louis Kronenberger (New York, 1953), p. 237.

[8] "I myself was never on bad terms with my mother: we lived together until I was forty-two years old, absolutely without the smallest friction of any kind; yet when her death set me thinking about our relations, I realized that I knew very little about her" (PMI, p. 30).

on a clinical context within which to proceed. The all-important nursing situation may be affected by numerous factors ranging from the child's genetic constitution, the urgency and strength of its drives, to the attitudes, moods, and availability of the mother, the family's economic security, and finally cultural traditions. So we proceed with more than a little modesty and caution.

Since there is no reason to suspect that in the earliest months there were instances of traumatic separation or that the mother was criminally or psychotically deficient in looking to the child's basic needs, I would expect that the moment of truth arrived for Shaw at about the same time as for most infants, that is, about midway into the first year. Up until then the infant attributes its gratifications to the offices of a "good breast," its hungers and frustrations to a "bad breast" (ways in which the earliest needs and the partial representations of the mother are expressed). But as the child begins to differentiate itself from the mother, he is given the task of perceiving that the good and bad breast hitherto kept safely apart in fantasy must now fuse in the same emerging ego structure and in the same object in order that the mother become the libidinal object for the later oedipal phase.

> [The infant] begins to realize, at first only intermittently, that the gratifying objects he needs and loves are but other aspects of the frustrating ones he hates and in phantasy destroys. With this discovery he begins to feel concern for these objects and to experience depression. This "depressive position" is so painful that to escape it he tends to deny either that his destroyed good objects are good or that they have been injured. In other words, he tends either to regress to the older persecutory position or to adopt a "manic defence" in which concern and guilt are strenuously denied. But so far as he can tolerate depressive feelings, they give rise to reparative impulses and to a capacity for unselfish concern and protective love. The extent to which

he achieves or fails to achieve this normal outcome determines the stability of his health, or his liability to illness.[9]

Winnicott has suggested renaming this period the "Stage of Concern," since previously the infant, ruthlessly pursuing its instinctual impulses, now begins to experience "ruth," an achievement, a sign of becoming established as a whole person, and not an indication of inevitable depression (only in instances where the mother completely withdraws after a relatively normal period of nursing does the term, introduced by Spitz [1946], "anaclitic depression," apply).

The issue before the infant is to fuse his contradictory conceptions. The degree of difficulty of the task will influence the defensive options taken. Regression to the "paranoid-schizoid position" being the least adaptive, the next serious possibility is to act as though the threat of losing the good breast does not exist. Manic denial flies in the face of reality by asserting that the good breast is not gone, it is safe inside and the bad impulses are outside. There is a germ of pretense here, even of the histrionic—the infant's trying to get away with something, a bit of an impostor—though I believe there are more cogent reasons than these first associations for assigning this alternative as the preferred one for Shaw, and I will return later in this and the next chapter to manifestations of denial as well as to manic states.

[9] Melanie Klein, et al., *New Directions in Psychoanalysis* (New York: Basic Books, 1957), pp. xii-xiii, 42f, 312f. The concepts followed in this discussion originate from the pioneering work in English psychoanalysis by Mrs. Klein. D. W. Winnicott, who worked under Mrs. Klein, has added to my understanding in his two papers, "The Manic Defence" (1935) and "The Depressive Position in Normal Emotional Development" (1954). These can be found in his *Collected Papers* (New York: Basic Books, 1958). Another related concept is that of the "phallic mother," a common distortion stemming also from the first year of life when the infant in his belief that the mother is perfect, assigns to her the presence of a penis. Disillusionment may begin to set in as early as the second year and is associated with the concerns of the phallic phase.

But now the influential role of Shaw's mother may be reconsidered. Shaw discerned that "her early motherless privation of affection and her many disappointments in other people had thrown her back on her own considerable resources," and it seems entirely reasonable to find a connection between these frustrations with libidinal objects and her withdrawal from her family on the one side and her son's presumed conflicts over sufficient maternal supplies on the other. It does not mean that the child identifies with the mother's depression, but it does imply that the mother, without necessarily intending to, sets up conditions that are suited to bring about cognate results. The "depressive mother blocks . . . normal development when she withdraws from the child into her depression," writes one close observer of early development. The "child follows the mother into the depressive attitude and so acquires her global incorporative tendency."[10] The object is swallowed whole, as it were, magically introjected and idealized instead of being "eaten, worn down, stolen from,"[11] digested, and made by degrees part of oneself as a continuing mother-child relationship would provide. And if the mother struggles with her plight by attempting a flight into reality—for instance into the world of music—the son may in time launch similar flights.

Since any number of things can go wrong and frequently do even in the most ideal nursing situations, Winnicott's concept of the "good-enough mother" nevertheless encompasses the vast majority of women. But I would speculate that a mother with her own problems surrounding loss and dependency ("everybody had disappointed her") would avoid overtaxing her patience with a child who might seek to draw out nursing and

[10] Rene A Spitz, *The First Year of Life* (New York: International University Press, Inc., 1965), pp. 261f. This last phrase means, "to take in as a whole without attempt to distinguish separate parts or functions," (*Comprehensive Dictionary of Psychoanalytic Terms* [New York, 1958]).

[11] Winnicott, "The Depressive Position in Normal Emotional Development" (1954), p. 276.

related sessions, or who might have trouble initiating what he cannot leisurely complete. Such a child may be seen by her as a "dreadful procrastinator," Mrs. Shaw's otherwise baffling description of her energetic, industrious son.

In any case, it may be very roughly surmised that, for Shaw, instead of need gratification along with graduated fusion, reparation, and object-love, the "bad" object was either denied or incorporated along with the "good" object and instituted as part of the developing psychic structure where they might reappear, as I hope to show, as early bad self-images and a stern but lofty ego-ideal.[12] Manic denial opposes object-loss and internal object-destruction; it acts, in other words, against rage and depression; it also interferes, as we shall see, with important later ego-functions, such as reality-testing.[13]

How much of this hypothetical account can be documented?

[12] A second crucial defense employed presumably around this time is "identification with the aggressor." Necessarily imperfect in her ability to adapt to the infant's every need, a mother normally compels this response, and when she is struggling with her own unmet needs it is stronger. The infant tends to interpret her neglect as opposition to his wishes, i.e., a "bad breast," which he then deals with by internalizing. Her presumed nursing inadequacies thus become the child's "No" to his unrelenting instinctual strivings, and since there is never a No in the unconscious, these very early internalizations announce the first signs of ego formation. Depersonalization and the feeling of not belonging may also be traced back to "discrepancies between opposing identifications," which produce "contradictions in the superego." Edith Jacobson, "Depersonalization," *Journal of the American Psychoanalytic Association* 7 (1959): 606.

[13] Winnicott ("The Manic Defence," pp. 132-34) lists the ways in which the manic defense is manifested:

> Denial of inner reality.
> Flight of external reality from internal reality.
> Holding the people of the inner reality in "suspended animation."
> Denial of the *sensations* of depressions.
> The employment of almost any opposites in the reassurance against death, chaos, mystery, etc., ideas that belong to the *fantasy content of* depression.

Following are some of the opposites. First in order, the depressive word, next the manic opposite: Empty/Filling. Dead/Alive, growing. Still/ Moving. Heavy/Light. Sinking/Rising. Low down/ High up. Serious/Comic. Separated/Joined. Many of these words enjoy a special place in the Shavian vocabulary, and we will be especially attentive when they are used.

Nothing like direct empirical evidence exists, and indirect means offer only a degree of probability. I will limit myself at this point to one argument. Winnicott (1935) mentions that "in manic defence mourning cannot be experienced." Mourning, which allows one to experience the ambivalent feelings of grief and anger, is a commonly accepted way of overcoming loss by internalizing the lost object and giving it up by degrees, piece-meal, memory by memory. To say that Shaw could not relin-quish the early mother in her capacity as the good breast is also to say that he could not mourn, for what cannot be mourned cannot be given up. Not only do funerals elicit his jesting mockery (by itself not deviant from Irish culture), but the loss of his closest family members, including his wife, summons manic denial. His father's death drew a two-line acknowledg-ment to his mother to the effect that the "governor has left the universe on rather particular business and set me up as 'The Orphan,'" and he sums up having his mother cremated as a "merry episode."[14] Just as denial opposes the acceptance of object-loss through mourning, so can the recognition of object-destruction be denied by opposing the sense of guilt. Along with

[14] "Whether it is a missed train," Shaw boasts, "or a death among his nearest and dearest, he shews this inhuman self-possession. No one has accused him of being a bad son: His relations with his mother were appa-rently as perfect as anything of the kind could be; but when she was cremated, Granville-Barker, whom he had chosen to accompany him as the sole other mourner, could say nothing to him but 'Shaw: you certainly are a merry soul.' Shaw fancied that his mother was looking over his shoulder and sharing the fun of watching two men dressed like cooks picking scraps of metal from her ashes. He is fond of saying that what bereaved people need is a little comic relief, and that this is why funerals are so farcical" (SS, p. 204).

No less remarkable was his behavior at his wife's deathbed: "It's a miracle. She is exactly as she was when I married her. The colour of her hair has gone back to auburn. Her wrinkles have disappeared and her feet look beautiful" (RM, p. 54).

Once, he wrote in 1927, "I used to feel sad when my old friends and even enemies began dropping around me. Nowadays I have got over that: I exult every time another goes down. I am a man of the most extra-ordinary hardness of heart" (PM, p. 177). But he proceeds to attribute this condition to having come of age in a hard-hearted period.

his refusal to mourn, Shaw disavows feelings of guilt, but he could allow laughter, and I believe, by way of qualifying my argument, that his sense of humor included a sense of loss. Jokes, as Nietzsche has remarked, are the epitaphs of emotions.

One psychoanalyst, who found in Shaw a "deep depression over maternal deprivation that haunted him all his life," has proposed denial as "one of his greatest weapons of defense," and has gone on to wonder if he might not be "hypomanic" (JS, p. 253). (Hypomania is a chronic, mild state of mania, marked by increased gaiety, affability, buoyancy, self-confidence, seemingly boundless energy, impatience, and flightiness. "Ascensive," says Winnicott, in getting at the feeling tone behind it —which is to say that the hypomanic person may strike others as a sprite who goes about claiming to have risen by sheer force of gravity. Such a type is to be distinguished from the manic-depressive mood swings of the cyclothymic personality.)

The outcome of these early processes may be taken as Shaw's first faltering step toward separation and civilization—his first self-creative, or Shavian, act. At this basic level of life one is first struck—perhaps a symptom of the amateur investigator's naïveté—by the sheer force of Shaw's early instinctual needs and the likelihood of their continuing claims and displacements (defenses are not final); second, one is struck by the stupendous amount of work the ego must carry on to maintain its measure of independence. For example, the phobic maneuvers regarding vegetarianism, vaccination, and vivisection apparently are very likely instituted to guard against a cannibalistic orgy—indeed, against the mere thought of it—that would jeopardize the internalized good object, and also probably to ward off many bad impulses that might stand in the way of self-esteem. And in spite of how well Shaw actually succeeded, his self-respect, sense of mastery, and self-image as an advanced man biologically and culturally, all rest on his inner conviction that he succeeded quite well. Instead of taking in spirits and "chewing on the dead bodies of animals," he proudly subsists on cocoa and porridge, macaroni and vegetables.

But the price he seems to have paid for his high measure of control was an enforced turning away from the original object in order to master his feelings over its widely split internalized components (the nurturing "good breast," the repelling "bad breast"), fostering an extensive reliance on fantasy and preserving a sense of union with the early "good" mother so powerful in some ways as never to be relinquished. And while fantasy may have succeeded in reducing instinctual tensions and contributing to control, it could not lead to true separation, though it could open the way to turn early loss to future gain by placing his attachment on other levels. After recalling how his mother thickly buttered his bread, he continues:

> Her almost complete neglect of me had the advantage that I could idolize her to the utmost pitch of my imagination and had no sordid or disillusioning contacts with her. (LM, p. 857)

This glorified image Shaw retained indefinitely in fantasy: he is not talking about infancy.[15] In the course of time, all he comes to require is her worshipful presence (or the sense of it). This, bleak as it may sound, was one thing the child could not be deprived of, and so he made the most of it. It is one reason why at twenty he follows her to London and takes a room in her house, although they continued to go their separate ways and had little to do with one another (HP, p. 204), and why many years later he can be in such exalted spirits at her cremation and immediately following have an experience of her

---

[15] It is clearly established," for Weissman, "that the early neglect by his mother promoted the perpetuation of the omnipotent and omniscient mother image. This image would be projected onto the real mother who then became indispensable and idolized" (p. 158). "In manic defence a relationship with the external object is used in the attempt to decrease the tension in inner reality" (Winnicott, "The Manic Defence," p. 131).

laughing ghost accompanying him. The real mother can vanish in the "merry episode" of the fiery furnace (serve her right and good riddance considering her cold neglect!) but the Great Mother of early infancy and childhood fantasy lives on in the man and crops up again in certain women; and thus, well may Shaw ask, "O grave, where is thy victory?" (PC, p. 204).

Never having had the mother except apparently in the early months at her breast and subsequently as a receding worshipful presence, he never truly succeeds in giving her up because she was never experienced in a humanizing relationship in which early loss could be eased, reparation could be accomplished by degrees, and sharply disparate perceptions could be integrated, but rather he retains her as a source of vital energy and an omnipotent object of worship. The accomplishment of this task is largely assigned to fantasy. Fantasy, with its memory, traces from the very dawn of life, predates the disruptions of the depressive position, and may be given an opportunity to preserve the integrity of early introjects, to heal narcissistic wounds, as well as to foster separation and build bridges to future developmental stages. These first important lineaments of fantasy may now be described.

FAMILY ROMANCE

An impetus to Shaw's fledgling fantasy life may have come from events around his fifth or sixth year. Mrs. Shaw had become acquainted with George Vandeleur Lee, who then lived a block away. Lee's entrance into the mother's life and thence into the family at a time when her son should otherwise be drawing the oedipal period to a close (repudiating incestuous wishes and identifying with father) could only have further altered the already irregular course of psychic events and must have further stimulated fantasy. For suddenly the mother is revealed as having another life beyond the family, her neglect is perchance explained, the steam is let out of the biparental pressure-cooker as the son's libidinal interest acquires new dimensions and thrives more intensely. Lee is elevated to a "genius" of "mesmeric force and vitality." And while a magical aura hovers over him, a "divinity" (LM) hedges about Mrs. Shaw, who had married one man, acquired another, produced three children, and was on her way to becoming a luminary in Dublin's music world. Certainly the recourse to fantasy already accentuated by the mother's neglect and the child's loneliness would be augmented by the seemingly realistic prospect that her formidable powers and availability might eventually incline her to the neglected son and reinstate an equivalent of the early pleasures of nursing so highly valued after their foreclosure.

Herein are the makings of the family romance singled out by Freud, Rank, Kris, and Greenacre as significant in the lives of artists and other highly gifted persons.[16] Freud had found that when a child feels slighted, and consequently that "his affection is not being fully reciprocated [he] then finds vent in the idea . . . of being a step-child or an adopted child" (V, pp. 74–78). In his imagination he frees himself from his parents, of whom "he now has such a low opinion," and replaces them with others occupying a "higher social station."

16 "Family Romances," pp. 74-78; MY; *Psychoanalytic Explorations in Art*; PA; PB. Components of the family romance inform a great deal of Shavian drama. *Arms and the Man* (Chap. 3) incorporates the outsider into the Aristocracy; *Getting Married* (Chap. 7) employs celestial imagery to increase the magnitude of a female Life Force figure; *The Devil's Disciple, Captain Brassbound's Conversion. The Shewing-up of Blanco Posnet* (Chap. 5) exploit the rescue fantasy, a family romance variant, as do *Pygmalion* and *Misalliance* (Chap. 7). *Man and Superman* expands the family romance to cosmic proportions. Shaw's real-life romances lean heavily on this material for their overdetermined significance, especially Mrs. Pat Campbell (below) and Ellen Terry (Chap 2 and Conclusion); his own "special type of object choice" in marriage was an Irish millionairess-with-a-romantic-past. To a far-reaching extent, he was, as he said, "at home in the realm of my imagination."

The "lowly" parents are replaced by "cosmic" ones or "Olympians" (PB). Indeed, we are such stuff as dreams are made of; and this fantasy material, the raw fabric of imagination, appears in the dreams of adults, confounds the lives of neurotics, but particularly affects the personality of the artist. While it often tends to enhance and prolong the oedipal situation, its first priority is to "help regulate self-esteem" and to protect omnipotence through projection. Socially, it may stem from an "experience of not belonging" and is often manifested as shyness (either directly by reticence or indirectly by adoption of a role). Projection invests other figures and objects with heightened significance; shyness shields "vivid fantasy activity."[17] Shaw's role-playing is duly celebrated, but his shyness has gone largely unnoticed, even though he confessed to being "mortally shy" during his youth and early London years, corresponded with Ellen Terry for years without a meeting, and insisted he belonged with the mighty dead.

Celestial imagery will certainly cluster around women in Shaw's life just as the mother was exalted in fantasy; indeed the Life Force itself, Shaw's conception of the Divine, may have first been imbibed at the mother's breast. Lee's magic being of a lesser degree is not so well sustained, nor are there any male Olympians to be found elsewhere. The godhead is within: the "kingdom" is "not of this world"; the Superman is still to come. As usual, it is easier to speculate than to confirm. "I cannot remember any time," he boasts, "when I did not exercise my imagination in daydreams about women" (SS, p. 176). The context of these daydreams becomes clearer in Frank Harris's biography, which Shaw oversaw and at times helped write.

[17] The first quotation is from "The Family Romance: Theoretical and Clinical Implications," by Linda Joan Kaplan, a paper pending publication in *The Psychoanalytic Review*. The following quotations are from Donald M. Kaplan, "On Shyness," *International Journal of Psycho-Analysis* 53 (1972): 440-41, 452.

> All through from his earliest childhood, he had lived a fictitious
> life through the exercise of his incessant imagination. . . . It had
> one oddity. The fictitious Shaw was not a man of family. He
> had no relatives. He was not only a bastard . . . he was also a
> foundling. (FH, p. 28)

Shaw may have been speaking more frankly through Harris
than he would have spoken in his own person. In any case,
to be a foundling is better than to be a lostling, and Mrs. Shaw's
having in effect "found" Lee may have spurred an obsession
with the foundling-child fantasy as a corrective to the sense of
abandonment in the superfluous child. Indeed, so strong is this
fantasy and so pervasive in his works is the treatment of the
foundling and of the son seeking to regain his rightful inheritance that one biographer was inspired to concoct a hypothesis
that Shaw doubted his paternity so far as to harbor suspicions
over Lee's collaboration in his own conception (BR), although
the evidence is nonexistent and a physical resemblance between
Mr. Shaw and his son has been noted. But no more than
Mr. Shaw, when one comes down to it, was Lee worthy of such
a far-reaching, Shavianizing act. Lee's otherwise disruptive impact may have opened up new possibilities for the rescue fantasy,
a family-romance variant (OC). And, as is true with so many of
Shaw's conflicts and quandaries, the question of paternity fans
out into the world of ideas—here of eugenics and evolution.

As a child, Shaw may have idolized his mother as his needs
dictated, but as a man he scrutinized her with a critical eye,
exposed the worship of woman as romantic nonsense, and
drove it from the temple of Art with the stinging whip of his
prose. (What he felt writing to his actresses in the privacy of
his study is something else.) Never a simple idolator, he nevertheless always remains involved with women. And, to be sure,
the child's idolatry of his mother stimulated dreams of the
"Uranian Venus" along with fantasties of the family romance,

which spread unchecked over the years of latency until at puberty the "dawning of moral passion" in him began to organize and transform his "mob of appetites" to prepare him for the mature conversions and commitments to come.

Thus three major stages emerge in this line of development. From early attachment and fantasy reliance, he advances to moral passion, and thence to championing the woman's cause and building a system of morality and religion on his high regard for life, just as the mother was first worshiped, then idealized and defended in his feminism, and eventually impersonalized into the mystical Life Force. And if these processes should be described from the viewpoint of Shaw's artistic genesis, they would encompass a deflection of instinctual impulses from the original object, being the mother, to the "collective alternates," comprising the artist's presumed "creative romance with the world" (PA, pp. 58f). It has been suggested that for Wordsworth, who at the age of eight lost his mother, "Nature" is the "cosmic concept" that "takes the place of the parental images" (PB, p. 41). Similarly, for Shaw the Life Force "sanctifies all life and substitutes a profound dignity and self-respect for the old materialistic self" (LS, p. 505).

While such an early overall view is valuable, it would be misleading to assert that Shaw's manifold endeavors are so simply all of a piece. But it can be proposed that from the obscure basis of a dangerous oral situation and the engagement of powerful primitive urges, fears, and countermeasures, Shaw's conceptions of Vitalism and Creative Evolution eventually find their way into consciousness as derivatives and representations of instinctual conflicts, with his "moral passion" at adolescence and his "evolutionary appetite" at maturity recounting in their very phrases the instincts' visissitudes as well as the ego's adaptations. And the more his feminism refuted the libidinal and economic exploitation of women through marriage and Capitalism, the more it endeared him to the fair sex, which was after all in keeping with the aim of the original impulse. He "trimphed" over desire by denying it. To a practical philanderer like Frank Harris, this made him the most vexing of enigmas: "In all my days I never met a man so eager to win women and so frightened out of possessing them as Shaw" (FH, p. 216). When his doctrine of the Superman inspired a beautiful actress to propose an experiment in practical eugenics with him, he was able to extricate himself only by warning her that the offspring might just as easily have *his* looks and *her* brain. While courting Charlotte Townshend, he altruistically took her best interest to heart and advised her to marry on principle, while she earnestly took his advice to heart and married him in fact. Clearly one key to Shaw's originality is in the comic dimensions of his defensive strategies.

NATURAL HISTORY

Shaw did not become merely a mother-fixated, *fin de siècle* Romantic, or "one of your suburban Love is Enough fanatics." His works are not written in adoration or adulation of women. They are not transparent attempts to come to terms with conventionally ambivalent feelings about the mother as the woman-with-a-past convention encouraged Dumas *fils*, W. S. Gilbert, Jones, Wilde, Pinero, and other well-made playwrights to do. There are no languishing Camilles, remorseful Mrs. Tanquerays, wronged Mrs. Arbuthnots, or any other Dark Ladies and shadowy Beatrices in his plays.

And yet the oedipal situation has been said to be the wellspring of artistic creation. Maurice Valency has shown, for example, that the woman praised in Troubadour and

Renaissance poetry is a re-creation of the oedipal mother.[18] Perhaps because Shaw's most important transactions with his mother were so early as to be experienced virtually at the level of biological energy, they were pre-sexual, pre-oedipal, practically pre-everything. Could there not be, behind the molding of the family romance and the promoting of creativity, the Primordial Mother as the Life Principle itself, less a person than a vital force? And if that should be the case, there would hardly be any eroticized Dark Ladies or romantic heroines of the kind that abound in the works of his contemporaries, but there could be a religion of the Life Force, and that distinctive kind of drama promulgating it, called Shavian.[19] This is not to say that women characters in their own right may not figure prominently in Shavian drama; but when the Life Force is incarnated and dwells among us, it is always in the flesh of woman.

As a dramatist, his strategy is to place woman in the setting of reality, Shavian reality, by converting the talents of his actresses (notably Janet Achurch, Ellen Terry, Mrs. Pat Campbell) to the dramas of the Life Force, just as his early impulses toward his mother had been transformed to serve other needs. These attachments to actresses—fixations if you will—were actually defenses against a much earlier fixation to his mother, who indeed serves as creative model. For just as she had made the best of a bad marriage by turning to music, Lee, and London, so the Shavian heroines are often pragmatic masters of their dire situations; and in both instances, this moral prag-

---

[18] MY; *Totem and Taboo;* Maurice Valency, *In Praise of Love* (New York, 1958); cf. Norman Holland, *The Dynamics of Literary Response* (New York, 1968), pp. 46f. Edmund Bergler and Arthur Wormhoudt have pushed it back to an earlier period, which also seems indicated here.

[19] As an adolescent Shaw once horrified his friend Edward McNulty by asserting that he would establish a new religion. McNulty managed to persuade him to become a writer. Shaw followed McNulty's advice, but he never relinquished his first goal.

matism may be mistaken by members of society or of the audience as immorality. But in Shaw's hands it becomes "natural history," where it proudly stands, along with the "higher morality" of the intelligentsia, squarely in opposition to conventional morality and popular romance.

Vitalism, realism, and skepticism inform his materials and forge his characters; eroticism, romance, and conventional idealization are left for the fools and buffoons, even as his burgeoning libidinal instincts are left behind (but not out) by his transformations. In *Arms and the Man,* the romantic, phallic hero, Sergius (SURGE) is bested by the "Chocolate Cream Soldier," BLUNTschli. Other early plays like *Mrs. Warren's Profession* and *Candida* examine the disparities between the names and the realities of relationships. "Wife" does not adequately express Morell's relation to Candida, who reminds him she is his mother, sisters, and much more besides (although much less from his temporarily disillusioned point of view). "Mother" fails to establish a viable relation between Mrs. Warren and Vivie. Names do not correspond to reality; they are deceptive screens or mere conventions, forms that fall short of life. Best expose them, Shaw argues from the roots of his own life. And if the plays do not embrace romantic passion, uphold conjugal devotion, or praise filial piety, and if the cracks in the virtues of home and hearth are permanently on display, there is also present a whole series of emergent relationships that are cemented by the Vitalist energy of the Life Force. Away from fulfilled personal bonds, Shaw's family romance is steered toward forms of cosmic integration.

Furthermore, since his family provided him not only with the makings of romance fantasy but with a domestic comedy situation (although it could just as well be called bourgeois tragedy or temperance melodrama)—a mother slamming the door on her marriage like Nora on her doll's house and asserting her independence as a New Woman while becoming a woman-with-a-past; and a father bankrupt of everything except gentility, producing a line of fatherless Shavian heroes whose fortunes were tied to wills and inheritances—it is not by happenstance that Shaw should become the consummate master and manipulator of stage conventions. In fact, he transmutes these theatrical conventions as skillfully through his dramatic art as his mother had mastered her plight through her musical talent. And whether we encounter a master of reality in Mrs. Shaw or in her son, in Candida or in Jack Tanner, a closer inspection of them will reveal the binding operations of the Life Force. However else it may fit into the greater system of Shavian thought, the Life Force fundamentally binds Shaw to society and to the cosmos through his mother. For better or for worse, it is the marriage bond of his unconscious to his conscious, the leaven of his mind, the mortar of his imagination, in sum, the apotheosis of the "good breast."

With the early mother's powerful image looming ever large in Shaw's unconscious mind and impelling him away from instinctual encounters toward independence and autonomy, woman is scarcely conceivable, much less adaptable as a future love-object to be possessed through sexual energy. That would be regressive, disturb repression, and provoke too much anxiety. The eternal feminine draws him, like Goethe's Faust, ever upward. Growth becomes an ongoing, ascending slope, not a circle or spiral, There is neither an oedipal defeat, nor an Odyssean quest for home and Penelope; in short there is no fusion or internal development of maternal components except perhaps into the Life Force itself. The evolutionary advance of life becomes the only ideal and acceptable goal, the one Shavian appetite to be glutted, but the inner evolution of the mother into a future love-object is not to occur.

The troublesome accommodation between instinct and object

that Shaw struggled with is reflected in his sexual relations. Ellen Terry he loved passionately by mail; he gave up his virginity at twenty-nine to an amorous widow of forty-four for whom he had no special feeling; he aroused married women only to frustrate them and bewilder their husbands by taking flight; and after a period in his thirties which reads in his diary like notes for Restoration Comedy (JE), followed by a "mystical betrothal" to May Morris, he wed at forty-three a woman of forty-two with whom sex was ruled out, only several years later to initiate an affair with Mrs. Pat Campbell which he would neither consummate nor terminate. Perhaps a psychoanalyst would conclude that Shaw was psychically impotent. Shaw once appeared to acknowledge as much in conversation, but he also denied it (SS, p. 175). Certainly our common plight stemming from the "long and difficult evolution" of the instincts imposed by culture to the degree that "something in the nature of the sexual instinct itself is unfavorable to the achievement of absolute gratification," was greatly magnified in Shaw's cleavage between desire and object. It is, up to a point, the familiar story : the few women he could make passionate love to he could not respect, and the women he could respect inhibited his sexual passion. He was both very sexy ("Irish gallantry," "Free Masonry of the theatre") and very repressed, which must have perplexed almost everyone. "You may count the women who have left me nothing more to desire on less than the fingers of one hand," he wrote to Frank Harris (FH, p. 221). "To these occasions I attach comparatively no importance : it is the others which endure" (an explanation that hardly would have set Harris's male mind at rest). Of course his solution ultimately is the very one that Freud pointed out in the paper on which this discussion is based.

> This very incapacity in the sexual instinct to yield full satis-
> faction as soon as it submits to the first demands of culture

becomes the source, however, of the grandest cultural achievements. (IV, pp. 203–16)

But in the area of sexual substitutes, try as he might, Shaw just
never made it.[20]

COLLECTIVE ALTERNATES

He never made it partly for the reasons described above,
but also because other forces were beginning to prevail in his
personality. From the interruption of his early demands and
the intolerable prospect of emptiness, he made necessary instinctual repudiations and identifications, but he also became in
his childhood an enormous consumer of, for lack of a better
word, reality. Put in different language, he may have invested
"peripheral objects" (or "collective alternates") with some of the
libidinal interest and the tendency toward global incorporation
derived from the "primary object" (the nurturing and with-
drawing mother) (PA). Here his father helped out in
encouraging him to read, to look at pictures, and to go to the

[20] Either the mark of trauma and repetition–compulsion are stamped
on Shaw's relations with women, or the arm of coincidence is uncannily
long. Can it all be accidental that he chooses for his sexual initiation a widow
of 44; begins his intimate, "completely satisfying relationship" of correspondence with Ellen Terry when she is 44; marries a woman of 42; becomes
involved with Mrs. Pat Campbell at 47; when his mother was 43 at
the time she deserts her family to flee with Lee to London? Perhaps, but
what about the fact that Shaw himself is 43 when he deserts the London
home of his mother to marry? And if there is a note of retaliation here, is
there not also a further sign of identification, because it was Elizabeth
Gurly who reacted by marriage against her father's abandoning her by
his second marriage, which in effect Shaw does also. Perhaps that is
what identification with the agressor means: doing to others what has
been done to you.
For more on the numbers game, see the exchange between Don Juan
and the Old Woman of 77 (double sum of 4 + 3), written when Shaw's
mother was 70 (MS, pp. 605f.). And as Shaw responds to his mother's
Dublin departure by teaching himself music (see below), so he deals with
his London desertion of his mother by composing the Mozartian "Don
Juan in Hell."

theater. "Shakespeare was like mother's milk to me" (AH, p. 30). Dublin's musical society, with his mother singing and Lee conducting, was rehearsing in his own parlor. Aesthetic objects became his real substitute-gratifications. "What power did I find in Ireland religious enough to redeem me from this abomination [his childhood] of desolation? Quite simply, the power of Art" (EP, p. 77). "Only the fictions of fine art gave me any satisfaction" (EP, p. 78). Art, music, and literature began feeding his boyhood hungers; politics, philosophy, and drama continued the process. He incorporated the things around him with the same ravenous appetite that used up the healthy qualities of his father's personality as well as Lee's and a Rabelaisian uncle or two. That is why in tracing Shaw's ideas, one ends up studying Carlyle, Mill, Ruskin, Arnold, Shelley, Nietzsche, Schopenhauer, Darwin, Bergson, Bunyan, and even Plato, to mention the more prominent authors his Gargantuan capacities devoured. In order to study the plays seriously, we need to know the English popular theater along with Shakespeare, Molière, Ibsen, Strindberg, and Chekhov. When William Archer gave him a French play to adapt, Shaw used up all the plot before he had finished his own second act and stunned Archer by asking for another play. In the course of time the redeeming "power of Art" will be called upon as the medium for representing the Life Force.

Like Walt Whitman he contained multitudes, and much of it started with the displacement of a powerful appetite seeking the pleasure of maternal love and nourishment, unable to accommodate itself to genital love, and settling in large part for the reality of the world.

> To most women one man and one lifetime make a world. I require populations and historical epochs to engage my interests seriously . . . love is only diversion and recreation to me. (LS, p. 801)

While we take this with a full shaker of salt, let us also agree that if he did not secure early satisfactions, their frustrations did lead him into the universe of art and hurled him into the affairs of the world where his creative romance could be played out to the fullest and where he kept himself too busy most of the time to dwell on early losses. An original person, if not an original thinker.

NARCISSUS, OR THE BIRTH OF EGO

When Shaw began assembling materials for his autobiographical work, *Sixteen Self Sketches,* he rummaged through some nearly century-old letters written by his father to his mother away on a visit to her father, when Shaw was a one-year-old Sonny. Excerpts from them open the book:

Poor whiggedie whellow was very sick in his stomach about 1 o'clock in the night, but he is all right and as brisk as ever this morning. Nurse attributes it to some currants he ate.

The young beggar is getting quite outrageous. I left him this morning roaring and heaving like a bull. I expect he will be able to run down the street to meet you when you are returning.

Nurse is in great blood about having the young chap able to walk when you come back. . . .

Bobza honors me with his company and we have walking matches together.

. . . Bob is growing very unruly. The *threshing season* is approaching and he had better look out or I'll flail him.

I will feel disappointed every morning that Bob does not stagger into me with a letter from you—and desperate fighting

there is to get it from him. The young ruffian tore the newspaper this morning.

Nurse said to me this morning that Bob has her nearly
broken down! And indeed he must be a very tiresome young-
ster to mind altogether without any help.

I delivered you kisses to Yup [the second oldest sister] and
Bob but contrary to your instruction I fobbed a few for myself
—you know how sweet a stolen kiss is!

Poor Bob is annoyed with his teeth. . . .

Leaving little Bobza teething in an aura of robust normality,
we may wonder what Shaw wanted to tell us, apart from his
thesis that genius is banal in its everyday perspective. Did he
want to expose his sense of being maternally abandoned, perhaps as symbolic of psychic events and his own self-sufficiency?
Or, simply that he walked and teethed and fell and was made
over, like most babies—in order to reassure himself of his
normality? The facts are tantalizing. The parents appear interested in his growth, take pride in his infantile achievements; but
what truly were their expectations for him? The mother's goal
for her family soon becomes making a life for herself apart from
it. From the father's calling his son "Bob" in order to catch the
fancy of Sir Robert Shaw, a second cousin and member of the
gentry, are betrayed the father's social aspirations as well as the
inept, "magical" manner in which he sought to fulfill them.
But realistic expectations for the "young beggar" either do not
appear (as evidenced in the way he was shuttled about from
school to school and finally to work as a cashier) or do not
survive the parents' increasing absorption in their own needs.
And so in a singular sort of way Shaw was loved, and in a
singular sort of way he was abandoned.

Piecing together the family romance along with Shaw's memories and the arrangement of these quoted letters, we may suppose he combined experiences of nurture as well as neglect of care as well as deprivation, into the parental images he incorporated into his emerging self. Certainly the internalized authority of an exalted and stern mother, with the favor of the one aspect being contingent on satisfying the demands of the other, would strengthen his defensive needs to overcome primitive oral urges. I propose this because without the mother's sustaining love more of the burden was thrust upon the child who perforce must rise gravitationally rather than climb anaclitically, and a severe and austere ego-ideal could better take command of the instincts and do so less by wooing them than by invading their domain and erecting strenuous controls and prohibitions on the flow of instinctual energy. The introjected "bad breast" begins as a sternly prohibitive "No" to the instinctual cravings, and soon very likely produces negative ego states or self-representations. However, it is in the nature of renunciations that one forgoes a "momentary pleasure, uncertain in its results . . . in order to gain in the new way an assured pleasure coming later" (IV, p. 18), and thereby one "expects to be rewarded by being loved all the more" (MO, p. 149). Hence if bad ego states and self-representations can be externalized, this time onto the real world—for example, school authorities, capitalists, theater managers, medical men, and so forth—the ego will then be purified, and the approving and bountiful "good breast" may step in to heal narcissistic wounds and promise satisfactions—in some indefinite future.

These intrapsychic operations bear one further look. First of all one notices Shaw's extreme reliance on mental control and his peculiar, manic life-style of improvisation and sternness: the exuberant sprite who preaches revolutions, or the self-styled ascetic who writes plays—either way the combination jars. It is as though his early superego treated the instincts much as the mother had appeared to treat the child, for her neglect would have been experienced as harsh and cruel, if not at times nearly murderous, and only later on be construed as liberating. In order to survive, his ego, holding up the mirror of the idealized parent image, necessarily deflected instinctual drives for its own ends and built up a formidable energy system at their expense. An inveterate reformer, this was possibly his first, albeit unacknowledged, reform—that, and ridding himself of negative self-representations. Both of these would have taken heavy tolls. The master-slave relationship of will to body, with the body turned into a machine proliferating various working parts, is described in *Back To Methuselah* (p. 253). And Shaw's habitual downgrading of the physical or the sexual, as well as the basis for the frequent criticism of the master puppeteer manipulating his stage puppets, may spring from these processes.

Whatever its components, the maternal image turns into the ego-ideal and subsequently the object of narcissistic libido. As he measured up to this ego-ideal, principally during a period of extended adolescence, he gave flesh and blood substance to his own ideal, and while giving the impression of sprite-like self-sufficiency, he reduced the frustrations from early object-relations along with the need to carry out later role identifications.[21] Thus

[21] Another way to express this process is that the "ego experiences the influence of the ego ideal ["the internalized image of perfection"] as coming from above and that of the narcissistic self as coming from below," so that one can say "man is *led* by his ideals but *pushed* by his ambitions." There are periods in the "lives of the very fortunate, in which ambitions and ideals coincide" (Heinz Kohut, "Forms and Transformations of Narcissism," *J. Am. Psychoanalytic Assoc.* 14 (1966): 250f). Because there appears to be so little dissatisfaction expressed by Shaw, and few recriminations or self-criticism either over his personal life or over his work in proportion to his undertakings and achievements, he may at least have nearly been one of the "very fortunate."

Certainly conflict subsides when ideals and ambitions converge, but do they dissolve into something new as well? Can this be what Shaw was getting at when he denied being ambitious ("my timid want of push") or competitive and took for granted the fact of his genius? And can his

the peculiar convergence of early instinctual frustrations, withdrawal from objects, and regression of libido back into the ego for mastery are processes that are going to reappear as an extreme overvaluation of the early instinctual object, a remoteness in future relationships, a search for purified ego states, and the persistence of grandiosity—broadly speaking, narcissism.

Narcissism floods through Shaw's life. It infuses his identity as writer and profoundly affects his concentration, be it critical or creative, on art, and what was intimated by Freud's descriptive sketch of obsessional narcissism (p. 17) may now be better filled in. Significantly, it is Shaw himself who from the outset institutes and enforces his ascetic measures. "I do not smoke. Tea I also bar, and coffee" (LS, p. 262), not to mention all stronger stimulants. This "I" is the ego speaking, not the will of the parent, nor the norm of society through the superego, but the "I," which may be proudly rooted in stern necessity but remains accountable only to itself. Having insufficiently internalized either parent as a sound basis for values and internal control, he formed a most unusual superego, one with its stern and forbidding side as well as its sustaining and loving side, and one that does not compel his ego to be answerable to parents, society, or, in effect, to any external authority. Partly because he does not succumb to paranoid projections of his early drives, he does not seem compelled to act out his defiance or to rebel against himself. And he never permits a fall from grace. A conjugation of Shaw's mind might run, "I can," "I will," "we

gravitational rise be a way of describing the upward pull of narcissistic libido by the ego ideal? See also "On Narcissism," IV.

"The development of the ego consists in a departure from the primary narcissism and results in a vigorous attempt to recover it. This departure is brought about by means of the displacement of libido to an ego-ideal imposed from without, while gratification is derived from the attainment of this idea.

"At the same time the ego has put forth its libidinal object-cathexes. It becomes impoverished in consequence both of these cathexes and of the formation of the ego-ideal, and it enrichs itself again both by gratification of its object-love and by fulfilling its ideal" (p. 57).

must," but never "I should," "I ought," or "I had better."[22]

His purified ego made him lovable both to himself and to others, or at least impervious to their criticisms. His executive and exhortative superego predisposed him to sympathetic rapport with the great minds of the century like Goethe, Schopenhauer, Nietzsche, and Carlyle, who one way and another were concerned with the preeminence of Will. His confidence in the intelligence of his adaptations inclined him to be more receptive to the Functional Adaptation of Lamarck than to the Circumstantial Selection of Darwin, and to the "inevitability of gradualism" in Fabianism rather than to the social analogues of Darwinism that he found in Capitalism or revolutionary Marxism. Shaw liked to quote Butler's indictment of Darwin as banishing mind from the universe, but Shaw would banish the irrational, either as chance or as instinct, from the universe in favor of the super-rationalism of Creative Evolution. His preference for Lamarck over Darwin signified a need for control from within to being controlled from without by a "senseless mob of forces" (PBM, p. viii); even so, his concept of the Life Force attempted to rescue the world from the damaging hands of man.

Perhaps what ought to be emphasized is that Shaw's control over himself was dictated less by society than by the prospect of instinctual urges and infantile fears overwhelming him. And although Weissman's assertion that "throughout his life, his ego was master of the situation" (p. 160) may be an oversimplification (Freud reminds us that the ego is not master of its own house), Shaw in many if not all ways developed a formidable ego. It seems to have taken over some functions of the superego, so that not only is there little tension between the two, there is also less of the usual resultant sense of guilt; and those stringent

[22] Robert Brustein in *The Theatre of Revolt,* p. 204, pursues the implications of Shavian imperatives.

oral prohibitions and taboos may be seen as an effective instance of Shaw's emerging self's exercising authority *in loco parentis* over instinct. Overdone the prohibitions may have been, but done they were with such finality of purpose, even though he was twenty-five before he consciously avowed his vegetarianism, that a liberation of energy from the draining away of anxiety and frustration over basic unmet needs resulted. This *coup d'état* for Shavian economy appeared to be so successful that he once warned against making saints of those who "abstain from the ordinary pleasures of society because they have no taste for them" (LS, p. 280). And because he was free to worship what he could not possess, he could say, "you do not lead the heavenly life by abstaining : you abstain because you lead the heavenly life" (LS, p.505). You do not go to church, you find your way to the "cathedral within." And it is precisely this sense of ego liberation, born of fusing with its ideal in the superego—and behind so much of what distinguishes Shaw's personality for us —that fulfills intrapsychically the manic defense's positive goal of achieving a purified ego state and re-fusing mother and infant in the blissful, pre-depressive nursing situation.

But his victories were costly. Possibly deriving from his earliest conflicts, there is an aversion to instinctual pleasures, an uneasiness with many emotions, and an inability to cope with loss. The first Shaw tended to denigrate as sensuality, the others to dismiss as sentimentality. Growing up, he feasted on art and was "overfed on honey dew" daydreams, but they nourished his imagination more than his instincts. His sexual diet had to make do with the foreplay of *billets-doux,* flirtations, and gallantries, as his stomach had to settle for carrots and cabbage. His ego turned the fatty tissue of narcissism into its own brain and muscle, and as the ego grew strong through the exercise of its manifold and unceasing projects and campaigns, the id suffered the withering effects of deprivation.

In its *loco parentis* capacity the Shavian ego redoubled its authority and vigorously presided over the conquered domain of the instincts. This autocratic strain provides one basis for his otherwise unaccountable affiliation with the political dictatorships of Hitler, Mussolini, and Stalin. Because his narcissistic blurring of the self-other differentiation fostered a like-to-like way of perceiving, he tended to see himself in them; like him they were not only strong-minded men but the magical children and "social nobodies" who had also, as he once claimed for Hitler and Stalin, risen by "sheer gravitation" (EP, p. 339). He attributed an "irrepressible sense of humour" to Stalin, and admired what he called his efficiency and sense of responsibility. After reading *Mein Kampf,* Shaw allowed, "Of course he's mad on some points, but who isn't?" (HP, pp. 208, 427). And like him, they were willing to stand up against the popular will, the "mob of appetites." Eventually historical events compelled him to change some of his political views, but by then the blind spots in the vision of the advanced thinker had become all too plain.

His staunch and rather insular ego, especially as it faced the public, became increasingly stern and peremptory with the years (HP, p. 469), perhaps as the wish-component behind his renunciations dimmed. Today we find cold comfort in the fact that in opposition to the brutality of Stalin's extermination policies Shaw advocated putting extermination on a humane basis (RR, p. 94). This has been called Shavian irony, but the cruelty is there all the same. The people, like the appetites and instincts, must be governed; the ruler will decide how. "Every civilized authority must draw a line between the tolerable and intolerable" (SS, p. 156). The day will come when the exterminating angel will descend to separate the "social nuisances" from the "social assets" (PSU, p. 538). (He also advocated the extermination of the Forsytes as a social type, and those who have been exposed to twenty-six televised chapters of the *Forsyte Saga* may desperately wish it had been done.) But on the other hand his good angel never allowed him to become too deeply embittered or cynical, and one can also detect a personally mellow tolerance lighting his sunset years.

It must be clear that in Shaw's case narcissism cannot be taken in the ordinary sense of passive, complacent self-love, or clinically as lingering autoeroticism. In large part it must have stemmed from fears of abandonment and a desperate striving for independence. The family romance having well-nigh eclipsed the real parents, he can proclaim that "the Life Force had given me in my boyhood an excessive regard for self-preservation" (SS, p. 170), and he never lost it. Outer reality, represented by his negligent parents and their insensitive servants, led him to say, "I was taken—and took myself—for what I was, a disagreeable little beast" (PC, pp. 52–53). He once confided that his treatment at home went beyond parental neglect. "When we misbehaved like untrained children . . . we were simply disappointing and inferior little animals with our father's weaknesses" (OB, by permission of the Harvard College Library). And when he went out it was no better. "The nurse-maid who took me out to exercise me just as she might have taken a dog, took me into the slums where she had friends instead of into handsomer and more salubrious places" (EP, p. 78). His earlier bad introjects were probably reinforced by these shame-laden experiences and became negative self-representations, further damaging self-esteem.

But if the voice of Reality thus spoke to the young Shaw, Reality could be changed. "Naturally," he continues, "I hated the slums and the dwellers therein. I still want to have the slums demolished and the dwellers exterminated." "Thus were laid," he affirms elsewhere, "the foundations of my lifelong hatred of poverty and the devotion of all my public life to the task of exterminating the poor and rendering their resurrection for ever impossible" (LM, pp. 856–57). The reader may take these remarks at face value or seek for further significance in them. I think that the poor, being socially rejected, are all too reminiscent of his own deprived ego state, and that he speaks of them as unlovingly as he himself must often have felt. Very likely he wanted to get rid of them as he wanted to get rid of his own poor—that is, both weak and bad—feelings about himself. Certainly if the Shavian reformer evolved from these early experiences as is claimed, it is not from any profound sympathy for slum dwellers, with whom he had relatively little contact, except for a time as a vestryman, or for the proletariat, in whom he had even less confidence and never idealized—the poor remaining largely an abstraction, a class, never touched lives—but more likely his reforming urges sprang from a need to wipe out his own early deprivations and unjust humiliations by externalizing them where they could be corrected or undone, and restore self-esteem. His contemporaries were shocked at the vehemence of his wishes to eliminate poverty by eliminating the poor and his refusal to grant them any dignity, but if there were no poor, he probably felt, then he was not impoverished, and in the meantime he could feel reassured by keeping the poor on the outside and by working against poverty. But he did not identify with them or with any class, except to a degree with his own Fabian circle, because it did not become his emerging nature to identify with others so much as to get others to identify with him and his causes. For beauty, not poverty, he reserved his empathy.

Intimately related to his narcissism is his exhibitionism. The one counteracted lack of object-love with self-love; the other warded off his superfluous decline into oblivion with self-display. It also probably shielded his shyness. Like the professional performer's, Shaw's exhibitionism is rather impersonal, impervious, and always controlled. It can be confirmed by an audience but never surpassed by public acclaim. Indeed, the presence of so much libido in the ego makes the self seem more real than the surrounding world, and the deeply felt conviction of the narcissist that he has himself if nothing else can be reassuring when it is not depressing. When the question of Shaw's receiving the Order of Merit was brought up by his admirers, he replied ruefully, "I have already conferred it on myself" (HP, p. 374). And speaking of himself as the real King Magnus in *The Apple Cart*, he confided, "Never having been offered a throne, I have had to seize one and crown myself." (HP, p. 381). In 1896 he told an interviewer, "I haven't the least doubt of my success. It may not be a commercial success. The public may fail in their part of the business. But I shall not fail in mine" (CR, p. 537). This blending of the impervious with the sense of the ridiculous underlies much of Shavian humor. It is the type that Freud referred to as the triumph of "narcissism, the ego's victorious assertion of its own invulnerability."

> It refuses to be hurt by arrows of reality or to be compelled to suffer. It insists that it is impervious to wounds dealt by the outside world, in fact, that these are merely occasions for affording it pleasure. ("On Humour," V, p. 217)

Inseparable from his imagination, Shavian narcissism is the opposite of Keat's "negative capability," which enters emphatically into the objective world; it is also antithetical to the strategy of the great modern writers who, as Stephen Spender has pointed out, suffer the modern world to work on them, forging their sensibilities.[23] Shaw went to work on the world. He drew everything into himself. The world of ideas and the real world around him—social classes, Capitalism, Christianity— are taken in but never quite felt as real until they become Shavian. He re-creates them as an imagination of reality; and

[23] Stephen Spender, *The Struggle of the Modern* (Berkeley and Los Angeles: University of California Press, 1963); pp. 72f.

this inner model, with its psychic energies, weights, tensions, and determinants, can be viewed as mediator between self and world, through which he related to his surroundings and at times to which he related instead of his surroundings.

In fact, there is a disturbing "borderline" quality about Shaw apparent in his overvaluation of a mental construct of the self at the expense of the physical being. It suggests deep narcissistic wounds when the self was little more than a body-ego and perhaps not fondled, but neglected and dropped, as it were. Within the purified "mental self," the fantasy of being loved may thrive and attempt in grandiose fashion to make things up. But without straying too far from the present context and poaching on R. D. Laing, one may sense a marked inner division nonetheless. To say, "I am a writing machine" is to express more than a comic self-body relationship. And consider again these remarks: "My kingdom was not of this world; I was at home in the realm of my imagination, and at ease only with the mighty dead." Not belonging to the society of man bespeaks depersonalization as well as shyness. Not to be at home in the world is not to be at home in the body and perhaps not to be loved in the body. It is more nearly to be an object. To be at ease only with the mighty dead may not be anything so patent as a death wish, but at least it may intimate that the hardy self-preservation forces in Shaw illustrate the Freudian paradox of the ego-instincts being indentured to the death-instincts, since the aim of life is to die *naturally*. And in this context the Life Force may serve as a safeguard against death-instincts.

On a cognitive level narcissism may disclose an underlying anxiety in differentiating between self and other. Certainly it made his perceptions as often perplexing as it marred the brilliance of his observations. For example, Shaw tries to incorporate Christianity into the scheme of Creative Evolution: ". . . the driving force behind Evolution is a will-to-live, and to live, as Christ said long before, more abundantly" (PBM, p. xxxii). But then, the problems of a universal genius are not everyman's (and more recently priests have tried to incorporate Evolution into Christianity).[24] Shaw's narcissistic *modus operandi* often tended to blur mental distinctions and gloss over real differences.[25] This may help account for his Shavianizing Ibsen and upgrading Brieux, while virtually ignoring Strindberg and Wedekind. His prolonged infatuation with twentieth-century dictators has been noted. He was asked in later years whether any place had impressed him during his recent globetrotting: "No. One place is very much like another." Had anybody impressed him? "No. They're all human beings" (HP, p.388). Nor did the differences among religions impress him. "The Creator, the Holy Ghost, the Word (properly the Thought), the Cosmic Energy, the *Elan Vital,* the Divine Spark, the Life Force, the Power that makes for Righteousness (call it what you will)" are all essentially the same human formulation when it comes to their fallibility (EP, p. 232).

He is most candid in the following conversation with Hesketh Pearson:

"All my plays are about myself . . . and my friends."
"Were you ever particularly fond of any of your friends?"
"I was with them, but when we separated I did not miss them."
"Then I will put it another way: Whose company did you most enjoy?"
"My own." (HP, p. 436)

Leonard Woolf said he was "personally the kindest, most friendly most charming of men, yet personally he was almost the most impersonal person I have known."

[24] Daniel J. Leary, "The Evolutionary Dialectic of Shaw and Teilhard: A Perennial Philosophy," *The Shaw Review* 9, no. 1 (Jan. 1966): 15–33.
[25] Richard Ohmann *Shaw: The Style and the Man* (Middleton, Conn., 1962).

> You might easily flatter yourself that you were the one person in Europe to whom at that moment the famous George Bernard Shaw wanted to talk, but if you happened to look into that slightly fishy, ice-blue eye of his, you got a shock. It was not looking at you; you were nowhere in its orbit; it was looking through you or over you into a distant world or universe inhabited almost entirely by G.B.S., his thought and feelings, fancies and fantasies.[26]

And who is G.B.S.?

> Oh, one of the most successful of my fictions, but getting a bit tiresome, I should think. G.B.S. bores me except when he is saying something that needs saying and can best be said in the G.B.S. manner. G.B.S. is a humbug. (SS, p. 89)

Whether viewed as mask, mental construct, or writing machine, G.B.S. enables a voice to speak through it, an "I" that had to create a "fantastic personality fit and apt for dealing with men, and adaptable to the various parts I had to play as author, journalist, orator, politician, committee man, or man of the world, and so forth" (LS, p. 801; IM, p. 670). G.B.S. strikes me as the omnipotent, fictional impostor of manic denial and a strategy for preserving vital fantasies, but the more honest "I" behind all the Shavian personae, postures, and roles is also the prodigious executive of mental energy, distributing it wherever called for and creating means for mediating between the vital center of life and the great world. As a young man Shaw found that "life only realizes itself by functioning energetically in all directions" (LS, p. 463), and apart from sexual generativity he lived his discovery in good faith. The writing machine becomes virtually a witty and wry ego-ideal in its rather manic wish to be self-sufficient and continuously productive, free from psychic conflict and reminders of emotional deficiency—for even in this protean omnipotence of the self, an alarming note sounds.

[26] Leonard Woolf, *Beginning Again* (New York, 1963), p. 122.

"I am the world's pack-horse," he once confided to Ellen Terry.
"And it beats my lean ribs unmercifully" (ET, p. 216).

Narcissism may be seen then as allied with defense, as
depersonalizing and leveling, as second best, as standing alone,
as signifying a failure in object-relations, but also as reservoir of
energy, adaptation, and forward step in the struggle for independence.[27] The large accumulation of libido within the ego
inevitably expanded into the true Shavian grandiosity, reversing

[27] Kohut holds that "while the exhibitionistic-narcissistic urges may
be considered as the predominant drive aspect of the narcissistic self, the
grandiose fantasy is its ideational content" (p. 253). It can be supposed
that Shaw's manic defense of denial had the purpose of preserving the
grandiose fantasy and the maximum or original narcissism. Kohut illustrates
this kind of fantasy from the life of Winston Churchill, in which a famous
escape is derived from the fantasy of flying. Shaw frequently employs
expressions of flight and ascent to color events with magical qualities.
Thus he rose by gravitation instead of climbing the ladder of natural
development. We will be discussing soon the celestial effects of certain
women on his volatile psyche. The two somewhat different approaches to
Shaw's development taken in this chaper may be reconciled by the persistence of grandiose material in the family romance, about which more is
said in the Conclusion.

In addition Kohut maintains that the "adaptive value of narcissism"
has not been given full credit. Of the transformations of narcissism he
lists the following: 1) creativity; 2) empathy; 3) capacity to recognize one's
mortality; 4) sense of humor; 5) wisdom.

In this light Ernest Jones's early paper "The God Complex" (1913)
makes amusing reading. Very roughly, it sketches the characteristics of
the individual who remains bound to his narcissistic condition. Jones's
type takes a great interest in language, poses as an authority on literary
style, and is fond of talking (monologuing), speech-making, and lecturing.
He sees himself as a prophet, while remaining aloof and inaccessible; he
shrouds himself in mystery. Though an atheist himself, because he "cannot
suffer the existence of any other God," he takes a great interest in religion,
particularly the mystical side. He has an "exaggerated *desire to be loved,*"
and is convinced of his own immortality. "The belief in self-creation, and
rebirth phantasies, are practically constant features." (This should be
recalled in the Conclusion.) He puts forth "far-reaching schemes of social
reform, He believes himself to be omniscient, and tends to reject all new
knowledge. Authority is viewed as intolerant through an association with
the "wicked father." All these traits can be found in Shaw, *mutatis mutandis.*
In a postscript Jones correlates his composite portrait with Melanie Klein's
emerging views of the manic phase (*Essays in Applied Psychoanalysis,* 2:
244-65).

But perhaps Winnicott should be given the final word. He notes that
flights into omnipotent fantasies do not so much present inner reality as
defend against its acceptance ("The Manic Defence," p. 130).

his cruel origins and early humiliations. After his "devil of a childhood," "it turned out later on that I was born a Shake-spearean genius" (SS, p. 170). Only becoming a genius would make up for such basic deprivations, and he became one. Along the way he was well served by his narcissistic qualities, especially the "independence of external factors" and the capacity not to be "easily overawed" by others, as when he was attempting to have his early novels published:

> Fifty or sixty refusals without a single acceptance forced me into a fierce self-sufficiency. I became undiscourageable, acquiring a superhuman insensitiveness to praise or blame. (IM, p. 676)

"During all these years," he wrote in 1896, underscoring the obsessional features, "I have acquired a certain power of work, and hardened myself to stand unscraped by many knife edges that cut ordinary folk" (LS, p. 625). Persevering without becoming self-serving, he can write:

> I sometimes dislike myself so much that when some irritable reviewer chances at that moment to pitch into me with zest, I feel unspeakably relieved and obliged. But I never dream of reforming, knowing that I must take myself as I am and get what work I can out of myself. (PMS, p. 515)

As a music critic he liked to boast that "never in my life have I penned an impartial criticism," and he held that "criticism written without personal feeling is not worth reading." More-over, when his "critical mood is at its height, personal feeling is not the word: it is passion: the passion for artistic perfection —for the noblest beauty of sound, sight, and action—that rages in me." The personal narcissistic element is merely a given and a point of departure; for once stimulated by a work of art, he becomes obsessed with one passion for perfection, and mere personal pleasure or disappointment is dissolved in the "higher" pleasures of serious work.

Considered as a desperately chosen and hard-won adaptation, narcissism is one response to possibly the most elemental of anxieties: abandonment, loss of love, helplessness. The worst suffering of the souls of the damned in Dante's Hell is their separation from Divine Love—a theological condition reinforced by psychological fact if not derived from it. Shaw's need to deny the emotional impact of death has been noted. "Our indifference to one another's deaths marked us as a remarkably unsentimental family" (SS, p. 149). One morning in 1943, he entertained some friends by trying to get them to say whether they noticed anything different about him. Was he wearing new boots? No. On and on it went. At last they gave up, and he told them, "I became a widower at 2:30 this morning" (HP, p. 418). He was not callous, and gregariousness can be related to mourning just as manic denial can be related to depression, but in any case he appeared unable to investigate the meaning of loss and to connect it with possibilities of further growth. His inappropriate levity and joking is an admission of this. Apparently there were emotional ties related to dependency that could not be severed, and a great deal of his compulsive activity may be seen as strivings to assure himself that he is independent and self-operating (an ideal machine) and not threatened by emotional deprivation or breakdown. Either woman must not die, or death must not be final. Joan of Arc, burned at the stake (as his mother was cremated?), is brought back to life in the Epilogue, where comedy has the best lines and immortality the last word.

His narcissism, from which so much followed, is all the more significant because it differs from the usual male defenses, which stem from castration fears. Since fuller treatment of this question awaits us in the next chapter, a few remarks here will suffice. First, the prior outlays of defensive energies. Second, the inadequacy of the parents as sustaining authorities. Their own lives were hardly models of propriety, and at some point they apparently stopped bothering. To their son they were "utterly uncoercive" (SS, p. 25). It might be added that a child needs a degree of exposure to genital attitudes or behavior from key figures in his life before he fully engages this new stage. I do not mean to compare Shaw to Harlow's apes, who cannot perform coitus unless they have previously watched it; I do want to suggest that growth is at least in part a learned process and that Shaw's development, while it may not have been limited by his surroundings, was inseparable from them. His father's and uncles' Dionysian antics, his mother's transplant of Lee, and Lee's exhibitionism may have formed a wildly phallic but plainly pre-genital society around Shaw. Instead of real organs there were musical instruments, bottles, and batons —pseudo organs that belied their owners' own problems in handling loss—stage props that were part of the larger play-acting, acting-out, and theatricalism of the Shavian household. These factors support the impression that the reality Shaw found himself surrounded by was itself rather fantastic, with a manic topography of its own that would reinforce a prolongation of his own fantasy-world, and as a result of these and other factors yet to be considered, his libido did not become genitally organ-ized to any great degree, for when his ego-ideal was formed, it apparently neither included sexual performance nor completely ruled sex out: its ideals and values lay elsewhere (PA, p. 59). The hypomanic sprite is to be implanted in the "mercurial mind that recognizes the inevitable instantly and faces it and adapts itself accordingly" (SS, p. 203).

In vain one scans his life for men he feared, revered, or even loved. There were many he liked, and his best and most enduring friendships (William Archer, Sidney Webb) were working ones. He was a singular controversialist who never sustained quarrels, personalized his attacks, or suffered litigation;

his aggression went into the vehemence of his verbal attacks and the creation of his iconoclastic plays. It cannot be proved, but it seems likely that the women in his life—especially those he kept at a distance or fled from—did not threaten him so much with castration as with the more primitive prospect of cannibalism. It may not be an infallible rule that castration anxiety will more likely be manifested interpersonally, whereas a certain remoteness of relationship and a diffusion of energies will reflect more basic anxiety, but it seems to hold for Shaw.[28]

[28] No one can get along in life without a certain amount of narcissism. And although much of it is normally retained, it is also used developmentally. Narcissism has been described as a "halfway phase between autoeroticism and object love" (Joseph Vrendenburg, "The Character of the Incest Object: A Study of Alternation between Narcissism and Object Choice," *American Imago* 14, no. 1 [1957]: 49. The author is summarizing the ideas of A. A. Brill). The psychodynamic role of narcissism is described by Freud:

> After the paternal function has been internalized so as to form the super-ego, the next task is to detach the latter from those persons of whom it was originally the psychical representative. In this remarkable course of development the agent employed to restrain infantile sexuality is precisely that narcissistic genital interest which centers in the preservation of the penis. (V, pp. 256-57)

In other works, the previously diffused narcissism becomes concentrated in the genital area, and after a period of latency, genital sexual aims begin to arise at puberty.

At puberty a series of interesting and puzzling events occurred in Shaw's life. He was thirteen when he became acquainted with Edward McNulty, also thirteen. They played cricket together; they acted in the school play of *Hamlet* (Shaw as Ophelia, McNulty as the Ghost); they visited art galleries, where Shaw admired the muscular masculinity of Michelangelo and expressed his own ambitions in art. During this period the boys were confidants; and when Shaw left school the next year, they corresponded fervently until Shaw left Dublin. By mutual consent they destroyed their letters as soon as they were read.

This kind of intense adolescent relationship seems unusual in Shaw's development partly by reason of its very normality and partly because McNulty stands alone as both a really intimate friend and a personal correspondent. Moreover, their ties seem based on pure affection rather than practical interests. We might interpret their friendship as reflecting a phase of phallic narcissism which can but does not necessarily take a homosexual turn before the parties move forward to female love-objects.

I assume that this is what happened in the life of McNulty, but it was not to be the path followed by Shaw. And McNulty records an incident that may have had a disruptive effect on Shaw. In a "queer little room" in Shaw's home where the boys often went to look at "prints and studies,"

However, one may insist that in the Freudian scheme of things castration fear is inevitable, because the child must in time notice the absence of penis on woman, usually mother or sister, and think to himself—ah-h, she is not so perfect as I thought, and if I pursue my incest wishes, father will inflict the same thing on me. In view of Shaw's intense involvement with his mother, we cannot avoid asking how he dealt with this situation, one so important that it must elude even the best of censors. In later life, he records the following experience:

> I well remember, when I was a small boy, receiving perhaps a greater shock than I have ever received since. I had been brought up in a world in which woman, the angel, presented to me the appearance of a spreading mountain, a sort of Primrose Hill. On the peak there was perched a small, pinched, upper part, and on top of that a human head. That, to me, at the period of life when one is young and receiving indelible

Shaw "proposed that I should pose as a nude model, and that he would do the same for me. I declined, because the door was close to and opposite the window, and I was afraid of catching cold" (EM, pp. 8-9). We can let pass whether it was a cold that McNulty was actually afraid of. But it does appear that Shaw was beginning to develop a phallic interest at an early, perhaps homosexual phase, which was frustrated at that point and did not, so far as anyone can determine, reappear until his genital interval from twenty-nine up to sometime before his marriage.

In any event the clandestine auspices under which Shaw conducted this abortive project suggest that the underlying intention was not solely for the sake of art.

It must have been broadly exhibitionistic; perhaps to compare his member with McNulty's, to ascertain if he was properly equipped, and to find out how the equipment was to be employed. McNulty's lack of cooperation did not frustrate Shaw's exhibitionism; it merely took a different turn following his "birth of moral passion," for as a young man his debating exercises, Hyde Park oratory, and lectures kept him continually on public display. He boasted of the personal bias in his criticism, and his prose in general has the purpose of exhibiting Shavian views. Certainly his plays are not unrelated to this disposition. In all these instances his generalized and far-ranging self-display seems to have more in common with the diffused bodily exhibitionism of the female than with the localized, phallic exhibitionism of the male—or perhaps, in view of the aggressive, energetic thrust of his prose, a singular combination of both sexes. See below (p. 100) where he pictures himself as a "sort of comet" [male], brandishing crystal tresses [female] in the sky."

These puzzling events, taken in the larger context of Shaw's life, raise doubts as to whether the "paternal function" was internalized.

impressions, was a woman. One day, when I was perhaps five years of age, a lady paid us a visit, a very handsome lady who was always in advance of the fashion. Crinolines were going out; and she had discarded hers. I, an innocent unprepared child, walking bang into the room and suddenly saw, for the first time, a woman not shaped like Primrose Hill, but with a narrow skirt which evidently wrapped a pair of human legs. I have never recovered from the shock, and never shall (PM, p. 173)

Clearly, the shock is determined by more than fashion styles, as Shaw would have us believe. The fact that it occurs at the crucial oedipal age of five will not go unnoticed, nor the likelihood that this is a screen memory and that he has distanced himself from a more acutely painful awareness by displacing the perception onto a "very handsome," transient, and anonymous lady. Castration is obliquely acknowledged, and we may take this early disillusionment as a sign that the existence of the phallic male must be accounted for and that in later years his mother will not be immune from his qualified criticism.[29]

[29] From this episode a more strictly psychoanalytic line of inquiry opens up. Shaw once explained that the wry face made by Eve when the serpent whispered the secret of reproduction to her was due to the "combination of the reproductive with the excretory organs and consequently of love with shame" (HP, p. 109). A further suggestion of the cloacal birth theory occurs in the portrayal of the "British home" as the "Holy of Holies," the "temple of honorable motherhood, innocent childhood, manly virtue and sweet wholesome national life," but which, "with a clever turn of the hand" can be "exposed as an Augean stables, so filthy that it would seem more hopeful to burn it down than to attempt to sweep it out" (PGM, p. 362). Certainly the sexual ignorance of the child who associates sexuality with dirt is given vent in Shaw's impertinent "marriage is legalized impurity," even though he professed the aim of making it "decent and reasonable." And while eventually I do work my way back to Shaw's sexual revulsion (in the Conclusion), I do not have sufficient confidence in the conclusion that Shaw was an "anally fixated child" as well as being a "latent homosexual" as has been argued by Lisbeth J. Sachs and Bernard H. Stern, "Bernard Shaw and His Women," *British Journal of Medical Psychology* 37 (1964): 343–50. Rather than simply stating that he was hostile to women, I would stress the ambivalence; rather than latent homosexuality, I would stress identification with procreativity. Rather than anal fixation I would prefer adjusting the reaction formations and the evident traits of super-rationalism, efficiency, and productiv-

Moreover, the Life Force itself will be depicted as flawed and imperfect, and he will consider himself when writing women's parts as a "first class ladies tailor" (PC, p. 15). For a woman is nothing less than a "man in petticoats," and his celebrated "secret of the extraordinary knowledge of women" is that he "always assumed that a woman is a person exactly like" himself (PM, p. 174).

IN THE GRIP OF HIS GIFT

We would expect Shaw's psychic energies for the most part to be organized in the area of his deepest concerns, that is, in the oral zone. It was there that he learned to master reality, just as his mother's talent for singing freed her from a hopeless marriage and enabled her to settle in London. And Shaw did not forget that it was Lee's mastery of teaching and conducting music that enabled him to mesmerize women, Mrs. Shaw included. Out of his oral concerns and from these oral models springs Shaw's lifelong and passionate involvement in speaking, in writing, and in language itself. The coincidence of his success in public speaking with his becoming a vegetarian may in fact signify that he had realized a more culturally advanced and acceptable oral activity. An ego that frowned on "chewing up dead bodies" could more easily countenance chewing up ideas and spewing out the dead systems of thought he found around him. Thus he once concluded a Fabian debate: "Marx is as dead as mutton. I, Bernard Shaw, have killed him."

So powerful is the word for Shaw that Henry Higgins can create practically *ex nihilo* a living person through speech exer-

---

ity, along with the splitting of good and bad objects (and their later externalizations onto economic systems) to fit onto the developmental paths already charted.

cises. The word made flesh is Liza, a recreation of Elizabeth Gurly Shaw, as pointed out by Philip Weissman when he reads the play backwards, or psychoanalytically.[30] Oral omnipotence displaced onto language re-creates and regains the love of the mother, while at the same time it permits weak, i.e., inadequate or "feminine" features in his personality to be externalized through the flower girl. She is the poor abandoned child whom Shaw rescues narcissistically (the rescue fantasy involves a self-rescue), and then separates himself from by reexternalizing as a full-grown woman, an oedipal love-object. But before incest can enter, the anti-romantic Shaw must break in. Knowing that one can not marry a fantasy of oneself any more than of one's mother, he has Higgins send Liza on her way to someone else, and then reinforces their separation with a prose epilogue. The play may also be a desperate attempt to deal with castration in Higgins's rescuing the lowly flower girl from the "gutter" and attempting to turn the little "guttersnipe" into a "duchess" by investing her via the family romance with the magic potency of language. But while language can finally only free Liza to assert her genuine femininity, fantasy can be made into autonomous art. For a creative artist such as Shaw, the externalized mother-image ultimately becomes the transformed work of art—the living sculpture of the stage. The act of love is the act of creation, but one does not live with it, one liberates it

[30] The psychoanalytic equation for the writer is words=milk, which derives from the nursing situation wherein sounds=liquid (Edmund Bergler, *The Writer and Psychoanalysis* (New York, 1954), pp. 69f; Arthur Wormhoudt is quoted in the passage cited). As interpreted by these authors, writing is an active defense against a passive need. This emboldens us to consider that the fount of Shaw's creativity springs from his profound identification with his mother, probably as aggressor. The artist, according to Tanner in *Man and Superman,* "steals the mother's milk and blackens it to make printer's ink to scoff at her and glorify ideal women" (p. 538). One of Shaw's precocious creative acts occurred when he "painted the whitewashed wall in my bedroom in Dalkey with watercolour frescoes of Mephistopheles" (IM, p. 666). It is almost as if this early self-image as a kind of oral demon emerges from and adheres to the "whitewashed wall" of the mother's body (see below, chapter 5; Norman Holland, p. 238).

for the world. Perhaps Shaw preferred the audience's applause for this feat rather than for a conventional love tryst.

The criticism that Shaw's plays are all talk and only talk is not well founded, although perhaps his worse ones seem that way. But in his best plays the overdetermined potency of language is qualified by the more potent Life Force, which can fling Higgins's "words, words, words" back in his face as Liza does, or can let the word-spinner weave his own trap as Ann Whitefield manages with Jack Tanner in *Man and Superman*.

Naturally, Shaw's lifelong concern with language cannot be separated from his playwriting, and a collection of his writings on language casts some light on their relationships.[31] It shows that an increasing obsession with language reform in the last years of his life, culminating in his will, which aimed at establishing a phonetic alphabet, may in some general way be in inverse proportion to the exercise of his creative powers. He first met the English phonetician Henry Sweet in 1879, the year of his first novel and his entrance into public speaking, but he did little publicly to further the cause of phonetics until after 1900. His interest seems to have reached a high water mark with *Pygmalion* in 1912 and then to have receded into the background until the 1940s. Perhaps it would be more accurate to say that throughout his life Shaw had deeply invested his energies in language and its uses; but in *Pygmalion,* when he took up the issue of phonetics in dramatic form and mythic parallel, allowing private psychological energies to enter into the construction, the result is his most pleasing and possibly enduring work if not his most serious and intellectually engaging one. His later works, like his early novels, are little read, and this may be in part because his obsession with language is split off from serious issues as well as psychological energies and is sidetracked into

31 Abraham Tauber, ed., *George Bernard Shaw on Language* (New York, 1963).

tedious repetitions of Shavian phonetics supported by too familiar, all-purpose polemics.

But if his argument for a revised "alfabet" of forty or forty-two letters based on sound rather than on custom, accident, or etymology is disappointing in itself, it does shed light on his conception of the artist. He eventually based his phonetic argument on economics. His system would save the writer up to twenty per cent of his time. This Shaw calculates would have enabled Shakespeare to compose another play, Dickens another novel or two. If Shaw is being disingenuous, he does not let on. What he overlooks is nothing so simple as inspiration breaking out of the confines of man-hours and work done, but that the artist from time immemorial has solved the problem of economy by unlocking the nuclear energies of image and symbol. An ounce of image is not worth a pound of prose because straight prose, no matter how torrentially poured on, can not produce an effect equivalent to that of an image. Criticism has long since alerted us to the radiating center of works of literature; and both Shakespeare's and Dickens's works have been described as expanded metaphors, and of course as much more. But it is probably because we sense in a Beckett play an extended metaphor of the human condition that we prefer *Waiting for Godot* to *Heartbreak House,* the play in which Shaw consciously attempts to give character, setting, and action metaphorical dimensions. But whereas the Beckettian metaphor expands to universal symbol, the Shavian metaphor is tied down to a virtually allegorical treatment of European society before the Great War and to a closed metaphor of the ship of state drifting onto the rocks. He is more successful when he attempts to allegorize the working of the Life Force in plays like *The Devil's Disciple*.

The three sources of universality in Shavian drama are: (1) the conventions of the popular theater that are perennial and often rooted in basic fantasies; (2) issues of lasting human concern that are variously presented by allegorical, musical, comical, or dialectical techniques; (3) modern parallels or inversions of myths. The myth can do for drama what the image does for lyric poetry. But however much Shaw enriched the myths of Don Juan and Pygmalion, he maintained a tight control over his use of sources and left them with a Shavian specificity of meaning. So far it appears that the nonverbal mode of primary process had as much difficulty gaining entrance to his work as direct instinctual gratification had difficulty gaining release in his life; but before we finish, this view may well be revised.

I can conclude this section by suggesting that owing to his early experiences, Shaw won great stores of mental energy for creative ends but became and to some extent remained depersonalized, as his late preoccupations with efficiency and economy for their own sake illustrate. To excel as a writer he must repeatedly wrest his energies away from the mechanical sphere of sheer verbal output into the creative; but there was a compulsive force behind his writing, which continually kept him favorably or unfavorably in the public eye, a defensive process possibly intended to overcome the polar fears of engulfment and abandonment. Although vast stretches in the last thirty years of his writing occur when the machine ran on after the mind had run down, the image of the Shavian machine perpetually feeding the mind of the British public is one I shall return to at the end of chapter 3. I will only note here that his writing machine was at best partially and intermittently under control, and with the years it may have become too nearly autonomous, just as he seems to have succeeded too well in imposing "G.B.S." on the English public. When he estimated near the end of his life that he averaged twelve words per minute, day in day out, year in year out, we can only wonder how far the machine prevailed over the genius. "As long as I live I must write," he wrote, nearing ninety-two. "If I stopped writing I should die for want of something to do" (PBB, p. 149). Too true, one may add, to be good.

THE SECRET OF GRAVITATION

Anna Freud has written that every individual from the outset of life is beset by three great forces, of which two engage us here. External stimuli bombard one from the real world and instinctual impulses strike from within. The one arouses objective, the other instinctual anxiety. The ego counters these threats with two basic defenses: denial deals with external dangers by reversing them through fantasy into something more acceptable and pleasurable; repression keeps dangerous instinctual wishes (e.g., to possess and devour) from consciousness. The neglect and indifference Shaw suffered from his mother would likely have aroused objective fears of loss of life, starvation, and abandonment, while the inadequacy and impoverishment of his father would have aroused other fears concerning his sense of worth; and all would have required denial. I have attempted to locate that defense during the differentiation process of the first year, and to specify it as manic denial against object loss and destructive rage. Now I want to provide for it more content and adaptive meaning.

Denial of reality leads to formation of fantasy. This went far to fill the emotional vacuum of Shaw's childhood and established a process that was to be fed by the family romance, reading, art museums, and the stage, eventuating in playmaking (although the completed work, whatever its origins in fantasy, assumes an objective position in the world as another order of reality). Repression is often assisted by reaction-formation, and his rescue-fantasies as well as his later alignment with women's causes and his oral taboos would have strengthened repression. Within the Shavian psyche the two defenses of denial and reaction-formation no doubt reinforced each other. His fantasy that his funeral would be attended by a grateful procession of all the livestock he had not eaten expresses the transformation of cruel, devouring wishes into sympathetic, saving ones.[32] By the same token, biting impulses are transformed into anti-vivisection and anti-vaccination campaigns (no half-measures for Shaw: even ordinary phobias are made into lifelong missions).

Given the realities of his "devil of a childhood," it is not impossible to reconstruct the kind of reversal fantasies that denial fostered. They could allow him to turn devouring drives into adoring dreams, to counter moribund starvation fears with the boundless Life Force, which could be pumped into the world instead of his waiting to have the world pump it into him and so eventually to feel that others needed him instead of his being dependent on them. The incestuous "I love her" can be narcissistically transposed into "she loves me" and "I am loved." Shaw can feel useful instead of a "feverish little selfish clod of ailments and grievances complaining that the world will not devote itself to making you happy" (PMS, p. 150); he can carry on like a genius instead of being treated like a "disagreeable little beast," and in short reverse his condition of being acted upon by acting. Reversal enables him to turn the tables on reality, to reclaim his narcissistic centeredness from the superfluous periphery, to control the mother in the rescue fantasy as he could not in reality, and to deny (also undo) his deprivation by rescuing the poor from their poverty. This would have

---

[32] Likewise Androcles, in converting to Christianity, befriends and feeds animals. Refraining from meat protects him from being devoured when he is beset by the afflicted lion in the forest. Being neither aggressive toward the lion nor fearful of him, Androcles is in a position to tame him by removing the thorn, thereby winning his everlasting gratitude.

connected his reversal fantasies with reaction-formation (which converts an "evil" impulse into a "good" one) and with his tendency to externalize, so that, being the strong one, he could champion the cause of the under-classes of society—the poor, women, children, and animals.

Denial became a pivotal defense for Shaw not only because it enabled him to master the conditions of childhood but also because in helping him to overcome the helplessness of infancy, it served through fantasy as a prerequisite for later creativity when "mother's milk" is made over into "printer's ink." And insofar as Weissman's study of *Pygmalion*, which treats Shaw as Higgins re-creating the oedipal mother in Liza, is sound, this feat was achieved by a reversal of roles with the child as parent and the mother as child; the deeper import of the fantasy may have been less a libidinal wish than a desperate means whereby a helpless child rescues himself from the fear of an overpowering mother. The process of reversal may be taken as Shaw's first creative act.

In his unstructured childhood begins the unlimited imagination. In the dreams of the superfluous child begins the Superman. In due time the reforming moral passion of the Socialist and feminist will be generated; and because destructive impulses are only denied and not eliminated, the iconoclast accompanies the reformer and directs aggression toward a disagreeable society instead of against the "disagreeable little beast" within.

Although denial is one of the commonest defenses—no family could long survive without it—in the Shaw family it seems to have been particularly prevalent. Despite his father's alcholism and social ostracism, his mother's uncertain infidelity, and the three more or less neglected children, Shaw relates that they all accepted one another in the "kindly Irish fashion" (SS, pp. 141–42). Mrs. Shaw, who "had plenty of imagination, and really lived in it and on it," denied her depressive sense of loss in various ways, including perhaps a flight into reality. Her neglect of her son was in effect a denial of her motherhood as well as of his maleness, a neglect that his sisters did not suffer so much from (HP, p. 435). And Mr. Shaw had attempted to deny his alcoholism and then through it to deny other failures, making trivialities of tragedies. Denial, along with manic tom-foolery and spritely playfulness, may not have been "learned" by Shaw, but it was ego-syntonic with his family environment. Too much denial is dangerous, as Anna Freud points out, and Shaw was not immune from the "excrescences" and "eccen-tricities" its excesses can produce in later life; indeed they con-tribute to the impudent charm of the G.B.S. character, affecting not only his manner, though, but restricting his affective life and stifling some areas of mental growth while spurring others on. How else but by denial and its correlative of magical think-ing could Shaw come to view death as an "acquired habit," and to argue that "if you can turn a pedestrian into a cyclist, and a cyclist into a pianist or violinist, without the intervention of Circumstantial Selection, you can turn an amoeba into a man, or a man into a superman, without it" (PBM, p. xxiv)?

Such a Shavian strategy of defense, ultimately coming to depend less on repression of infantile needs than on a denial of the basis for them, amounts to a massive counterforce against the instincts as such, while heightening in him the basic human conflict between instinct and civilization, for his defenses repudi-ate instinct as his plays renounce pleasure. Further, it clarifies some of the countrarieties in a nature that could be obsessed with women and at the same time personally ascetic, that could be a source of public iconoclasm and militant reform to his fellowmen yet urbanely even-tempered and privately modest.

His exercise of denial and reversal also explains the odd effect on the reader who opens his *Collected Letters* to find a nineteen-year-old son advising his mother and sister in London in a most matter-of-factly paternal way. Another piece of his early writing, *My Dear Dorothea* (New York, 1956), discusses child education from the point of view of a seasoned and sympathetic uncle to a favorite niece. Given their realistic context, the air of confidence in these pieces is hardly convincing, and Shaw's fanciful self-image must have become even more fragile when he was depending on his mother for much of his livelihood around this time in London. But he did not abandon the defense even after his novels, written from the author's omniscient point of view, were unanimously rejected.[33] Fortunately, during these years he was beginning to gain a reputation as a public speaker and to find ways to substantiate his fantasies of strength and adequacy by mastering revolutionary economic and political theory, so that in time, when the world began acclaiming his genius and the "impecunious younger son" became a wealthy capitalist, it was indeed reality that had reversed itself. Nor was his reputation for standing ideas, institutions, and social and artistic conventions on their heads won by accident or because he was merely a clever wit. It was the way he saw things. The mechanism of reversal became part of his character along with the iconclasm he wore in his Mephistophelian features and the visionary gaze of his eyes.

> All human progress involves as its first condition the willingness of the pioneer to make a fool of himself. The sensible man is the man who adapts himself to existing conditions. The fool is the man who persists in trying to adapt conditions to himself. . . .

[33] In the late 1890s Shaw depicted Irving and Shakespeare, his formidable rivals for control of the English Stage, as children, and placed himself at least implicitly in the role of competent adult (cf. chapter 2). In addition, see "The Phantasy of the Reversal of Generations," in *Papers on Psychoanalysis* by Ernest Jones (Boston, 1967). On the basis of this article, it may be speculated that Shaw could have preferred to remain childless because in his fantasy of reversal in which he is the parent to his family, having a child of his own would, according to the fantasy, return him to the position of a child before it. In other words he could reverse the situation once, but a double reversal would be disastrous; it would rob him of the magic of his fantasy.

When I first began to promulgate my opinions, I found that they appeared extravagant, and even insane. In order to get a hearing, it was necessary for me to attain the footing of a privileged lunatic, with the license of a jester. Fortunately the matter was very easy. I found that I had only to say with perfect simplicity what I seriously meant just as it struck me, to make everybody laugh. My method, you will have noticed, is to take the utmost trouble to find the right thing to say and then to say it with the utmost levity. And all the time the real joke is that I am in earnest. (CR, pp. 530–31, 539)

THE HEAVENLY COUNTRY

In his heart of hearts Shaw did not mind that "G.B.S." was a fiction and contrivance based on denial and reversal yet well suited for dealing with the world and releasing energies. He told Ellen Terry that she "went straight through the imposter to the real man and nursed him like a baby . . ." (ET, p. 13). And so he felt with her, but that she really did baby him in her letters is not apparent to the reader. Shaw's continual redefining of their roles on a parent-child model leaves a strong impression that denial was reworking reality and allowing him to project omnipotent wishes onto this renowned actress whom he did not really know. After mentioning to her in a letter written aboard a late evening train his "devil of a childhood . . . rich only in dreams, frightful and loveless in realities," he continues, "and *still* I have to dream of my Ellen and never touch her" (LS, p. 773, my italics). Their correspondence with its maximum play of fantasy and minimum of realistic contact (their first personal encounter in 1900 was an awkward anticlimax) remains interesting because she awoke in him such profound feelings of transference that even his marriage halfway through it had little effect on them. Because he could "idolize" her as he had his mother to the "utmost pitch" of his imagination without any "sordid or disillusioning contact," she reinstates the family romance and becomes an intermediary between the early un-resolved feelings for his mother and the virgin-mothers he put on the stage. The son-mother relationships in his early plays are as important as the father-daughter reversals that follow in later plays. These two combinations, which in a psychological sense are fundamentally related, out of all other human possibilities engaged him most deeply and recur most frequently. Therefore a more precise definition of the basis for them must be attempted.

It is conceivable that Shaw's manic denial, as well as his early identifications with his mother and continuing idealization of her, reveals a tendency to reestablish a state of symbiosis with the mother as a refuge from oral conflicts of cannibalism or abandonment and remote from genital confusion. Traditionally this state is the realm of "oceanic feeling," of oneness with the universe, and of flights of ecstasy best expressed in poetic or mystical terms. Psychogenetically it is rooted in the early months of bliss when the infant does not distinguish itself from the all-important source of oral supplies.

Should this apply to Shaw, then the need to preserve the physical integrity of the mother and himself in order to insure the symbiotic union, the basis for the grandiose fantasy of original narcissism, could also be at the root of his oral taboos, his subsequent energetic protests against vaccination and vivi-section, and his adherence to feminism. In other words, symbiosis may be the deep root out of which grows the trunk, branches, leaves, and blossoms of Shaw's life, but precisely in the sense that the root alone does not explain the total tree.

There is very little solid evidence to go on, but if the necessity for biological rapport with the maternal organism survived in Shaw's later life, his need to maintain a sense of his mother's presence and its continuation in the long line of feminine corres-pondents can be viewed along with his dramas and the structure of his thought as symbiotic derivatives. For even such a profoundly unconscious need as the one I am supposing was regulated by Shaw's ego. Denial may have gotten things off to a flying start, but its effects were not totally blinding. "You are a figure from the dreams of boyhood," Shaw wrote Mrs. Pat Campbell. "I will hurry through my dream as fast as I can; only let me have my dream out" (PC, p. 131). This double awareness kept certain lines open for growth and adaptation. In an early letter to Ellen Terry he wrote, "I *must* attach myself to you somehow . . . ," and later, "I must be *used,* built into the solid fabric of your life . . ." (LS, pp. 610, 676). In order to prevent such an urgent need from being foredoomed of sheer physical necessity, Shaw attached himself to her by discussing the theater and her acting career, and in the course of time she became attached to him by acting parts in plays he wrote for her. In other relationships the passive need to be loved is taken over by its active, outgoing opposite; and the overall result was that Shaw's hyperinvolvement in the affairs of the world guaranteed that the world would never leave him abandoned. Nor would he ever really be alone. In view of his many private and public relationships, his unending correspondence, and his hundreds of created characters, one would have to conclude that one way or another he was almost always relating. He manned a frantically busy writing factory, his prose became a crowded marketplace of ideas, his residence a shrine. Solitude was as nearly absent from his life as the soliloquy from his stage. In a sense he cathected the world.

The great value and perhaps ultimate justification of his correspondence with a lifelong series of women was that it provided just enough to stimulate, without destroying, a sense of symbiotic presence.[34] It also preserved the early combination

---

[34] Although the idealization of the parent image is a direct continuation of the child's original narcissism, the cognitive image of the idealized parent changes with the maturation of the child's cognitive development" (Kohut, p. 247). Shaw's "cognitive equipment" undoubtedly changed in

of the worshipful and increasingly remote mother. When Ellen Terry was replaced by Mrs. Pat Campbell, whom Shaw did get around to visiting, she acquired some "predestined adorability" reawakening "the bond of the child with the dark lady" that he suddenly recalled dreaming about forty-three years ago at fourteen (PC, pp. 90–91). And when that bond was threatened, the pain and rage were acute. "What are you, miserable witch, that my entrails should be torn asunder hour after hour?" (PC, p. 154). But for all that, Shaw was considerably more successful in controlling the affections of his actress-mothers than the unresponsive heart of his real mother. Frequently he composed his letters late at night, and the flights of fantasy bordering on ecstasy testify to rare feelings indeed. Writing to Mrs. Pat Campbell he could be "quite sensible, quite able, quite myself, yet a lad with you on the mountains and unable to feel

some ways as he matured, but his "idealization of the parent image" in other women enabled him to preserve much of his "original narcissism." It is immediately following this state—during the give and take of gratification and frustration—that the mother is gradually perceived as a separate object from the child, and it is here that I have posited Shaw's departure from the model. The cognitive image of the mother evidently split in two. The rather heartless mother he describes matter-of-factly parallels his own cognitive development. But the glorified image of the idolized mother remained, and it was this image that wielded so much influence on his development, object relations, and art.

It would be well to add a word about the use of certain concepts. Original or primary narcissism strictly speaking refers to the "psychological state of the infant" before the "I-you differentiation" has been established between itself and the mother (Kohut, p. 245). Now, because this state may have intra-uterine sources and may continue through the idealized imago, we may divide primary narcissism into three phases. Of these only the first would be symbiotic, strictly speaking. But I would like to extend the term more broadly to include the three phases of primary narcissism. Secondary narcissism begins when the idealized imago draws instinctual energy into the ego. This is the "transformation of object-libido into narcissistic labido which thus . . . implies an abandonment of sexual aims, a desexualization—a kind of sublimation, therefore" (*The Ego and the Id,* p. 30).

In describing Shaw as narcissistic, I refer to the secondary stage, but I believe that it was pre-oedipal and that he had access, perhaps through it, to the primary narcissism, which enabled him to experience states of ecstasy described above.

where you begin and I leave off" (PC, p. 116). She became his Stella whom he fancied a star, and he a "sort of comet" split off from the star, brandishing his "crystal tresses in the sky" (PC, p. 215).

He wrote to Janet Achurch that she "recreates me with an emotion which lifts me high" above sexual fascination. "I become a saint at once and write a drama in which I idealize Janet" (LS, p. 506). The drama was *Candida,* and he later identified Candida herself as the "Virgin Mother" (LS, p. 623). If Shaw founded a new religion based on the Life Force, it is in this area that we must look for its source and inspiration. "Super hanc Stellam will I build my church," he punned to his Stella (PC, p. 173).[35] Clearly Freud did not reckon on Shaw when he said that "all religions have evolved . . . as a substitute for a longing for the father," for Shaw's religion is related to the other sex. His superego arises not from the internalized paternal phallus but from the breast; his religion springs not from the stone decalogue but from the flaming fount of life-energy.

Although such inferences may always remain uncertain, what clearly matters is that Shaw retained access to some kind of profound union at least partly under his control and transferable under certain conditions, thereby relaxing the need for a permanent maternal presence, and that this union profoundly influenced his character and creativity.

It is this felt union with Candida that enables Marchbanks to go out into the night with its secret in his heart. And because the ecstasies are converted into visions of future possibility ("realities as yet unexperienced"), Vitalist figures in other plays either attach themselves to the Life Force or are swept along

[35] "Unfortunately this Christian Church, founded gaily with a pun . . . has become the Church where you must not laugh; and so it is giving way to that older and greater Church to which *I* belong; the Church where the oftener you laugh the better, because by laughter only can you destroy evil without malice, and affirm good fellowship without mawkishness" (AH, p. 44).

by it in order to carry out the work of Creative Evolution. In fact, the plays trace the path of the symbiotic situation as it climbs into trackless regions of mystical vision and mathematical essences, so that apart from the precise source of this union, its purposes are made clear once the ego has transformed it into something else.

> What I like is not what people call pleasure, which is the most dreadful and boring thing on the face of the earth, but life itself. And that of course is the genuinely religious view to take, because life is a very wonderful thing. Life is this force outside yourself that you are in the hands of. (RS, p. 5)

> As for my own position, I am, and always have been, a mystic. I believe that the universe is being driven by a force that we might call the life-force. I see it as performing the miracle of creation, that it has got into the minds of men as what they call their will. (RS, p. 33)

Which means that with the force of life working as will in the minds of men, the cosmic and the human are profoundly and inseparably related. Moreover, this union is no respecter of families, classes, nations, or of other religions.

Along with his iconoclasm and his reforming moral passion, the visionary aftermath of ecstasy is the third component of creative energy behind the distinctive content of his plays. It summons the "evolutionary appetite" into being, and charts "higher" purposes for instinctual life. "Every dream is a prophecy," and there is an "indescribable levity" and "something spritelike" in discovering the whole truth of things (JB, p. 611; SS, p. 87). If Shavian ecstasy is a leavening and even soaring force of imagination, his pragmatic ego still keeps it sober, antiseptic, and at times prosaically explicit. He felt that "ability does not become genius until it has risen to the point at which its keenest states of perception touch on ecstasy, untainted by mere epilepsy or drunken incontinence, or sexual incontinence."

This conviction he addressed in 1896 to Janet Achurch, the drug-prone actress who had inspired and acted in *Candida*; and he added more realistically, "Well, in the rose valleys, on the plains of heaven, I was not continent; but I was ecstatic . . . and I never lost the ground I gained afterwards" (LS, p. 625).

The swelling, exhilarating effect of these ecstatic states[36] enlarged his ego by a rush of pleasurable energy (narcissistic libido before the ego redistributed it) sufficient for him to feel this expansion physically, confirming the rise by sheer gravitation and making the reversals seem realities. "The step up to the plains of heaven was made on your bosom," he continued to Miss Achurch. And the same metaphors are called into active service twenty years later when he is writing to Mrs. Pat Campbell:

> you must still be the Mother of Angels to me, still from time to time put on your divinity and sit in the heavens with me . . . you on your throne in your blue hood, and I watching and praying, not on my knees, but at my fullest stature. For you I wear my head nearest the skies. (PC, p. 137)

Up to the "highest summits" Candida lifts Marchbanks where he "wanted nothing more than the happiness of being in love." And indeed after an encounter so sacred, down-to-earth sex would be anticlimatic.

In closing this section, I would like also to close the dis-

---

36 I hesitate to refer to them as peak experiences, for their precise nature remains as elusive as the surrounding circumstances are obscure. Cf. "Psychodynamic Aspects of the Peak Experience," William H. Blanchard, *The Psychoanalytic Review* 56, no. 1 (1969): 87-112. In his nineties Shaw is comparing creative pleasure with the sexual orgasm when he suddenly recalls "moments of inexplicable happiness" that "have only come in dreams not oftener than every fifteen years or so." They have an "exalted chronic happiness, as of earth become heaven . . ." (PBB, p. 751). More than manic states, these vivid memory traces, so they seem to me, stem from the infant's experiences of fusion with the mother. For more on the relation between elation and religious esctasy see B. D. Lewin's excellent *The Psychoanalysis of Elation* (London: The Hogarth Press Ltd., 1951), pp. 144-50.

cussion of denial, so crucial a defense for Shaw, but one I do not wish to reduce him to and about which the reader must now feel he has heard quite enough, and simply note its three-fold activity. First, of course, it kept at a safe remove devastating fears of loss, emptiness, and destruction, but it also blocked the development of important affective states (grief, sadness, guilt, empathy), and impaired the ego function of reality-testing. In order for maternal integrity to be protected, castration is to be denied, or perhaps displaced onto the ineffectual father. Second, it had the adaptive function of consolidating libido for main-taining fantasy, spurring flights of mental activity, and repairing damage to self-esteem. It also contributed to the peculiar Shavian life-style and the formation of character traits. Third, it may be thought of as a portal that opens onto oceanic feeling and grants it regulated entry into the ego. Finally, it did not entirely shield him from the stresses it opposed. He claimed for himself the "infernal" inspiration of his Caesar's admission, that "he who has never hoped can never despair" (SS, p. 204).

THE FORCE BEHIND THE LIFE FORCE

If the ecstasies induced by the women of Shaw's manhood, about which he is so effusive, were a continuation of the period of union with and worship of his mother, about which he is more reticent, then it seems probable that from these related expansive experiences his transforming and reforming ego con-ceived of the Life Force as the animating principle and driving power behind all reality. The evolutionary energy of biological development that Shaw finds in the cosmic environment is a continuation of that same energy that nurtured—as well as thwarted—emotional growth in his earliest environment. For instead of allowing the Life Force to be merely a mystical flight from reality, he structures it rather consistently on the conditions of actual experience. If the Life Force is beyond human reason and indifferent to human sentiments, mystical and everlasting, in and of itself it is imperfect and incomplete. Pursuing an evolutionary course, it stumbles along blindly through trial and error, dependant on its inventions for vision and intelligence, the latest and best of which is man, who is now challenged to cooperate with it to produce an "executive organ of godlike knowledge and power" (HP, p. 280), elsewhere called the Superman. Most recently the Life Force has gotten bogged down in one of its unhappiest strategies, namely, Capitalism.

Thus the Life Force incorporates Mrs. Shaw's primordial divinity along with her faltering roles as daughter, wife, and mother. Shaw maintained that after "innocently" getting her father arrested, she had to return either to his wrath or to the iron-willed aunt, and that out of this desperate dilemma she fell into the arms of her future husband. Shaw further reports that following the honeymoon disclosure of her husband's alcoholism, she ran off to the docks to seek employment as a stewardess, only to be roughed up by dockworkers and forced to return. Whether this last account is fanciful or not, it projects a vision of will thwarted on every side by external circumstances, which could be seen in the larger context of bourgeois marriage and capitalistic economies: woman as the prisoner of society, yet surviving. The concept of the Life Force further encompasses her mastery over circumstance and her imperfect solution in forsaking her family. Her unconventional conduct becomes a basis for his pragmatic morality, and as the suffering she caused her family is real but accidental, so the evil in the world is the unfortunate but unavoidable by-product of the Life Force. In fact, her whole wandering course in and out of marriage could serve as a model for the trial and error method of the Life

Force, and more important, it could argue the value of attaching brains to its energy, which, in making evolution creative, would also have the effect not of terminating but of transforming symbiosis and elevating it to an ideal and permanent working relationship.

For just as his mother never quarreled and never forgave, Shaw probably never expressed anger toward her and certainly, for forty-three years, never left her. He emerged from the oedipal struggle, such as it was, more closely aligned with her than with his father. Shaw was preserved from her maladaptive unforgiving, grievance-collecting traits, but he had enough anger and blame to wage unrelenting warfare on a society dominated by the male sex, and he never forgave Capitalism its injustices. His self-image was one of inner remoteness, which she may have either induced or reinforced, and he impressed others as impersonally looking through and beyond them.

"The real process is very obscure," Shaw once mused on his creativity, "for the result always shows that there has been *something behind* all the time, of which I was not conscious, although it turns out to be the real motive of the whole creation" (TT, p. 65). And so, having bought our consistency with reductionism, we can ponder how intimately the son is bound up with his mother; how much his early relationship with her affected the mode of his creative work as well as the direction of his thought—and, most simply put, the extent to which his family life formed a paradigm for his vision of reality.

For, whether or not Shaw is telling the truth when he informs us flatly that his feelings for his mother were never responded to, we can believe that they were never resolved. The repetition compulsion is stamped on his relations with women. Ultimately unmet needs cannot be denied, nor can one renounce what has not been enjoyed.

> "Would you call your mother a good mother?" my wife [Hesketh Pearson's] asked him.
> "The worst in the world."
> "Would you have changed her for a better mother?"
> "I would not have changed her for any other mother in existence." (HP, p. 435)

The role of Mrs. Shaw in her son's development (as are so many artists' mothers') is a dual one. Consistent in her singular indifference as she may have been, she is for him the source equally of deprivation and idolatry, of skepticism and Vitalism. These tensions and contradictions made his adherence to the Life Force all the more fervent and unshakable. He must have religion, "for the religious people . . . are not empty" (LS, p. 504). He may be "detestably deserted," he once wrote to his future wife Charlotte, but, "lonely—no, by God never lonely" (JD, pp. 138–39). Not if you are creative as well as religious, it may be added, and can people the emptiness with living characters as Shaw reported doing on such occasions, for it is precisely out of such loneliness that the sacred fount of the family romance springs (LS, p. 98; PB, p. 35).

Nor is his ascetic ascent without its blessings. "You cannot act on beans and water alone,"

> but there is always religion, if you can reach it—the religion of Beethoven's ninth symphony, the religion which rediscovers God in man and the Virgin Mother in every carpenter's wife, which sweeps away miracle and reveals the old dogmas as the depth of which everyday facts are only the surface, which sanctifies all life and substitutes a profound dignity and self-respect for the old materialistic self. This is the most creative of all religions : with it you can live on half a bean a day, if that is all that your bodily well-being requires. (LS, p. 505)

Asceticism seems to make possible in another form the very pleasures it had once opposed because the Life Force is not irrevocably anchored in the maternal object but moves through all of creation. "Recreation is the secret of the religious life," so long as one can rediscover and re-create in later life semblances of pleasures that began at the dawn of life. "You need no stimulants, no meat, no spirits, no enjoyments: you live the heavenly life, and die at a stupendous age, unexhausted in spirit," he prophesied in 1895 (LS, pp. 504–5). And although he was on an exhilarating crest of growth and awareness at this time, there was the necessary undertow simultaneously taking its toll.

In the safety of his seventies he could look back and observe that while "all young people should be votaries of the Uranian Venus to keep them chaste," the difficulty is that "she can also sterilize us by giving us imaginary amours on the plains of heaven so magical that they spoil us for real women and real men. We may become celibate through a surfeit of beauty and a excess of voluptuousness. We may end as ascetics, saints, old bachelors . . . " (SS, pp. 176–77). If he recognized the dangers by then, did he sense them in time to ward off the fate he so well articulated? He did not turn into an old bachelor, but a celibate marriage at forty-three does not weigh heavily in his favor. And although he did not rule out sex between real men and real women, sex as personal experience or as erotic passion does not exist in his works and probably was never experienced in that mature and rare coalescence of sensuality and tenderness, recommended by his Viennese contemporary.[37] One of Shaw's spurned women noticed that his gallantries were a substitute for sexual passion and his verbosity a defense against amorous activity. "Frequent talking, talking, talking," about finances and

[37] "Shaw was in pursuit of the Uranian Venus, the classic love of the aesthetes. In the Galatean myth, Venus sanctions the womanhood of Galatea for its creator, Pygmalion. Shaw had no quarrel with the world in its pursuit of direct sexual gratification (giving the misleading impression that it was true of him), but his major personal pursuit was a desexualized aesthetic one" (WA, p. 160).

marriage, including "his dislike of the sexual relation and so on, would create an atmosphere of lovemaking without any need for caresses or endearments . . ." (JD, p. 118). His pleasure in debating and arguing with women, which had the "avowed object" of "vivisection" failed, according to Beatrice Webb:

> He idealizes them for a few days, weeks or years—imagines them to be something utterly different from their true selves— then has a revulsion of feeling and discovers them to be inutterably vulgar, second-rate, rapscallion, insipidly well-bred.

"He never fathoms their real worth, nor rightly sees their limitation," Mrs. Webb concludes (JD, p.123).

In the solitude of his nineties Shaw wrote his last play, a "Little Comedy," which opens in the woods with a "lady, good-looking, well dressed, and not over thirty . . . being conducted along the path by a burly and rather dangerous-looking man, middle-aged, ugly. . . ." The man starts to rob the woman; he wants the pearls from around her neck. A "young male voice" is heard: "Can I help?" A man in working clothes but with a "well-bred" accent frightens off the robber and rescues the young woman. She turns out to be Miss White of Four Towers, the granddaughter of the chairman of the board of the "greatest timber merchants and woodmen in the country." The young man, who describes himself as an "upstart tramp,"[33] reveals his name to be Henry Bossborn and claims as his reward a position in the carpenters' shop, but on his own terms, that is, with unspecified hours and duties. This is done and in time he has replaced his superiors, turned the business to even greater

---

[33] The phrase is rich in condensation. While still largely unknown, Shakespeare was referred to as an "upstart crow." Shaw speaks of himself as the "downstart son of a downstart." Thus "upstart" reverses his birth and connects him with genius, while "tramp" apparently refers to the orally deprived outsider whose inner reality is Henry (possibly an allusion to Henry Irving, the powerful actor-manager) Bossborn: the man who is born to rule. Miss White's first name, Serafina (Seraphim), places her with the angels.

profits, left, and formed his own realty agency. He has torn down the old family estate of Four Towers (emblem of Family, Business, Church, State, and symbol of the woman's body), and rebuilt a modern, efficient home for Miss White. And so the only question left in this family-romance, rescue-fantasy is marriage. But it turns out that Miss White is not very pleased with all the progress, and tells Bossborn that "your way" is not "our way." He implies that he has merely served the Life Force; nevertheless, she will not marry him (sexual love not being the goal of the Life Force), and they settle for friendship. The title of this dramatic sketch, which compresses much of Shaw's life and conflicts, is, "Why She Would Not." Why indeed—well may this have been his first as well as his last question. There is some uncertainty over whether the play as it exists is finished; it seems that Shaw may have intended one more scene, but died first (AH, pp. 664–65).

Finally, it hardly needs to be said that not every woman in Shaw's life or every woman's part in his drama is derived from symbiotic sources, although some of the most important women in his life and works are. For him the symbiotic situation was not so much symbolized by the safe harbor, or the serene island amid stormy seas, or the Rock of Gibraltar, images in which the Great Mother may appear in the works of other Irishmen, such as Yeats, O'Neill, or Joyce, but by a great ball of fire sending off flaming comets in orbit. For she is above all a source of productive vital energy. She may be as solid and stable as any other earth mother, but she has been divested of her earthiness and is glorified as a celestial body on the "plains of heaven." And like a flaming star she has the power either to repulse or to attract, to liberate or to envelope and consume other orbiting bodies. This potential for self-annihilation is the dark side of Shavian ecstasy and the reason for the derivative comet, that is, the male offspring, to maintain distance and conceive schemes of cooperation for survival. Or, as King Magnus says to his would-be Queen, Orinthia, in the "Interlude" of *The Apple Cart* (a transparently autobiographical sequence based on Shaw's afternoon dalliances with Mrs. Pat Campbell):

> Every star has its own orbit; and between it and its nearest neighbor there is not only a powerful attraction but an infinite distance. When the attraction becomes stronger than the distance the two do not embrace; they crash together in ruin. (p. 289)

Magnus's description of his relations with Orinthia as "strangely innocent" also defines Shaw's with Mrs. Pat, and echoes Mrs. Shaw's "blameless *ménage à trois*" with Lee.

Although in *Farfetched Fables* (1948) the projection of human evolution into invisible "thought-vortexes," suggesting minute particles in a vast cosmic sea of energy, does betray a regressive tendency toward some kind of embryonic nirvana, the more usual emblem of Shavian symbiosis is the brilliant comet liberated to produce dazzling patterns in the presence of an eternally fixed star. And in *Man and Superman,* when the philosophy of Creative Evolution is set into motion, intelligence is intended to guide energy, and the prospect of productive reciprocity between the sexes is envisioned in opposition to the danger of an engulfing and annihilating union.

This threat of engulfment Shaw once expressed in his characteristically jesting fashion by reassuring us that his comical assaults would not plunge us mutually into a "majestic Atlantic where we might perish tragically," but merely into a harmless "sea of ridicule amid shrieks of derisive laughter" (SS, p. 187). Since this protective sea of laughter, a sort of anti-sea into which one may sink without drowning, rises from his identifications and disillusionment with his father, this relationship will next engage us.

2

IMPECUNIOUS SON

Shaw is as merciless to himself as to us. He does not kick us overboard and remain proudly on the quarter deck himself. With the utmost good-humor he clasps us affectionately round the waist and jumps overboard with us, and that too, not into a majestic Atlantic where we might perish tragically, but into a sea of ridicule amid shrieks of derisive laughter. (SS, p. 187)

You are wrong to scorn farcical comedy. It is by jingling the bells of a jester's cap that I, like Heine, have made people listen to me. All genuinely intellectual work is humorous.
                                   Letter to Florence Farr (LS, p. 332)

A man learns to skate by staggering and making a fool of himself. Indeed he progresses in all things by resolutely making a fool of himself. (LS, p. 465)

DANCING SKELETON

Curiosity begins early in the life of a child. It is usually in the second or third year, in the process of separation from the mother, that he begins hatching speculations about his own origins. Sonny, as Shaw was referred to in his early years, no doubt entertained such quandaries. Looking around for an answer, his eye inevitably took in George Carr Shaw, his father, and his mother's "hopelessly disappointing husband." His father's class was the "Shabby Genteel, the poor Relations, the Gentlemen Who are No Gentlemen" (LM, p. 858). Their plight was epitomized by the younger son doomed to come after and take what was left over, compensated by dreams of grandiosity and headed for failure. "If you would know what real poverty is," Shaw remarks, meaning not just economic conditions but poverty of mind and inner resources, "ask the younger son of a younger son of a younger son" (IM, p. 659). "The Shaws were younger sons from the beginning," and Sonny was a "downstart son of a downstart" (IM, pp. 657–59). Taking these statements in the context of genetics and eugenics, which is the way Shaw's mind viewed generation, we get the picture of a species breeding itself out of existence. Recessive genes cluster to form the diminishing line of the downstart. His father "had no inheritance, no profession, no manual skill, no qualifications of any sort for any definite social function." He "spoke and dressed like an Irish gentleman" (SS, p. 74) and maintained his snobbery with alcohol.

These observations about Mr. Shaw lead one inevitably to conclude an absence of male vigor, or impotence, says Erik Erikson, in analyzing a Shavian screen memory (presently to be considered), which is offered as an indication of Shaw's rejection of his father when he should have been identifying with him. In the long run Erikson may be correct, but there was a considerably more complex interaction between Sonny and the man he once called "Papa in the fullest sense" (SS, p. 142). Moreover, Shaw's preferred mode of development within his family was identification, which, in view of his family, hardly prepared him to get along in what we now call straight society. At home he was not a "difficult" child. For the most part he was quite willing to avail himself of all the strengths of his father's personality and did so in various ways, but there was not much there to use, or at least not nearly enough for Sonny. Nevertheless, what was there, he did use.

Up to a point, conditions for identification obtained: Sonny ran his father's errands, accompanied him to his mill to play on the surrounding grounds, took walks with him, and even acquired an early dose of his father's Protestant snobbery. He appeared to Sonny as a harmless and humane man who never attempted to "impress children in the manner that makes awe and dread almost an instinct in some children" (LM, p. 668). Shaw's "natural civility," which prevented him from intentionally offending people, may have been his father's legacy. "People who met me in private," Shaw recalled after he had made his reputation as an iconoclast, "were surprised by my mildness" (IM, p. 670). In any case, identification was permanently disrupted by his father's alcoholism. When Sonny was as "tall" as his father's "boots" (LS, p. 773), Mr. Shaw

> pretended in play to throw me into the canal, he very nearly did it. When we got home I said to my mother as an awful and hardly credible discovery, "Mama: I think Papa is drunk." This was too much for her. She replied "When is he anything else?" (SS, p. 28)

This experience Shaw described as a sudden and violent "wrench from my childish faith in my father as perfect and omniscient to the discovery that he was a hypocrite and dipsomaniac" (SS, p. 28). "There the scoffer began" (LS, p. 773). No doubt this is part of the story; certainly it provides an autobiographical basis and rationale for the direction of his later iconoclasm. "I shall carry traces of that disillusion to the grave" (OB). "Traces" is an important qualifier, for his "derisive incredulity" is part of his identification with his father, and while traces of it remain, it also undergoes a sea-change with the dawning of "moral passion" (OB).

Shaw preferred to blame the disintegration of the marriage on his father's "drink neurosis" rather than on his mother's behavior or on Lee's intrusion, and even admonished a biographer, "If you had been through that time with me you would not see anything in it to joke about" (SS, pp. 146, 148). But Shaw in the 1930s was forgetting or disregarding what he had written in 1921 : "It would have been unendurable if we had not taken refuge in laughter" (IM, p. 668). The following incident is the one Erikson has interpreted as Shaw's recognition of his father's impotence.

> A boy who has seen "the governor," with an imperfectly wrapped-up goose under one arm and a ham in the same condition under the other (both purchased under heaven knows what festivity), butting at the garden wall in the belief that he was pushing open the gate, and transforming his tall hat into a concertina in the process, and who, instead of being overwhelmed with shame and anxiety at the spectacle, has been so disabled by merriment (uproariously shared by the maternal uncle) that he has hardly been able to rush to the rescue of the hat and pilot its wearer to safety, is clearly not a boy who will make tragedies of trifles instead of making trifles of tragedies. (IM, p. 668)

"It had to be either a family tragedy or a family joke," and it followed that, "if you cannot get rid of the family skeleton you may as well make it dance." Thus, by making the family skeleton jump on the strings of comedy, the Shaws apparently adapted to the situation; and Shaw firmly maintained, "All my comedy is a Shavian inheritance" (IM, p. 667). Again, there is more to it.

Alcoholism tells us little about a person, since in itself it is a response and a temporary solution to a preexisting conflict; it is a symptom that becomes an illness. More often than not it is a poor solution, and one that aggravates the causes while anaesthetizing the pain. Shaw described his father as a teetotaler in theory but a "miserable drunkard" in practice, who was racked with "shame and remorse even in his cups" (IM, p. 661). He was evidently burdened with an idealized self-image that demanded the perfectionism of total abstinence. His drinking subverted this untenable ideal by summoning the miserable drunkard to disarm it through mockery and debunking. He upheld "conventional observances . . . associated with the standing of the family," and then proceeded to get himself miserably drunk at family gatherings until he was invited no more.

Certainly neither parent was on easy terms with either external or internalized authority, and while such interlocking of traits may help explain why the marriage survived in some residual form for twenty years, it also meant that the unconscious of the parents was virtually on continual display to Sonny, whose exposure to it hardly assisted his own efforts at self-control and probably fostered his diabolical self-image and subsequent Mephistophelian appearance. But most important of all is the emerging pattern of identification through reversal expressed most succinctly here: "I work as my father drank." The father regains the oral object by passively imbibing it, the son by actively defending against it in the kind of writing that reproduces various maternal figures in his plays and draws actress-mothers into performing in them. As different as these processes between father and son are, Shaw prefers to stress their compulsive kinship: "I am a pitiable example of something much worse than the drunk craze: to wit, the work craze" (SW2, p. 3).

Of immediate interest is Mr. Shaw's attempts at dealing with conflict through humor. "He was," Shaw informs us, "in the grip of a humorous sense of anticlimax."

The more sacred an ideal or a situation was by convention,

the more irresistible was it to him as the jumping-off place for a plunge into laughter. Thus, when I scoffed at the Bible he would instantly and quite seriously rebuke me, telling me, with what little sternness was in his nature, that I should not speak so; that no educated man would make such a display of ignorance; that the Bible was universally recognized as a literary and historical masterpice; and as much more to the same effect as he could muster. But when he had reached the point of feeling really impressive, a convulsion of internal chuckling would wrinkle up his eyes; and (I knowing all the time quite well what was coming) would cap his eulogy by assuring me, with an air of perfect fairness, that even the worst enemy of religion could say no worse of the Bible than that it was the damndest parcel of lies ever written. He would rub his eyes and chuckle for quite a long time. It became an unacknowledged game between us that I should provoke him to exhibitions of this kind. (IM, p. 666)

This complex transaction involved more than the simple handing down of the gift of humorous anticlimax from father to son. Mr. Shaw reveled in lighting the fuse concealed in these exaggerated and idealized constructions assembled for the occasion. Requiring little from Sonny, the game was mainly self-contained and locked within Mr. Shaw.

What can be easily overlooked is that in Mr. Shaw's repeated building up and tearing down there was a strong destructive element turned against the self.

He was full of self-reproaches and humiliations when he was not full of secret jokes, and was either biting his moustache and whispering deepdrawn damns, or shaking with silent paroxysms of laughter. (SS, p. 141)

He set fire to internal strawmen, took magical revenge on the world, and detonated intrapsychic images of family, society, and religion; and instead of fostering a separation from their dominance or providing a useful sort of ground-clearing iconoclasm, the process is repeated for its own sake with no prospect of replacing what is mentally demolished for the moment with anything better for the future. Self-deprecating and self-destructive like his alcoholism, and equally passive, it functions in service of his illness rather than in service of his ego. At best it was, as Shaw realized, an exhibition; but what was being exhibited?

Despite its private functions, anti-climax displayed his father's inability to cope with social, religious, and other more practical realities. In sexual terms, anticlimax is equivalent to impotence, and that, through the games they played, may have been what Mr. Shaw was conveying to Sonny. Indeed Shaw may have come to realize, although for very different reasons, that genital sex *was* rather anticlimactic compared to those celestial trips he recorded.

Whether alcoholism produces impotence or whether it is the other way around, does not matter for our purposes. What does matter is that the alcoholic consumes pleasure in its earliest form and manner, which is orally, and that the powerful oral dependence it reveals or induces does lead to a state of sexual indifference. Seen through the eyes of Sonny, his father must have been a painfully clear object lesson in the evils of pure consumption. Sonny became a practical teetotaler, and he went so far as to rule out even the milder stimulants of coffee and tea. His father enjoyed a clay pipe; Shaw never smoked. He may well have been addressing his father when he warned that "if you must hold yourself up to your children as an object lesson (which is not at all necessary), hold yourself up as a warning and not as an example" (PMI, p. 11).[1] In Shaw's plays drunkenness is nearly always associated with anti-social behavior or weakness of character. It is one instance where he is quite conventional.

---

[1] In fact, the following passage make the connection clear. "When he [Mr. Shaw] caught me imitating him by pretending to smoke a toy pipe he advised me very earnestly never to follow his example in any way. . . . He taught me to regard him as an unsuccessful man with many undesirable habits, as a warning and not as a model" (SW1, p. 25). Shaw goes on to say that he found this quite admirable, and in that sense Mr. Shaw was a "model father."

One aspect of his father's fixation was this derisive but ultimately sterile sense of anti-climax, a symptom of his impotence and failure. But if anticlimax unconsciously conveyed these facts to Sonny, it was also a vehicle for laughter, which could help him master the effect on him of his father's condition. Mr. Shaw's sense of humor must have signaled somewhat masochistically to Sonny: Look, I may be a drunkard and a failure and a cuckold and a wretched provider and all the rest, but never mind, I'm all right, I'm getting along, it doesn't matter. Shaw's adopting his father's sense of humor may have been one way of adding substance to the emerging manic disposition and reassuring himself of his psychic well-being. The "humorist acquires his superiority," Freud wrote, "by assuming the role of the grownup, identifying himself to some extent with the father, while he reduces the other people to the position of children" ("On Humor," V, p. 218). But it can also be a way, Freud goes on to show, that the internalized parent in the superego can reassure the fearful child in the ego that things are not as bad as they seem. The humorist, according to Ernst Kris, "banishes man's greatest fear, the eternal fear, acquired in childhood, of the loss of love. The precious gift of humor makes men wise; they are sublime and safe, remote from all conflict" (p. 216). Thus the emerging manic pattern may have been sanctioned by the father. If we return to this chapter's first epigraph, we may find that Shaw's description of the operations of his humor, wherein "he clasps us affectionately round the waist and jumps overboard with us," is modeled on these comical interchanges with his father. Shaw may be carrying out on his public what had been carried out on him. And he may have staved off perishing in the maternal "majestic Atlantic" by leaping into the paternal sea of "derisive laughter."

In the long run Shaw's humorous superego may have comforted his ego with the prospect that life holds many pleasures apart from those all-important early ones, which perforce had to be prohibited. In any case, the father's sense of humor is for his son a psychological area in which identifications are made and denial reinforced, but the real interest centers on Shaw's mode of adaptation. In his hands anticlimax may have initially offered derisive detachment from conventional morality, but it eventually became a method of deflating the heroic postures and romantic attitudes played in melodrama and cherished in life. For Shaw these are analogous to the oral fixations occurring when trauma forces the pleasure principle into repetition-compulsion efforts aimed at mastery. Romantic fixation and alcoholic addiction alike are not only mindlessly repetitious but, bound to the passive mode of wish-fulfillment, they are ultimately illusory pleasures.

Sergius and Raina in *Arms and the Man* are straw figures of romance set up for a disillusionment that is dramatically executed by means of the family gift of anticlimax. But Shaw goes further. In a letter (LS, pp. 427–28) attempting to clarify his intentions in the play, he wrote that because Sergius, once bereft of his illusions, can only declare that "life is a farce," the audience had mistaken the play as a type of Gilbertian farce, which inverted truth and illusion in a "mechanical topsyturvy-ism." Shaw contended that this cleverness led nowhere, because Gilbert "accepts the conventional ideals implicitly while observing that people do not really live up to them. This he regards as a failure on their part at which he mocks bitterly." Implicitly associated are Mr. Shaw's futile anticlimax, Gilbert's inversion, and Sergius's disillusionment, which result in a "perfectly barren position: nothing comes of it but cynicism, pessimism and irony." "Barren" is enough like "impotent" to suggest the parallel predicaments of the father, the farceur, and the phallic fool, Sergius, although he is rewarded, after his exposure and ridicule, not unkindly with Louka. (Barrenness, or emptiness and disillusion, may also be connected with the issues stemming from the "depressive position" that Shaw would unconsciously associate with his father's conflicts.) Shaw proceeds to explain that he does not accept "conventional ideas." "To them I oppose in the play the practical life and morals of the efficient realistic man," Bluntschli.

> Sergius is ridiculous through the breakdown of his ideals, not odious from his falling short of them. As Gilbert sees, they don't work; but what Gilbert does not see is that there is something else that does work, and that in that something else there is a completely satisfactory asylum for his affections. It is this positive element in my philosophy that makes *Arms and the Man* a perfectly genuine play about real people, with a happy ending and hope and life in it.

It is precisely here at the Gilbertian phase that some good Shavians have gone astray. It is also here that the basic dialectic in the Shavian play emerges. The action proceeds from 1) illusion (acceptance of conventional ideals), to 2) exposure and loss of them (Sergius, Mr. Shaw, Gilbert), to 3) a new element that is in touch with the real world and in the service of life. (This sequence may be seen to have its model in the earlier one of 1) possession of the love-object, either in symbiotic bliss, or oedipal aspiration; 2) depressive position or phallic disillusionment; 3) manic defense and mechanisms of reversal that attempt to restore (1) on a more realistic level, though not exactly a genital one.

Shaw's purpose in his early plays is to "substitute natural history for conventional ethics and romantic logic." Natural history is what Bluntschli offers Raina, what Candida offers Morell and Marchbanks, and what Dick Didgeon offers the Andersons. This dialectic, which is compatible with but not identical to the one Eric Bentley has worked out (EB, pp. 107f.), is in the Shavian personality before it takes on Hegelian, Marxist,

Fabian, or any other conscious ideological construction. The state of ilusion is like the innocence of the child who still believes in the simple goodness of his introjects and, by extension, of the world at large, as Shaw had once believed in his father and mother. Then following disillusionment, his father helped him to turn the tragedy into a triviality by anticlimax. But his ability to transform reality by looking at it in a different way meant for Shaw not the depressive mockery of a drunkard's dance but "an indescribable levity—not triviality, mind, but levity— something spritelike about the conclusions of the writer who will face the labor of digging down to them" (SS, p. 87). In short, a way of seeking the inner nature of things. "When a thing is funny, search it for a hidden truth" (BM, p.247). Perhaps through the manic defense, the ego may raise the id's symbiotic treasures from the sea of ridicule and derisive laughter.

Although laughter, in recovering the triumph of narcissism, may be leveling, Shaw wanted it also to be discriminating, and, after iconoclastically leveling conventional distinctions, to make new ones available. In terms of Shavian religion this meant that when the omnipotent Christian Deity was reduced by Darwin to Blake's "Old Nobodaddy," despair need not follow because this imposter could eventually give way to the Life Force.[2]

---

[2] Freud, in his study of jokes, provides a way to understand this three-fold process psychodynamically. Mr. Shaw's exhibitions, which undermined the repressive systems of morality and religion by anticlimax, represented a victory over the reality principle by invoking the pleasure princple. And indeed his exhibitions affirmed his own triumph, and perhaps reaffirmed his sense of omnipotence, over the frustration of his situation. At that point he stops. Shaw subjects what he considers the undesirable rule of estab-lished values temporarily to the "liberating pleasure" of anticlimax. But the pleasure principle is his strategy, not his end; and once he had dis-armed his audiences into laughter, he would exhibit a new sense of reality for them. "My way of joking is to tell the truth. It's the funniest joke in the world" (JB, p. 533), for "every jest is an earnest in the womb of time" (p. 611). In addition it cannot be overlooked that the exhibitions of his cleverness must have gratified his narcissism and confirmed a manic sense of omnipotence for him no less than for his father. And in this sense they are one, and the "Shavian inheritance" a fact (*Jokes and Their Relation to the Unconscious* [New York, 1960], pp. 134f., 143).

In his first novel, *Immaturity* (1879), Shaw's alter ego, Smith, becomes a frequent theatergoer and develops an infatuation for a popular dancer. For a time he idealizes her from a distance, but he is soon disillusioned when someone tells him that she is no angel but a distinctively real Biddy Muggins sending her sons through college by dancing. Smith is staggered by this anticlimax to his fantasies, but the omniscient narrator steps in to assure us that the dancer is neither an angel nor Biddy Muggins, but rather a different and presumably more interesting and mysterious person named Erminia Pertoldi, who neither appears nor is mentioned again. But the implication that reality is something else is clear enough. (Biddy is but one of several diminutives of Elizabeth, Shaw's mother's name, to be found in his works.) And it is equally clear that this early manifestation of dialectical structure must have been imbedded in the Shavian psyche. At twenty-three he just did not know to what use to put it, so the structure had to await its content.

Freud discovers in the mechanics of the joke (the joke-work) a compromise between the demands of responding to a given situation with "reasonable criticism" and the "urge not to renounce the ancient pleasure in words and nonsense" (p. 204). This formula could be applied to the "Shavian inheritance" of humor, for the sense of humor was one of Mr. Shaw's ways of adapting to his alcoholism and one of Sonny's ways of adapting to his father.

"The pleasure of humor," Freud writes, "arises from an economy in the expenditure of affect" (pp. 228-29). Language replaces motor activity (Kris, pp. 223f). For Mr. Shaw this may have meant a means of ridding himself of troublesome, frustrating realities without dealing with them more directly and necessarily more exhaustingly. But for Shaw economy and efficiency are adapted to serve the interests of his art. They enable him to gain the concentration of effect and liberation of energy that other artists had discovered in image and symbol; they become a kind of aesthetic ideal.

My passion, like that of all artists, is for efficiency, which means intensity of life and breadth and variety of experience; and already I find, as a dramatist, that I can go at one stroke to the centre of matters that reduce the purely literary man to colorless platitudes. (LS, p. 463)

Freud does not consider anticlimax as such. But it might be added to his list of caricature, parody, travesty, and unmasking as sources of comic pleasure under the heading of "degradation of the sublime" (pp. 200f.).

But he must have long since come to the conclusion that his parents' indifference did not determine his identity and that his father's failure did not signal his own destiny. He was more than the "multiplication of his parents' faults and an accumulation of his own earlier selves."[3] About his mother he could be coldly matter-of-fact, and usually was; but he never accused her, for all her bohemian anarchy, of disillusioning him. The image of the mother found vent in the family romance and remained unbroken. But not so with the father. And whether he transferred feelings of disillusionment with his mother onto his father and identified not with him so much as with his mother's contempt for him, or whether Shaw arrived at his conclusions in other ways, he had little sympathy for men who fail to deal with the world on its own terms. "The lot of the man who sees life truly and thinks about it romantically is Despair." What Sergius, Morell, Roebuck Ransden, and Marchbanks up to a point all have in common is not only that they are romantically conventional men of the day but that their worshipful posture toward women is seen as a kind of fixation associated with childhood dependency.[4] Embodying the "hedonism of the *status quo*," they are defenseless against the natural superiority of Louka, Candida, or Ann Whitefield. For Shaw, perhaps for everybody, despair means abandonment by the love-object without hope of recovery. The skeleton in the Shavian closet, the man who is either betrayed by his early dependencies or deceived by his phallic vanity, inspired a string of dancing *alazons* (imposters) in Shavian comedy.

Shaw had come up from the disillusionment and despair of

[3] Erik H. Erikson, *Young Man Luther* (New York, 1958, 1962), p. 19. The author is not speaking about Shaw, but about a fatalistic view of the individual often fostered by psychoanalysis.

[4] Norman Holland, *The Dynamics of Literary Response* (New York, 1968), pp. 249-51, touches on this point. The quoted phrase immediately following comes from Hans J. Morganthau in *New York Review* (Sept. 24, 1970), p. 39.

his family. The dismal apparition of the drunken family skeleton was mastered by making it dance and later on by leaving it behind. Such a past does not offer hope for the future; despair has no spiritual or creative function in life. Loss cannot be healed by mourning, nor is one better off for encountering despair existentially and emerging on the other side, as Sartre prescribes. Rather, the comic eye renders it foolish and unreal by anticlimax, so that one can proceed to serious things. Shaw was a creative thinker, but not an introspective one. Because he was unwilling to explore the dramatic possibilities of despair, *le néant*, the abyss, his work must suffer a certain attenuation. The closest he comes to despair is in *Heartbreak House* and Captain Shotover, that ancient Shavian whose dubious visionary powers and faltering hold on reality are served by rum—a despairing self-projection had Shaw gone his father's route.

INTRUDING LOVER

In addition to bettering his father at his own defenses, Shaw acquired certain discernible traits from male adults—the father's comic sense, an uncle's scoffing Rabelaisian humor, Lee's mesmeric power over voice and music—and made them his own by enlisting anticlimax and irreverence in the service of realism, and by structuring his writing on musical principles (". . . if you don't know Mozart you will never understand my technique" [YA, p. 11]). He went on using whatever was available, and consumed plots, ideas, systems, reworking them all into the authentic Shavian article. But he could not acquire what was not there.

It is not that he was biologically incapable of the sexuality that every man, as Jack Tanner reminded Roebuck Ramsden, is capable of. He was, but it did not gain precedence for reasons as yet only partly clear. He maintained a strange innocence about the whole area of sex and underestimated the strength as well as the integrative value of adult sexuality. Nor did he conceive of the sex relation as a way of releasing aggression, or grasp the close association between sex and sadism as Strindberg, Wedekind, D. H. Lawrence, and many other contemporaries did. For Shaw sex usually meant trivial sensuality to be abandoned as one outgrows calf love; for woman it was nature's great imperfect means to fulfil her procreative purpose.[5] "Of the two lots," he confided to Ellen Terry, "the woman's lot of perpetual motherhood, and man's of perpetual babyhood, I prefer the man's, I think " (LS, p.645). Nevertheless, despite his attempts to ignore or belittle sexuality, his behavior and his plays will show that he was continually in an uneasy state of conflict over it.

His excursions into society in his first years in London strikingly reveal the extent of his sexual confusion. In the course of extended visits to married friends, among them the Charringtons, the Joyces, the Blands, the Sparlings, and the Webbs, he busied himself in their affairs, ostensibly helping out but often leaving either the couple baffled, or the wife aroused and the husband suspicious. What motivated Shaw in these repeated performances may stem from Lee's intrusion in the Shaw family ostensibly for the purpose of helping his mother and sister in their musical careers, but one continues to wonder, and just as the extent of Lee's involvement was never clear, neither was

---

[5] Or it could serve as a preview of better things to come for the higher faculties:

I was never duped by sex as a basis for permanent relations, nor dreamt of marriage in connection with it. I put everything else before it, and never refused or broke an engagement to speak on Socialism to pass a gallant evening. I valued sexual experience because of its power of producing a celestial flood of emotion and exaltation which, however momentary, gave me a sample of the ecstasy that may one day be the normal condition of conscious intellectual activity. (SS, p. 178; HP, p. 408)

the purpose of Shaw's after he had descended on some family
for a while :

> "You invite him down to your place because you think he will
> entertain your guests with his brilliant conversation," com-
> plained one of his hostesses; "and before you know where you
> are he has chosen a school for your son, made your will for
> you, regulated your diet, and assumed all the privileges of your
> family solicitor, your housekeeper, your clergyman, your doctor,
> your dressmaker, your hairdresser, and your estate agent. When
> he has finished with everybody else, he incites the children to
> rebellion. And when he can find nothing more to do, he goes
> away and forgets all about you." (HP, p. 141)

This fragmentary identification with Lee,[6] which appears more
like imitation, reappeared when Shaw invaded the professional
relationship of Ellen Terry and Henry Irving, and eventually it
faded entirely from his behavior if not from his creative sublima-

[6] The question of the extent of Shaw's identification with Lee is an
extremely difficult one. Weissman writes that "Shaw's childhood and early
adult life bear testimony that he identified himself with Lee." The testimony of facts seems a great deal weaker to me than to Weissman. It is
based on several factors. The fact that Shaw's vegetarianism and abstinences "were imitative of Lee," who liked brown bread and sleeping with
open windows seems unlikely. Nowhere have I found a suggestion that
Lee was himself a vegetarian, nor does Weissman turn up any evidence.
The second factor, Shaw's overdevotion to General Robert E. Lee and his
identification with the " 'weak' child the South, in its rebellion against
the 'parental' North" as evidence that George V. Lee was an early hero
to Shaw, seems merely farfetched. Shaw's brief stretch as a "ghost writer"
for Lee could best be attributed to practical necessities of earning a living,
and Shaw did not wait till Lee's death in 1886 to begin writing in his own
name, as Weissman asserts. On the other hand there is clearly something
to the suggestion that "Lee's mastery over Shaw's mother via voice training
was the area of choice in which Shaw could exploit has own fantasies to
win his mother." It should be added that Lee was an ardent vivisectionist
(he cut up birds to study their larynx), which would not have endeared
him to Shaw; nor did the way he painted whiskers on Sonny at their first
meeting encourage a bond of trust. Nonetheless, Lee was an important
early figure in Shaw's life. His arrival on the scene during Shaw's childhood
must have made him a sexual rival. And his intrusion in the family no
doubt merged with the superfluous child as an intruder, and Lee clearly
offered a solution by oral and verbal mastery. Enlisted into fantasy, he may
have also served as a prototype for the melodramatic hero-villain.
For more on the mysterious Mr. Lee see *Shaw and the Charlatan Genius,*

tions (the child as intruder in the lives of married adults is worked out in *Candida*).

Angel or demon—what was the young intruder? Probably just a sprite; for he would always fly away before one could say. However, a closer look at these activities discloses not only a tendency to repeat, but compulsive reenactments of what must have been a much earlier trauma. As father, Mr. Shaw would unavoidably have intruded on the already tenuous mother-child relationship, and Lee's later intrusion would have served to recall the earlier situation and summon further attempts at mastery through identification, this time with the male aggressor, while simultaneously placing the father in the same helpless position the son had earlier found himself in. The original intruders being phallic, castration fears must have arisen, and their intensity must be matched with the preexisting anxieties stemming from the troubled relationship with the mother in order to discern which were stronger and influenced character formation the more. It is safe to say that both contributed to a pre-genital cast to the Shavian personality. My guess is that the idealized figure of the mother had to be protected from thoughts of loss or injury from phallic invaders, with concomitant fears of castration (hers or the child's) in any respect, a dangerous situation his manic denial may have sought to obscure. Thus, it may be that castration anxiety strengthened his earlier identification with the mother, leading to phallic disavowals and a downgrading of the male sexual role as such, which the inadequacies of the father did little to offset. In fact, the need to revise sexuality is so overwhelming that in the course of time Shaw will undertake heroic efforts to remove it from the human sphere entirely. Nothing less will serve.

A Memoir, by John O'Donovan (Dublin: Dolman Press Ltd., Dufour Editions Inc., 1966).

OPPOSING SPRITE

We now come to a central problem in the formation of Shaw's personality. Not only is the question of guilt a serious one for Shaw, but for all of us it seems to be the toll levied by Freud for entering the gates of civilization. There are several things to be considered in speaking of Shaw and guilt. To begin with, his father was hardly a formidable rival who would provoke identification to offset aggressive impulses aimed at his removal. Drink had pretty well taken care of that anyway. Yet Shaw's insisting that "nobody could hate my father" (SS, p. 146),[7] must oversimplify his feelings, while converting the father's addiction into work habits pays him a certain dubious tribute. Mr. Shaw must often have been reduced to childishness and more so in some ways than his precocious son. Moreover, Shaw's disillusionment with his father coincides with his mother's expression of contempt for her husband, and it must have been increasingly difficult for Shaw to discern with whom, if with anyone, his mother really belonged.

"I have no competitive instinct . . ." (IM, p. 671); "in the ordinary connotation of the word I am the least ambitious of men . . . " (IM, p. 675). It is easy to arch a skeptical brow at these statements. But with whom should a self-declared Shakespearean genius compete? Certainly not Arthur Wing Pinero. And if one insists that Shaw was ambitious, who would call it ordinary? His strong investment in self-preservation may have lessened hostile wishes toward a rival, while his ambitions could more readily be nurtured by the family romance. In any event,

[7] McNulty, Shaw's boyhood friend, disagreed and held that Shaw hated his father; but Shaw's Irish biographer disagrees with McNulty (JE, p. 35). McNulty was there, however, and St. John Ervine was not. Without doubt, sharing his father's first name caused Shaw no end of annoyance and prompted his attempts at suppression: G. Bernard Shaw Bernard Shaw, G.B.S., Shaw.

his aggressive drives do not get locked into a protracted oedipal rivalry where they could be resolved.

Lee's role in the family is on the whole idealized. Shaw was impressed with his energy and originality, his nonacademic approaches to music and medicine. He insisted that Lee was a genius, and liked to boast of having three fathers, for the Rabelaisian uncle, Walter Gurly, also left the imprint of his ribald views. But although each in turn provided him with an education in skeptical irreverence, derisive humor, and anti-professionalism, none of them took a genuine paternal interest in him. At most they sparked partial and provisional identifications. The impostor, the rake, and the self-taught conductor may loom up at various times in the Shavian psyche as the humbug, the philanderer, and the eccentric genius.

But equally to the point, these men served as objects for Shaw's earliest reality-testing of male society. Apart from Lee, who receives special treatment in the family romance, he was not impressed. And when he exclaims that "even the black-guardism of my maternal uncle was a liberating influence" (OB, by permission of the Harvard College Library), he may well have meant that he was relieved of any debt of obedience or bond of loyalty to these father-figures and, by extension, to patriarchal authority in general. His exposure to them and their mainly anti-paternal influence may also have emboldened him during these boyhood years to indulge the powers of his imagination over the shortcomings of reality. He did not experience the "slightest remorse in telling lies whenever they seemed likely to help me out of a difficulty : rather did I revel in the exercise of dramatic invention involved" (IM, pp. 665–66). And so, throughout this period from about four to fourteen, Shaw is pretty much left to his debunkers and his daydreams, while his conscience is left largely unformed—a condition satisfactory neither to Shaw nor to us, and one to which we will return.

The sense of guilt, in the context we have been viewing it, is the typical product of castration fears that have been overcome by internalizing the father-castrator as superego, so that an internal agency is set up to prohibit and punish the ego for entertaining forbidden incest wishes toward mother and death wishes toward father, and, by extension, many other socially unacceptable impulses. It is this sense of oedipal guilt that appears weak in Shaw, but the more archaic sense of shame —especially the fear of being shamed for narcissistic greed—as well as the concept of oral guilt, which an infant contends with over the imagined damage his rage may have inflicted on his introjects, have also found a place in psychoanalytic theory. And I am urging that Shaw's presumed exercise of identification and denial during his earliest experiences set the tone for later stages. Toward both parents he appears to deny any feelings of guilt, and the only acknowledged injuries appear to be inflicted on his own ego, spurring acts more on the order of self-reparation than object-reparation.

Candida has been taken by Eric Bentley as presenting Shaw's oedipal conflicts, viewed from the point of view of Marchbanks (MD). A closer look discloses that the three main characters add up to the complete Shavian personality at that time. Marchbanks is the woman-worshiping child and budding creative talent at the Shelleyan stage, which for Shaw was late adolescence; Morell is the Shavian orator (a "talking machine") and religious Socialist, beloved of the ladies; and Candida is the pragmatic realist who rejects conventions for natural history. It is Shaw's production of the oedipal situation, with Narcissism casting characters and directing an action of revenge and reparation of self-esteem. The poet Marchbanks departs the stronger male, as well as the recipient of Candida's understanding and affection.

If, as described earlier, the Shavian ego had forcibly invaded the id, taken over and desexualized sizable quantities of energy, this seems to have happened without its submitting to the complicated network and inhibitions of male development. This is only an impression, perhaps the illusion cast by our hypomanic individual, but an enormous amount of energy, call it desexualized ego-libido, which Freud felt went into the building up of civilization, and which Shaw directed in his maturity into the instinctually neutral spheres of art, politics, literature, philosophy, and even religion, without the usual encumbrances, is undeniable.[8] The result in any case is the distinctive force of Shaw's "intellectual passion," which surges into cultural areas and makes him the reverse of the normal, genital male, who is pretty much a buffoon of his culture, and will not complain so long as he can secure a continuing sex relation and professional sports on T.V.

The disposal of psychic energy for culture is usually referred to as sublimation; yet to me the term somehow fails to convey the strength, the urgency, or the real meaning of Shaw's involvement in society, not to mention the force of his creativity.[9] Moreover, sublimation has fallen on evil times. Norman O. Brown finds that it leads man to seek in culture the "pale imitation of an imitation," the "shadow of a dream."[10] Shaw viewed culture as the ongoing work of the Life Force—a mystical and irreducible power for him that relies on biological (woman's) and mental (man's) energy; while for a psycho-

[8] "The reaction of the artist to the collective object(s) also involves utilization of the most primitive but acute empathic responses to an extent greater than is true in relation to the personal object" (PA, p. 68).

[9] While sublimation may describe the art of writing or the work of art itself, the "instinctual derivatives that act as its motive force" are not "subdued or neutralized." This distinction has been applied to Shavian drama (JS, p. 254). In a more general vein, Phyllis Greenacre is convinced that "creative activity is highly libidinized" (PA, p. 67).

[10] *Life Against Death*, pp. 163, 165. In *The Writer and Psychoanalysis*, Edmund Bergler describes the result of sublimation as the "grandchild of the original conflict": *"the defense against the defense* against a conflict originating historically in an Id wish" (p. 37).

analyst the Life Force would present itself as the derivative of an earlier conflict. But perhaps for Shaw too, man's energy, being mental and being displaced, must be—the term seems inescapable—sublimated.

On the other hand, Shaw's energy taken in total can only be called titanic. And perhaps the "mighty dead" he felt at home in the world with were the mythic race of Titans, Mother Earth's own sons, who derived their strength from her and used it in her cause against the Olympian male deities. I am not being literal, but Shaw should be attended to when he claims membership in "that older and greater Church" of "laughter" and "good fellowship." When the archaic is reintroduced into society, it may first be received as novelty.

But Shaw must be seen as a special type of Dionysian sprite, a spirit of life-energy, who paid for this strength by relinquishing his sexual aspirations the better to serve the source of all life. In addition, he seems to be a discontented Titan who aspired to scale the Olympian heights of Creative Evolution.[11] He once wrote to Ellen Terry:

> You say I'd be sick of you in a week; but this is another boast: it implies you could entertain me for a whole week. Good Heavens! With what? With art?—with politics?—with philosophy?—or with any other department of culture? I've written more about them all (for my living) than you ever thought about them. (LS, p. 623)

But Mother Earth is also the Virgin Mother, and Shaw hastened to add, "One does not get tired of adoring the Virgin Mother." He could worship the Virgin Mother in Ellen Terry, Janet Achurch, Mrs. Pat Campbell; he could serve them by writing

---

11 It may be noted, without drawing the parallels too fine, that when the Greek gods climbed the patriarchal Mount Olympus, Dionysus underwent a reformation. He was subjected to a second birth from the fertile thigh of Zeus. Shaw's self-creation and instinctual conversions amounted to a kind of second birth, for which, however, he owed nothing to the patriarchal powers of his day.

Vitalist plays for them to act in; but he could not live with them, and his other commitments insured him against their dangerous appeal.

In a certain sense Shaw's life took on the shape of an elaborate campaign aimed at removing certain flawed institutions from society—bourgeois marriage, Capitalism, third-rate theater, and the "Crosstianity" of Paul from the Christianity of Jesus. Capitalism was corrupted by profiteering businessmen and slum landlords. The theater was dominated by either hack writers or limited ones like Pinero and Jones, by aimless bardolatry, and by actor-managers like Henry Irving who excluded quality for popularity. The Christian God, sharing the defects of Blake's "Nobodaddy" and Shelley's "Almighty Fiend," became a "Koepenick Captain of the heavens" (PBM, p. lxvi). All of these structures and systems suffer from patriarchal contamination, some misuse and failure of male authority. In so striving, Shaw was not only undoing conflicts created by the phallic intruder, but he was acknowledging his father's impotence and disavowing a phallic function for himself. Thus his many roles and identities may obscure the lack of the important sexual one. It was fortunate, and not a little coincidental, that the very elements in society that he warred against were manifestly in need of reform as well as being vulnerable to criticism, so that his instinctual energies are transformed as they find roles in the service of society at large. Very possibly the means that brought this about is by now a familiar one. If Shaw's early disagreeable self-representations could be disavowed, in part by externalization, perhaps also early sexual wishes along with their representative, the father, disagreeable both for his felt invasion and for his real failures, could be expected to receive similar treatment. A recent book on Shaw has the appropriate title *The Chucker Out,* supposedly a tribute, but a succinct and telling epithet, since it is one that he himself suggested.

Shaw's evident by-passing of his father as a masculine model, leaving him without a standard male superego, meant that he had to depend more on early identifications, but it also meant that he was relatively impervious to the Damoclean sword of castration anxiety and many of its attendant cultural mores and restrictions, which he made out to be "artificial" or irrelevant, and that he could proceed to create his own, as it turned out, alternative values. He viewed this preliminary and destructive phase of removal positively as a necessary ground-clearing to enable Creative Evolution to operate unhampered by present artificial systems. He became a sort of Vitalist John the Baptist, making straight the way, as his Don Juan expressed it, for the greater one whose shoe straps he was unworthy to touch—not the divine Jesus but the mystical Life Force. This campaign becomes virtually a lifelong drama. In fact, it is set up specifically to continue indefinitely.

It is hard to avoid concluding that because his parents did not perform as parents and allow him to work out his impulses and feelings with them, he proceeded to displace conflicts onto whatever seemed suitable around him at the time. In so doing he served not himself alone but affected large sectors of society, because the oedipal situation had been transferred to reality in the widest sense. We cannot be certain that on some sort of vast primitive scale he programmed his later life, but if it cannot be proved, its operations in the world of the theater can at least be reconstructed.

Shaw's profoundest experience growing up in his family was finding himself a superfluous child, an intruder in an unloving world. His narcissism counteracted this somewhat, but self-sufficiency alone was not enough, nor in the long run was the reliance on fantasy. His strongest need remained:

> the being used for a purpose recognized by yourself as a mighty one; the being thoroughly worn out before you are thrown on

the scrap heap; the being a force of Nature instead of a feverish selfish little clod of ailments and grievances complaining that the world will not devote itself to making you happy. (PMS, p. 510)

This lifelong obsession with usefulness, which accounts for much of the energy expenditure, reveals his deficient sense of inherent self-worth. His narcissism was after all an early response to what he had missed from his parents. And hence he must work at becoming useful if the missing self-esteem is ever to be regained. Moreover, he tended to view reality according to his emerging inner model, valuing man for his evolutionary appetite, society because it could improve, life on the basis of further biological development, and God as the future of Creative Evolution.

The superfluous child rose by sheer gravitation only to find himself the outsider in London:

I was outside society, outside politics, outside sport, outside the Church. If the term had been invented then I should have been called the Complete Outsider. (IM, p. 680)

Consequently the new setting can provide him with opportunities for new displacements of his energies. He goes on to say that in music, painting, literature, and science he was the true insider. More accurately, these endeavors offered ways for him to get inside, and it took several years before he actually made it and the world had confirmed it. With the English language as his weapon (IM, p. 674) and the dominant posture of his prose expressing the self-appointed opponent, Shaw, like Jack Tanner in *Man and Superman,* assumed a kind of giant-killing and woman-rescuing vocation for himself.[12]

The theatrical world at that time was dominated by two giants. The style, taste, and economic control of the actor-managers had a strangulating hold on the theater, the strongest

[12] "Throughout his life Shaw wrote as an *opponent* . . . ." Richard Ohmann, *Shaw; the Style and the Man,* pp. 74-90. For the ways in which Ellen Terry fulfilled certain requirements for the rescue fantasy, see OC, p. 196.

grip of all being Henry Irving's. He acted the popular melodramas of the day and tailored to his talents the plays of
Shakespeare, who was the other giant. Irving's acting partner
was the incomparable Ellen Terry. Shaw's attachment to her
made him write:

> I must be used, built into the solid fabric of your life as far as
> there is any usable brick in me, and thrown aside when I am
> used up. (LS, p. 676)

The manner in which he set out to be useful was to pit himself
against the dual domination of Irving and Shakespeare in order
to rescue Ellen Terry for the New Drama of Ibsen and G.B.S.
As a critic, "Shaw dismissed the entire London drama, from
Shakespeare at its head to his own contemporaries, as too childish to claim any intellectual character whatsoever," he wrote
of himself in the third person, "and he seized every opportunity
to revile Irving and Daly for wasting the talent of such great
gifted actresses as Ellen Terry and Ada Rehan on pre-Ibsenite
plays." Better "to have tied him [Irving] up in a sack with
every existing copy of the works of Shakespeare and dropped
him into the crater of the nearest volcano," he declared in his
criticism, where he consistently attacked Irving (OT3, p. 38).[13]

The rivalry involved the authority of the actor versus that
of the author.

> The history of the Lyceum with its twenty years' steady cultiva-
> tion of the actor as a personal force, and its utter neglect of the
> drama, is the history of the English stage during that period.
> Those twenty years have raised the social status of the theatrical
> profession and culminated in the official recognition of our

13 Sir Augustus Harris, occupying in the musical world a position similar
to Irving's in the theater, was repeatedly challenged by Shaw to perform
the new music of Wagner. To the English public, Ibsen and Wagner were
social nobodies whose cause as unacknowledged geniuses Shaw sought to
advance to some extent, at least as surrogates of his own genius. In making
them acceptable, he would become accepted. Open the door to the new,
and the intruder would disappear inside.

chief actor as the peer of the President of the Royal Academy, and the figure-heads of the other arts. And now I, being a dramatist and not an actor, want to know when the drama is to have its turn. (OT3, p. 39)

Shaw's attitude, however, was not simple, nor did he intend to compete with Irving as actor-manager. He greatly admired Irving's talent and its potential use. He had first seen the actor years earlier and was "struck by the acting of one Henry Irving, who created a modern realistic character named Digby Grant in a manner which, if applied to an Ibsen play now, would astonish us . . ." (OT3, p.145). He repeatedly appealed to Irving to do Ibsen, and even tempted him with his own *Man of Destiny,* which had a Napoleon part for him and a mysterious-lady part for Ellen Terry. Irving held onto the script, preventing others from producing it, without giving Shaw an answer for several months. When Shaw finally met with Irving, he found he liked the old actor, even though Irving finally preferred to do a mediocre Napoleon play by Sardou. Shaw's play was not a vintage piece anyway, and possibly he wanted equally to tempt Irving with a light sampling of the New Drama and to enjoy the emotional benefits of bringing Irving and Terry together on the Shavian stage as his parents never came together in their real-life drama.[14] The total sequence may appear as: initial identification, followed by an internal reversal wherein the

[14] "I am myself the fruit of an unsuitable marriage . . . as an example of parental competence to guide, educate, and develop children it was so laughably absurd that I have been trying ever since to get something done about it" (EP, pp. 75-6). Although this passage could scarcely serve to support the above assertion, it does contain within it a non sequitur—unusual in a writer so logical and correct as Shaw—that may be a Freudian slip. Shaw means to say that since coming to some negative conclusions about his parents' marriage, he has been trying to "get something done about" the instituion of marriage, but the antecedent of "it" is his parents' marriage and may therefore imply that he is displacing onto society a wish to correct their marriage and thereby undo its harmful effects on him; the same wish may easily have been activated temporarily by the Irving-Terry partnership. It would then be the positive side of a wish of which the negative side soon followed.

revered objects are turned into aspects of the disagreeable child, and then chucked out.

To describe Shaw's realistic and constructive aims of helping Irving realize his talents in mature drama as a defence against aggressive wishes toward a rival or the unloved part of oneself, is not to deny the validity of these aims. We can see in retrospect that they were strictly in keeping with the needs of the theater at that time. But their sources have nothing to do with the reform of the theater. For the captive Ellen Terry could provoke him into writing:

> What do you mean by Hampton Court? Have you a place down there? or do you only drive about with H. I.? I once or twice have met you on Richmond Terrace or thereabouts with him, like two children in a gigantic perambulator, and have longed to seize him, throw him out, get in, take his place, and calmly tell the coachman to proceed. (LS, p. 646)

He reminds Ellen Terry that "your Henry is not a hero off the stage" (LS, p. 760), and reinforces the idea when he passes onto her the rumor that "Henry *was* drunk in Richard." Shaw is then reminded of his own disillusionment over his father's drinking: "There the scoffer began: then was sown the seed which so annoys Henry when it comes up in my articles" (LS, p. 773). So Sir Henry must pay for Mr. Shaw's alcoholism.

Irving remained impervious to the New Drama, insulated perhaps by his own narcissism ("his self-absorption makes him as incapable as a baby of suffering the slightest cross without petulance" [LS, p. 761]); and as Shaw came to realize that he could not unite Irving and Terry on a Shavian stage, he increasingly wrote the man off as failing "to create a new drama . . . and cutting himself off from all contact with the dramatic vitality [read Shaw and Ibsen] of his own time" (OT3, p. 145). Years later, in 1906, when Shaw succeeded in getting Ellen Terry to act commercially in his plays, the New Drama had already succeeded in loosening Irving's grip on the stage, relegating him increasingly to playing the provinces, where he died in 1905. And to that extent Shaw effected his removal along with Ellen Terry's rescue. A similar dualism marked Shaw's attitude toward Shakespeare. If the princess Ellen was a captive of the creaky theatrical apparatus of the "Ogre's Castle" (ET, p. xxv), she was also confined to playing in the archaic contrivances of the Bard of Avon. Once again the rivalry is established:

> With the single exception of Homer, there is no eminent writer, not even Sir Walter Scott, whom I can despise so entirely as I despise Shakespeare when I measure my mind against him. The intensity of my impatience with him occasionally reaches such a pitch, that it would positively be a relief to me to dig him up and throw stones at him, knowing as I do how incapable he and his worshippers are of understanding any less obvious form of indignity. To read Cymbeline and to think of Goethe, of Warner, of Ibsen, is, for me, to imperil the habit of studied moderation of statement which years of public responsibility as a journalist have made almost second nature in me. (OT2, p. 195)

The operative word in the passage is *mind*. Shakespeare's mind is found wanting because it has not been formed by Darwin, Marx, Nietzsche, *et al.*, and is therefore not concerned with modern issues. He lacked Nietzsche's conception of the Superman, fell short of the *engagé* that the "terrible Norwewgian" Ibsen was then felt to have had.[15] His plays

---

[15] "We have got so far beyond Shakespeare as a man of ideas that there is by this time hardly a famous passage in his works that is considered fine on any other ground than that it sounds beautiful" (OT 3; SS, pp. 200-201). For Shaw, to express despair is to yield to it, and that is why he took Macbeth's "tale told by an idiot" speech as Shakespeare's own confession (HP, pp. 162-63). Shakespeare had "no creed and no programme," whereas Shaw was a "social reformer and doctrinaire first, last and all the time." Life was not a "brief candle" for Shaw but a "splendid torch" (HP, p. 217). They shared a "sensitiveness to social, political, and religious injustices and stupidities," but as Shakespeare "saw

were quarrels with God for not making humanity better, instead of assaults on the idle, ruling classes for tolerating inhuman conditions. Incidentally, he is also guilty after the fact of producing generations of worshipers. It is not that Shaw wanted Shaviolatry to replace Bardolatry, but that any form of idolatry wastes time and energy and prevents people from grappling with the real work of bettering life. Shakespeare was the opiate of the people and Shaw was the Marx of the theater. Shrines immortalizing the past can overshadow present realities, and Shavian iconoclasm had its constructive purpose. Furthermore, his efforts toward restoration of the complete text to replace acting versions are well known, as are his acute perceptions of Shakespearean character and of the music in his poetry. His admiration comes out in the same passage :

> I am bound to add that I pity the man who cannot enjoy Shakespeare. He has outlasted thousands of abler thinkers and will outlast a thousand more.

Shaw encountered Shakespeare and Irving as rivals and obstacles in his path, but in no sense as ominous, threatening, or superior. They were often coupled unflatteringly in his mind; he places Irving in a child's perambulator and states that we are "growing out of Shakespeare." Being his senior

---

no way out it drove him to a Swiftian pessimism in which he saw man as an Angry Ape, and finally into a cynicism made bearable by the divine gaiety of genius" *(Ibid)*. But Shakespearean genius, just like Gilbertian topsy-turvyism, is not enough. The complete playwright must see a "way through the Valley of the Shadow" and believe that "when men understand their predicament they could and would escape from it" *(Ibid)*.

It should be added that just as Shaw anticipated modern editors in his recognition of the need for restoration of the whole Shakespearean text, he was also part of the general reaction by the proponents of the New Drama against the loose, episodic structure of Elizabethan drama. Foremost among these was William Archer, and he has left behind in *The Old Drama and the New* a testament of the extremes to which criticism based on the well-made formula can be carried.

in years and reputation, both initially fostered identification, but the young intruder proceeds to reverse the situation, expose their deficiencies, and chuck them out, so that as the true adult he need not compete with children. He explained to Ellen Terry that he could not get along with Irving because "he would have behaved like a baby sooner or later; and *I* shouldn't have spoiled him" (LS, p. 761). He dealt with Shakespeare by trying to rescue him from becoming a mere object of pleasure and with Irving by trying to rescue him from the pleasure-mongering of a public too easily gratified. From this aimles expenditure of energy he would enlist them in the service of present-day reality. They were not permitted to be objects of inherent worth but instruments of Shavian strategy and subject to the same transforming energy that operated on society as a whole. Plainly stated, the worship of the Bard and the acclaim of the actor were too reminiscent of the fateful self-regard of the narcissistic child (or the self-indulgence of the alcoholic father); they had to be disavowed and reformed as Shaw's narcissism had to be turned useful. Many years after his critical onslaughts he quietly admitted that "nobody can be better than Shakespeare, though anybody may now have things to say that Shakespeare did not say, and outlooks on life and character which were not open to him" (SS, p. 190). Shaw, then, did not pretend to be better than his rival, for he knew that culturally, and he felt that psychologically, he was more advanced : he was content to be the Bard's successor. And to put it more clinically, the oedipal rivalry, though strong, was secondary to and much less intense than the prior need to control the instinctual object, whose current incarnation was Ellen Terry. Control by utility becomes here, as it does generally, one of Shaw's major adaptive strategies. It may help account for the agility of his "mercurial mind" in shifting from critic to playwright.

Finally, as Shaw's friendships were never intimate, so were his hatreds never personal. As Oscar Wilde observed, he "has no enemies but is intensely disliked by all his friends." Irving drew Shaw's anger because the actor wasted his talent, emasculated the Bard, and monopolized the stage, which included Ellen Terry. Irving the man never really entered into it any more than did Henry Arthur Jones, a beneficiary of Shavian criticism and support who broke with Shaw later on. But the vanity of these men and their vulnerability led them to take Shaw's attacks personally and underestimate his seriousness. It is the difference perhaps between the everyday garden variety of narcissism and Shaw's more extreme kind, which carried him beyond sensitivity to personal offenses and rendered him far less vulnerable and far more serious. He could not afford to be sensitive in the ordinary way because his personality had become too enmeshed in the world around him to allow individuals to disturb him. Like his Don Juan, he sought reality over happiness; and now reality, in a sense being all he has, comes to matter most and personal feelings least. And yet, even when he turns to reality, he tries to make it conform to his idea of it, which is also his fantasy of it.

Moreover, there is the difference between aggression as a natural drive in life that enables the organism to grow and expand by overcoming obstacles, even as a plant must break through the earth's crust, and the kind of aggression with a hostile component usually intended for a definite object (PA, pp. 62–3). In actual life these necessarily overlap, and for Shaw they are as inseparable as his iconoclasm is from his evolutionary appetite. There are, however, more particular aspects of Shaw's aggression. Just as he foreswore all carnivorous habits and opposed vivisection and vaccination as an assault on sacred flesh, women for the most part are delivered from his wrath; his skepticism and idealization maintain a balance of safe distance.

Men, on the other hand, are fair game. The rules are that the anger be verbal, purposeful, and only minimally personal. The better Shaw can level his sights on classes (the British public) or groups (doctors, vivisectors, clergymen), the more potent is his volley. It is directed neither at certain sitting ducks nor at the whole shooting match; it operates on the structure of society, which is often why it is so effective.

We would ordinarily regard the mixture of positive and negative impulses brought into play by the joint tyrannies of Irving and Shakespeare, as ambivalence, and trace it back to Shaw's family situation. The fact that he had a double oedipal conflict with a father and a mother's "lover" may have been coincidental, or it may have reinforced his involvement in the parallel situation he found Ellen Terry in. But although aggression and reaction-formation played some part in his relationships, the concept of ambivalence leads to a discussion of neurotic conflict and guilt feelings, which does not take us far enough. Rather we see him as exhibiting a characterological phenomenon in which his hypomanic destiny derives from his narcissism. "I was entirely free," he somewhat too simply declared, "from the neurosis (as I class it) of Original Sin" (SS, p. 175). He continually embarrassed his friends by violating their confidences, especially in matters of the heart. He seemed to have nothing to hide and averred, "It never occurred to me to conceal my opinions" (IM, p. 660). And, making allowances for self-dramatization, we may see that many of his innermost feelings —tenderness, rage, jealousy, adoration—are contained in his letters to Ellen Terry, who insisted on having them published and let him write the Preface. Yet, he remains shy, and his shyness hid much.

But now I may seem to be blundering toward a contradiction. We have seen that Shaw was able to direct great resources of psychic energy into those cultural spheres that advance civilization. During the energetic years of the 1890s, he viewed himself as an advanced man both biologically and intellectually. And yet Freud measures civilized advance by the sense of guilt. It is one aspect of Freudian dualism that makes modern man still capable of tragic conflict. In other words, we want to ask: does this mean that Shaw, being no Eugene O'Neill, can get away with anything, and is so super-civilized as to be beyond guilt as his plays are immune to tragedy? And what about conscience? Can its function be separated from the sense of guilt? "We cannot get away from the assumption," Freud insisted, that

> man's sense of guilt springs from the Oedipal complex and was acquired at the killing of the father by the brothers banded together. On that occasion an act of aggression was not suppressed but carried out; but it was the same act of aggression whose suppression in the child is supposed to be the source of his sense of guilt . . . . His aggressiveness is introjected, internalized; it is, in point of fact, sent back to where it came from —that is, it is directed towards his own ego. There it is taken over by a portion of the ego, which sets itself over against the rest of the ego as super-ego, and which now, in the form of "conscience," is ready to put into action against the ego the same harsh aggressiveness that the ego would have liked to satisfy upon other, extraneous individuals. The tension between the harsh super-ego and the ego that is subjected to it, is called by us the sense of guilt. (CD, pp. 78, 70)

This model suits mankind in general, but it does not suit Shaw, less because he was a born genius than because of his "manic solution." Edoardo Weiss describes what occurs when the "ego identifies with the superego" by usurping the "function of the superego, while it externalizes the portion to which the superego objects." Specifically, the ego acquires such superego functions as observing, controlling, forbidding, commanding, and punishing, and exercises them "in respect to people of the external world." Those who follow this developmental route are the hypomanics. They feel the impulse to persecute and to punish other people, whom they accuse of all sorts of misdeeds; they accuse them of being godless, dishonest, of undermining social morals, of betraying their country, of committing subversive acts, etc. . . they are not afraid of persecution; rather, other people should be afraid of their persecutions. It is noteworthy that they themselves feel free to behave in an objectionable and dishonest way.[16]

Add a qualifier about dishonesty, change a few of the targets in society, and how clearly has Shaw's likeness been captured! "I like fighting successful people," he wrote to Ellen Terry (ET, p. 34), "attacking them; rousing them; trying their mettle; kicking down their sand castles so as to make them build stone ones."

During his latency years, Shaw admits to typical anti-social attitudes. "My hero in fiction was the rebel, not the goody-goody citizen, whom I despised" (PBM, p. 103). And these attitudes evidently carried over into behavior. "When I associated with other boys in secret gangs it was to do mischief for the fun of it, to wreck and steal and circumvent law and to emulate Dick Turpin and Jack Sheppard, and generally to defy the commandments and do whatever our teachers and the police told us we must not. do." As noted above, he once painted his bedroom wall with "watercolor frescoes of Mephistopheles" (IM, p. 666), a step away from being dominated by a bad self-image but one that in this instance does not lead to disavowal so much as reversal: the good opponent against a bad society. At around fourteen, when he was experiencing the "dawning of moral passion," he recorded this incident:

I had only one conflict with the school discipline. Some offence was committed; and the master, to discover whom to punish, asked each boy in succession whether he was the culprit. I refused to answer on the ground that no boy was legally bound

16 Edoardo Weiss, "The Phenomenon of Ego Passage," *Journal of American Psychoanalytic Association* 5 (1957): 280-81.

to criminate himself, and that the interrogation was a temptation to boys to lie. A day or two passed during which I was supposed to be doomed to some appalling punishment; but I heard no more of it; the situation was new to the teaching staff. When authorities do not know what to do, they can only do what was done the last time. As I had created an unprecedented situation, they did nothing; but there were no more such interrogatories. It was my first reform. (SS, p. 51)

Shaw's refusal—indeed his indifference—to allow an appeal to an inherent or acquired sense of guilt to intimidate him can be appreciated by recalling the comparable situation of a gifted youth in conflict with the Dublin teaching authorities that James Joyce gives us in *A Portrait of the Artist as a Young Man*. Authority with its pandybat morality bears down so heavily on Stephen Dedalus that he must either defy or submit. The authoritarian device of controlling behavior by playing on guilt is partly responsible for Stephen Dedalus's resorting to "silence, exile, and cunning"; while for Shaw the outcome is contempt, confidence, and reform. External authority is ineffectual unless it can count on an internal responding agency in the recipient. Perhaps because of Shaw's disorganized family, wherein values of authority are mocked, scoffed at, or flaunted, he never associated authority with goodness, only at times with necessity. His personal civility and mildness, his sense of anticlimax, even his snobbery, are all traits that he very likely acquired from his father, but they fall short of "internalizing the paternal function."

So we return to the likelihood that he was far more intimately aligned with his mother's character and pragmatic mastery of situations. In fact, one may wonder that if superego means internalizing the "paternal function," whether Shaw had not rather internalized more of the female function, providing him with a super-conscience instead of a superego. Certainly his creativity, his Vitalist morality and Creative Evolution, his interest in life processes, eugenics, rearing children, not to mention his garrulity and dietary concerns, all have their analogy with feminine life and those aspects of procreation which include fertility, gestation, and nature.

Did he have a conscience, then? Conscience: the heir of the oedipal period, the "embodiment, first of parental criticism, and subsequently of that of society" (IV, p. 53). Although Shaw's "utterly uncoercive" parents did not speak to him in such a capacity, he himself warned against a simplistic view of this question. Summing up his family's influence on him, he remarked that the "children of Bohemian Anarchists are often in such strenuous reaction against their bringing-up that they are the most tyrannically conventional of parents" (SS, p. 34). The principle does not literally apply to one who was neither parent nor conventional, though the implicit point about tyranny as a reaction to anarchy is apposite. In less extreme terms, overly permissive parents often end up with the most militantly moral, Red-guard kind of children. But Shaw's stringent asceticism, as we have seen, places him on the extreme side.

In view of his atypical and inattendant parents, his conscience had to be something of an improvisation, and it must have had unusual unconscious precursors. We may distinguish the archaic commandments against cannibalistic urges, which later appeared as phobic avoidances or reaction-formations in the forms of vegetarianism, stimulant abstinence, his "cutting" mind, and so forth, and attribute these operations to the early defense of identification with the aggressor. During the energy transformations of adolescence there occurs a second stage of ego-ideal fulfillment, which Shaw designates the "birth of moral passion." Culminating around fourteen, these processes put a check on his aimless "romantic day-dreaming," and his boyish disregard for truth. A few years earlier the Shaw family had dropped all conventional religious observances, although Sonny continues to formulate and recite prayers partly for his own delectation and partly to cast a magical, "protective spell" during thunderstorms (IM, p. 665). But by fourteen "intellectual integrity synchronized" with "moral passion," and he stopped praying as he had already stopped believing. In fact, it is no exaggeration to say that by this time his disillusionment with his father, the effects of Lee's dubious morality, and uncle Walter's derisive debunking had spread through all the patriarchal orders up to and finally including the "Koepenick Captain of the heavens" worshiped as the Christian God. But as this line of influence leveled off and declined, the new sun of moral passion was on the ascent.

Rising out of symbiotic concerns over fusion and separation and from needs to protect the integrity and the early mother image, it denies and externalizes guilt, rejects male sexuality along with patriarchal value-systems, and works toward the affirmative morality of the Life Force, the true north on the compass of Shaw's conscience in his maturity. More modestly, it provided a desperately needed self-respect as well as the beginnings of an identity-within-himself. It organized the unorthodox influences of his three fathers into the defiant Rationalism that would try to satisfy itself with atheistic Darwinism for the next few years. His first published writing, a letter to a Dublin newspaper when he was eighteen, is a provisional combination of iconoclasm and idealism. It is a very civil and well-phrased Rationalist attack on an itinerant evangelist. In it Shaw is anxious to expose the appeal to base motives, but he is not yet ready to promulgate any alternative (AH, pp. 47–48).

As his mental awareness sharpens into the "cutting edge that everybody dreads," and his moral passion begins searching for ways of combining the idealization of the mother with outlets of social usefulness, he advances toward the fusion of science and mysticism that will be called Creative Evolution and toward that wedding of biology and magic which will be called the Superman and serve as the replacement for phallic-man.

Aside from other implications, this advance meant that Shaw was equipped with a different defensive alignment from his contemporaries and consequently with different ways of perceiving reality. It set him at odds with the various patriarchial structures of his day, not as the underdog who may identify with women as victims of male oppression, but as the outsider who could see through the essential weakness, cowardice, and hypocrisy of these structures as embodied in the characters of Morell and Roebuck Ramsden, two classical Shavian examples of official Victorian morality and authority. Their beliefs and principles were merely conventional signs of their "artificial system," and overturning them, exposing the "hedonism of the *status quo*," may have been a kind of retaliation, but in his drama it made for nothing more serious than comic iconoclasm.

However, his contemporaries' defenses were certainly real to them and performed vitally in maintaining their psychic equilibrium. Anyone who grasped that from the inside would think twice before tampering, but Shaw preferred to view their defenses as mere conventions. His purpose was to show that if stage conventions could be manipulated or overturned without disastrous consequences, then so could the conventions men live by. "If you take people seriously off the stage," he asked in *The Philanderer*, "why shouldn't you take them seriously on it, where they're under some sort of restraint?" (PH, p.147).

> The tragedy and comedy of life lie in the consequences, sometimes terrible, sometimes ludicrous, of our persistent attempts to found our institutions on the ideals suggested to our imaginations by our half-satisfied passions, instead of on a genuinely scientific natural history. (PL, p. 121)

Moreover, Shaw did not tamper with theatrical conventions

merely to bring about clever anti-romantic inversions. We have seen that quite early he dissociated himself from the "mechanical topsy-turvydom" of W. S. Gilbert. Shaw wanted to expose these conventions as unnecessary, arbitrary, and detachable so that they would yield to the realism of Bluntschli, the pragmatism of Candida, the Vitalism of Ann Whitefield.

The trouble was that the majority of his fellowmen did suffer from loss, castration-anxiety, guilt feelings, and the rest of the complaints our flesh is heir to, which all added up to much more than "Victorian sentiment" and "romantic convention." Even allowing for some dead wood among the Victorian rococo of their defenses, they were not all that arbitrary or detachable. Those "half-satisfied passions" were stronger, and in their own way more vital, than he from the heights of manic cerebrations estimated.

But he came at least close to doing so in two instances. In *The Quintessence of Ibsenism* (1891), he dismisses the man who idealizes his marriage in order to conceal feelings of discontent and frustration. However, when Shaw writes a play about the idealist of home and hearth, his Morell may find it necessary to be away from home much of the time, but he does in fact deeply need Candida and will cling to her on any terms he can. Consequently, the drama contains a certain artificiality of its own. Nor is there any hint of a Strindbergian duel to ensue after the final curtain, as some critics have insisted. That drama has been concocted by the Morells on the other side of the stage.

Twenty years later Shaw wrote that the bourgeois clings to his conventions (i.e., ideals) because he wants certainty, security, consensus, and not to be bothered. "His dread and hatred of revolutions and heresies and men with original ideas is his dread of disorientation and insecurity" (BX, p. 120). The terror felt by the ordinary respectable man "when some man of genius rocks the moral ground beneath him by denying the validity of a convention" is as real as the terror of an earthquake. This is acutely perceptive, but it tells us more about Ibsen's plays than about Shaw's, and more about Nietzsche's philosophy than about Shaw's Creative Evolution. Anticlimax, discussion, and the Vitalist alternative conspire against the Shavian earthquake. Only *Mrs. Warren's Profession* and possibly *Widowers' Houses* set off really disturbing tremors in society.

To return once more to the question of guilt, we know that the laws, restriction, and punitive measures of the parentally derived super-ego become agents of inner moral authority in most individuals. Freud believed that ill-fortune and external frustration "greatly enhance the power of the conscience in the superego" because "fate is regarded as a substitute for the parental agency." Therefore when an individual suffers misfortune, "he searches his soul, acknowledges his sinfulness, imposes abstinences on himself, and punishes himself with penance" (CD, p. 73). When Cusins in *Major Barbara* objects to a prayer service because Lady Britomart "would have to say before all the servants that we have done things we ought not to have done, and left undone things we ought to have done, and that there is no health in us," he is speaking in Shavian accents. "As for myself," he stoutly declares, "I flatly deny it : I have done my best." For Shaw, failures lacked their fateful meaning. Frustrations tended to reinforce his self-preservative energies, causing him not to withdraw but to redouble his efforts and to render his faith in the Life Force all the more unshakable. For what else but the antithesis of Fate is the Life Force?

If we encounter little expenditure of genital sexual energy, we do not find sexual perversions laying claim to his libido, and whatever inhibitions we encounter do not appear to lead to symptom-formation and a damming-up of libido so much as a redirecting of it, a very curious redirecting of it at times, one hastens to add. To say that his compromises were more often productive adaptations than neurotic symptoms may polarize the issue into a false dichotomy. And do we consider his works as creative solutions or as presentations of unresolved conflict? It is too soon to say. But some things are becoming clear. The great resources of energy at his disposal, coupled with his Vitalist morality, his deliverance from genital aims, his peculiarly diminished castration-anxiety, personal animosity, and sense of guilt, his self-sufficiency along with his self-possession—all contributed to the conviction that he could get away with almost anything he attempted and suffer neither a recoil from reality nor a collapse from inner conflict. Thus while he may seem to many today to be receding behind the frame of a rather inhibited Victorian neurasthenic, his impact on his own society must be kept in mind. Anthony Burgess in 1969 has written him off as "sexually frigid," while a contemporary in 1896 wrote of him as "intellectually full-blooded" (CR). The views are not mutually exclusive. Shaw made love to a merry widow and probably to one or two actresses besides; he marched with the workers to Trafalgar Square, lectured and argued vigorously in parks and public halls, fought with censors for banning his plays, whipped his actors into peak performances, and sent his audiences away shocked when his plays were allowed production; he attacked his countrymen for their insularity, patriotism, and hypocrisy, scolded the medical profession for its cruelty, and the Church for its barbarism. In his nineties he kicked up quite a row with Bertrand Russell. But he always conducted himself in a civilized manner. And the fact that his reputation for philandering far exceeded his performance, or that his exercise of aggression was always carefully administered, does not mean that he was utterly asexual or that his social indignation was a bluff. He abhorred violence, while he thrived on controversy. He triumphed over his enemy in debate without humiliating him and patched up quarrels among his fellow Fabians without alienating them (SS, p. 112). He even elicited Yeats's grudging admiration:

> I delighted in Shaw the formidable man. He could hit my enemies and the enemies of all I loved, as I could never hit, as no living author that was dear to me could ever hit. (*Autobiography*, p. 188)

Lingering feelings of shame or guilt diminished with his turning to Socialism. He regarded this movement as a way of losing one's *"mauvais honte"* by discovering larger causes affecting individual life and by projecting responsibility and blame for individual malaises onto the Capitalist system, whose greedy masters will henceforth be put to shame. "Yet even I cannot wholly conquer shame," Jack Tanner confesses, before turning it back onto Roebuck Ramsden: "The more things a man is ashamed of, the more respectable he is" (MS, p. 528).

But before we get ahead of ourselves, we should be able to conclude that if guilt is inevitable for civilized man, Shaw managed to minimize it in himself as well as to exploit it in others. "All you mean," Tanner concludes, "is that you think I ought to be ashamed of talking about my virtues. You don't mean that I haven't got them." And since we are interested in the interplay between personality and plays, we may find in the results a paradoxical sort of freedom. The virtual absence of guilt feelings and of a sense of the past as pregnant for the future may well have robbed his plays of grappling with the deeper causalities that underlie the human condition and deprived his artistic vision of a sense of fate or finality. His childhood was far from shameless; his first years in London reveal a shy, awkward young man, and an accident proneness, usually on a bicycle, no doubt belies a certain anxiety over failure and castration.

FORMIDABLE MAN

In fact, the image of a writing and talking machine mounted on a bicycle and careering through London, if it can be imagined, is not entirely absurd, although it may look more Beckettian than Shavian. Once on his own, Shaw was constantly on the go. And if he did not literally write letters while pedaling along, he was probably mentally composing them. Many letters, speeches, and dramatic scenes he did manage to pen while riding trains and during pauses walking. *"Arms and the Man* was mostly written on a bus"* (CR, p. 537). He was seldom still, and when he was not traveling about London to attend meetings or give speeches—for we have now taken leave of the Dublin youth—he was visiting friends, invading their marriages, intruding in the careers of theater people. He was intruding everywhere. Even his writing continues his intrusive mode. The novels are about social intruders. His criticisms intrude on the staid world of the arts. His plays dramatize intrusions and manic flights, not all of them ideas. He is all energy, he is useful to society, he is needed and no longer the superfluous child. But how this comes about is by no means simple. It will take at least a chapter to explain.

3
FATHERLANDLESS FELLOW

Telegram just received to say that the governor has left the universe on rather particular business and set me up as
The Orphan. (LS, p. 132)

The Germans . . . denounced me as a fatherlandless fellow. They were quite right. (IM, p. 642)

IMMATURITY

The superfluous child in the Shaw family back in Dublin became the twenty-year old "Complete Outsider" in the London of 1876, where opportunuities for using resources of energy unavailable to him earlier made it possible for Sonny eventually to become G.B.S.

It is not easy to get a clear image of this "mortally shy," "unknown, and shabby, and penniless, and awkward, and at the same time fastidious and proud" (LS, p. 279) young man who possessed what remains when one eliminates all the dazzling, engaging, and eccentric qualities of the great G.B.S. he was to become. He relates that instead of throwing himself on the world, as young men on the make were supposed to do, he threw his mother. "My timid want of push kept me a penniless burden on my harrassed parents until I was nearly thirty" (SS, p. 144). He worked intermittently at some minor jobs and turned out a few pieces of journeyman prose, including ghost writing for Lee. But his modest disclaimer that "for the first couple of years of my life in London I did nothing decisive" (IM, p. 675) seems justified. From 1879 to 1883 he resolutely ground out five novels, which were resolutely refused by nearly sixty publishers.

These novels, which eventually found their way into print, provide oblique and partial portraits of this unformed young man trying on various personae, vocations, and social roles. Smith in *Immaturity* (1879) is a self-composed young Rationalist and scoffing agnostic, aspiring to poetry but employed as a clerk. He becomes interested in an independent young woman residing in his rooming house but doesn't intervene when she makes a conventional marriage. At the end he is alone, with his Rationalism intact, having lost neither his temper nor his virginity. In *The Irrational Knot* (1880) Conolly, an efficient-minded inventor and part-time musician, is a matter-of-fact man who carries the Rationalist mode into respectable marriage. His wife soon betrays him; but when the cuckold confronts the lover, the expected fireworks are dampened by an anticlimax put to an ineffectual and unintentionally self-incriminating use. Conolly is merely composed and sensible about the whole mess, while the lover is conventionally outraged at being deprived of a duel. But when nothing appears to perturb Conolly, we conclude he is not superior to love and jealousy but deficient in feeling; not a true Rationalist but a fool, or perhaps somewhat schizoid—as indeed Shaw particularly seemed in these early, pre-Shavian years.

Cashel Byron's Profession (1882) is a pleasant account of a loquacious prizefighter who entertains society with his theory of "executive power" as the key to the art of fisticuffs while he is freeing himself from an unloving mother and winning a respectable girl. Within its family-romance context and its romantic-comedy convention it is a farly successful novel.

Each novel is a variation on the interchanges between a gifted outsider and the normally moribund world of English society,[1] which "believed in nothing except good manners; and the essence of good manners is to conceal a yawn. A yawn may be defined as a silent yell."[2] The common assumption running through the novels is that certain skills and energies will enable the hero to break into society by demonstrating his social usefulness. Owen Jack in *Love Among the Artists* (1881) is an energetic composer of Beethoven-like proportions who drops into and out of society while living a shabby bachelor's life much as Lee had in London. In fact, Shaw may have been giving the Lee personality a trial run, but finally it too is discarded. In the last of these novels, left unfinished, *An Unsocial Socialist* (1883), Sidney Trefusis lives alone as a gentlemanly Socialist and discourses on Marx as Shaw perhaps was beginning to do, or as his friend and rival H. M. Hyndman, the wealthy Social Democrat, could better afford to do. And finally there is a fragment referred to today as *An Unfinished Novel* that establishes the situation of a capable young physician moving in to help an older and conventional doctor whose restless young wife begins to—

But enough. Even when we combine all the heroes' qualities of Rationalism, inventiveness, pugnacity, creative energy, Socialism, and healing powers, we do not quite get the essential Shavian personality. Of all six portraits, Owen Jack's is the most realized and informative. Like Lee he was a musical

[1] This and other similar conclusions have been reached by Alick West, *George Bernard Shaw: "A Good Man Fallen among Fabians"* (New York, 1950).
[2] G. K. Chesterton, *George Bernard Shaw* (New York, 1956), p. 189.

instructor of young ladies, and Lee's dynamism as a conductor is matched by Jack's genius as a composer. But Jack's foremost quality is his speaking voice, described as powerful, commanding, thundering, and resounding. It is his real strength in society, his means of asserting himself and holding attention. "By the power of sound, I would pulverize you," he informs a gentleman being cruel to his daughter in a train compartment where Jack has recently intruded. The "power of sound" is futher revealed as a basis for his musical genius. Upon finding himself alone in the house of a family he is tutoring, its members being away at a party, he is inspired or rather provoked into an outburst of creative activity:

> Jack was alone, seated at the pianoforte, his brows knitted, his eyes glistening under them, his wrists bounding and rebounding upon the keys, his rugged countenance transfigured by an expression of extreme energy and exaltation. He was playing from a manuscript by imitations of the instruments. He was grunting and buzzing the bassoon parts, humming when the violoncello had the melody, whistling for the flutes, singing hoarsely for the horns, barking for the trumpets, squealing for the oboes, making indescribable sounds in imitation of clarionets and drums, and marking each sforzando by a toss of his head and a gnash of his teeth. At last, abandoning this eccentric orchestration, he chanted with the full strength of his formidable voice until he came to the final chord, which he struck violently, and repeated in every possible inversion from one end of the keyboard to the other. Then he sprang up, and strode excitedly to and fro in the room. (LA, p. 36)

This extraordinary passage reveals perhaps better than any other account Shaw's psychological state at the point of development he had reached by the early 1880s. Jack's exclusion from London society was tantamount to the superfluous child's experiences of infantile abandonment. Jack's performance reproduced a kind of tantrum wherein the child's wounded cry of rage is reproduced in the adult, and, gathering great energy around it, acquires a creative trend.

Although only informed guesses can be made so far about the impetus of Shaw's creative drive, there is an intermediate biographical link between his early deprivations and later adjustments. When his mother and Lee forsook the Shavian household for London, Shaw responded to the resultant emptiness by learning to accompany himself on the piano. With his "banging, whistling, roaring, and growling" (LM, p. 859), he replaced the departed figures.[3]

For both Shaw and Jack, abandonment and emptiness are counteracted by a creative use of energy strong enough for an orchestra to fill an auditorium. "I had not then tuned the Shavian instrument to any sort of harmony" (IM, p. 679), he remarks of these indecisive London years. When he eventually keys up, the emptiness will not be filled with musicians playing Jack's compositions but with actors playing Shavian pieces on countless stages.

Shaw does not identify with Lee to the extent of becoming Owen Jack, but the oral concentration of Shavian energy remained latent or appeared only fitfully, making him seem "insufferable, aggressive, impudent" (IM, p. 662) to others, until the possibilities of power and mesmeric mastery opened up by Lee could be satisfactorily organized, and the genius who described himself as a "word musician" could be realized. If Lee was a Shavian model, it was very likely in the area of creative transformations of energy, which Shaw was experiencing around this time. His moral passion had already dawned during puberty, and this gauche youth, hesitating diffidently outside the London salons, contained all the energies that would enliven a sixty-year career of oratorical, philosophical, polemical, creative, and possibly prophetic endeavors. He is seething with energy and quite

---

[3] In the years following the death of his wife, Shaw occasionally awakened the servants in the middle of the night with his renditions of Mozart, Beethoven, and old music-hall songs (RM, p. 148).

uneasy, because it is all there but still not effectively organized for distribution. And thus a great deal of his early shyness derived from the danger of energy's prematurely breaking out :

> I presented myself to the unprepared stranger as a most irreverent young man. My Mephistophelean moustache and eyebrows had not yet grown; and there was nothing in my aspect to break the shock of my diabolical opinions. (IM, p. 669)

These opinions are perhaps the first social manifestation of Shaw's unusual system of defenses and identifications. At this time he is irreverent only by conventional standards (calling on God, if He exists, to strike him dead, while he times the experiment at a party), and at all times his lack of restraint is verbal. But he eventually found more suitable roles than that of the party atheist to offset his shyness and to release his irreverent impulses. As critic, politician, playwright, and prophet he could damn the deadly virtues of the status quo because he had found a higher cause. Who would dream that beneath the mask of Mephistopheles breathed the shy saint of the Life Force? Yet even saints have diabolical impulses. And what shines from the red whiskers and arched eyebrows will in time radiate from a new kind of dramatic structure.

FABIAN FELLOWSHIP

When Shaw's novels are discussed—which is rarely, and probably justly so—they tend to arouse more partisan loyalty or patronizing nods than impartial analysis. Whatever twists of plot and passages of effective dialogue he brought to the genre, the fact is he left it exactly as he had found it, because he was not concerned with form as he later came to be with drama. He evidently viewed the form of the novel courteously and catered to it cautiously, as a gentleman learning the rules of society does not want to be caught in violation of them. For the shy young Shaw, novel-writing was a way of getting into society, not of disturbing social structure. His backward-sloping handwriting at this time is perhaps symbolic of his attempts to lean over backwards not to offend.

The fashions in content, which excluded any explicit treatment of sexuality, he implicitly accepted. Energy itself he banished except in Owen Jack's episodes. This obsequious and rather undifferentiated handling of fictional materials is symptomatic of vitality and thought's not having penetrated structure but rather remaining harmlessly confined within character, as they do in Owen Jack's rough genius, Cashel Byron's fists, and Sidney Trefusis's Socialism.

When his creative forays of the 1880's were not editorially welcomed, he did not persist in his mistakes; he suspended his creative work for nearly a decade. And when in the fullness of time Shavian drama is engendered, it has been lifted from concentration on character to generate ideas, and then both thought and creative energy join to forge a new and more fitting structure. Since the conventional novelist had been discarded in 1883 and the revolutionary playwright does not appear until 1892, decisive changes should be expected during that interval. "I do not proceed by crises," he wrote a friend in 1889 (LS, p. 229). But if there were no crises, there were at least some rather dramatic conversions, and not only in the order of thought, because he had already changed from Rationalism to Socialism without improving his last abortive novel, but these conversions also involved new organizations and displacements of psychic energy. Moreover, they began to be manifested in 1879, the year of *Immaturity*; and the fact that they coincided with his experiments as a novelist suggests that the real resources of power enlivening his plays were within him but not yet matured or creatively accessible, as the stillborn novels testify.

Although Shaw explicitly refers to only two conversions, these were spaced out in four phases. In 1880 he was "dragged" by a friend to a debating society, where he felt compelled to take part :

> I could not hold my tongue. I started up and said something in the debate, and then, feeling that I had made a fool of myself, as in fact I had, I was so ashamed that I vowed I would join the Society; go every week; speak in every debate, and become a speaker or perish in the attempt. I carried out this resolution. (SS, p. 94)

The meeting was clearly charged with deep meaning for Shaw. But the involvement it initially excited led to shame and wounded self-esteem. He then proceeded to master the painful situation not by a retreat into fantasy, but by a pattern of behavior suggestive of Conrad's "to the destructive element submit," and referred to previously as identification with the aggressor. Here, as in earlier instances, it meant aligning himself with the source of pain as a future protection against it.

> I persevered doggedly. I haunted all the meetings in London where debates followed lectures. I spoke in the streets, in the parks, at demonstrations, anywhere and everywhere possible. In short I infested public meetings like an officer afflicted with cowardice, who takes every opportunity of going under fire to get over it and learn his business. (SS, p. 96)

But in internalizing the causes of unpleasant experiences he does not so much identify with them as reverse and transform them into peculiarly Shavian attributes. He masters reality less by adapting to it—except perhaps outwardly—than by subjecting it to his transforming mechanisms, which is an adaptation of another kind. The superfluous child advances in society to become the spokesman of the new and the opponent of the status quo. It is a maneuver that at once pays tribute to his distinctive genius and betrays a certain rigidity of character.

The increasing sense of power he felt in discovering an appropriate outlet for his energies through oratory and debate was qualified at this time only by the limitations of his essentially negative Rationalism. Hence, the effect on him of the "handsome and eloquent" Henry George, "American apostle of Land Nationalization and Single Tax," was to convert him from "barren agnostic controversy to economics" (SS, p. 96), a source of vitality and faith, as his statement implies. Equipped with Henry George's economics, he speaks up at a meeting of Hyndman's Marxist Federation only to be "contemptuously dismissed as a novice who had not read the great first volume of Marx's Capital."

> I promptly read it, and returned to announce my complete conversion by it. Immediately contempt changed to awe. (SS, p. 96)

By 1884 he is an accomplished public speaker, a self-taught economist and a Socialist, "sufficiently known to have no further need to seek out public debates: I was myself sought after" (SS, p. 97). Having turned to reality as his defense against pain, reality was now beginning to come to him.

Nor, having by then met Sidney Webb, did he long remain a devoted disciple of Marx, for later on in the same year he completed his series of conversions by joining the

> newly founded Fabian Society, in which I recognized a more appropriate *milieu* as a body of educated middle-class intelligentsia : my own class in fact. (SS, p. 97)

These English Socialists he depicted as

> intensely serious and burning with indignation at very real and very fundamental evils that affected the world; so that the reaction against them bound the finer spirits of all nations together. (IM, p. 673–74)

This hyperbolic tone is not mere Shavian grandiosity; rather, it locates the deeper meaning behind the Fabian movement. These finer young spirits, notwithstanding their social position, were actually a relatively small and obscure circle, Ann Fremantle's "Little Band of Prophets," whose great strength rested on their whole-hearted and informed assault on Capitalism. No less serious were they, though, than the original and apparently legendary band of brothers who had joined forces in order to overthrow the Primal Father. With their striped vests and green eye-shades, their civil-service and accountants' backgrounds, the Fabians were taking on Adam Smith and the Wealth of Nations, John Calvin and the Protestant Ethic, Macaulay and the Empire. Their aims were as grandiloquent at Napoleon's, their industry stupendous as a military campaign. Yet they were armed only with facts and proposals, and rode around on bicycles instead of on horseback. The most urbane of revolutionaries, their "inevitability of gradualism" would never excite a mob to storm the barricades; but their motto kept the struggle alive, and it was the perfect social analogue to Shaw's discovery that the "method of the Life Force" is "Evolution" (PBM, p. 73), which could be accelerated by intelligence but not forced by violence. Nonetheless, the mythic prototypes of the Fabians were the Titans, sons of Mother Earth pressing against the Olympian deity her claims that the land and its wealth should not be consumed by a monopolistic few, but that it be redistributed among all her sons by means of an enlightened Socialism. The new order was the unconscious revival of an older one. This underlying psychological coherence experienced by Shaw and his fellow Fabians goes far to account for their unshakable convictions, their remarkable tenacity, their capacity to surmount internal strife, and their ultimate vindication, after sixty years, in 1945.

The practical value of these conversions was that for Shaw

the arena of action was no longer seen as closed-off in the salons of English society, as his novels had indicated, but in the future, with its key in his own vital being. The great psychological value was that clear and coherent economic facts could relieve the burden of disturbing emotional material. By internalizing Socialism he was demonstrating that the good objects (introjects) were inside, in part by consigning the bad objects to the system of Capitalism. Henceforth, his father's fate will be described in socioeconomic terms; the harmful influence in his childhood from bad servants will be linked to wages ("What can you expect for £8 a year?"); his prolonged celibacy and delayed marriage will be attributed to his impecuniosity. It would be an exaggeration to say that his conversion to Socialist economics enabled him to deal with his vexing family background and his sexual uncertainties on a more clearly defined plane; yet something on this order occurred. In fact the responsibility for poverty, disease, vice, and unhappy marriages will all in the course of time be dropped on the doorstep of Capitalism. The "young man" who gets rid of his *"mauvais honte"* by converting to Socialism comes to see that

> property is theft: respectability founded on poverty is blasphemy: marriage founded on property is prostitution : it is easier to go through the eye of a needle than for a rich man to enter the kingdom of heaven. He now knows where he is and where this society which has so intimidated him is. (IM, pp. 663–64)

The integrative value of these conversions he summed up in the following Credo :

> Socialism is not charity nor loving-kindness, nor sympathy with the poor, nor popular philanthropy with its something-for-nothing almsgiving and mendicity, but the economist's hatred of waste and disorder, the aesthete's hatred of ugliness and dirt, the lawyer's hatred of injustice, the doctor's hatred of disease, the saint's hatred of the seven deadly sins : in short, a combina-

tion of the most intense hatreds against institutions which give economists a strong pecuniary interest in wasteful and anarchic capitalism, artists in venality and pornography, lawyers in injustice, doctors in disease, and saints in catering for the seven deadly sins or flattering them instead of denouncing them. (EP, p. 78)

In 1885, the year after becoming a Fabian, Shaw initiates his first sexual affair by yielding his virginity to the amorous widow Jenny Patterson. Being "intensely curious on the subject," as he put it, he permitted her to seduce him. But compared to the foregoing conversions, it was anticlimax. The event took place on his twenty-ninth birthday, an occasion he did not ordinarily celebrate. Four months earlier he had been orphaned by his father's death at seventy-one, and in the course of the same year he finally began earning his own way.

I AM A POLITICIAN

Shaw's erratic sexual episodes during these years may be read as seismograms of ongoing, deeper troubles. For the integration of energy and purpose is not organically assimilated any better in Shaw's personality than its implications are entirely worked through in his writings. His iconoclastic and reforming drives are perfectly fitted to the Fabian enterprise; but what of the driving energies and visionary powers of his ego that conceive of the Superman? There is no place, and one would at least expect there to be one—for the Superman under Socialism. Shaw indeed affirmed his belief that from among the political supermen (Cromwell, Peter the Great, Napoleon, Mussolini, Hitler, and Stalin), "only Cromwell with his Bible and Covenants of Grace, and Stalin with his Marxist philosophy, had any principles and these two were the only successful rulers" (EP, p. 339; AH, p. 843). So perhaps it is the Superman plus, that society needs? Or is Socialism the "Democracy of Supermen" he refers to in the "Revolutionist's Handbook" (MS, p. 705)? And does Creative Evolution cease with Socialism? Shaw never said as much. Nor does he propose that the Superman perform the titanic but preliminary feat of freeing society from its present system of oppression, although this accomplishment appears to be at the base of his admiration for twentieth-century dictators. The trouble with such a view, as Shaw realized, was that violent upheavals easily lead to a worse system or merely to another swing of the pendulum. And such lack of purpose he could never tolerate. Nevertheless, the Fabian Society was central to his political theories, and its "inevitability of gradualism" philosophy disposed him to rely more on selective breeding than on revolution. Besides, Shaw is far from clear in his various uses of the Superman concept. It can stand for the "accidental supermen" of the past, like Shakespeare, Goethe, and Shelley, as well as for Christ, and a new species yet to be evolved.[4]

Norman O. Brown has written that "conventional Anglo-Saxon political theory is all patriarchal."

> The minority opposition to the orthodox line of patriarchal interpretation has clustered round the hypotheses of a contrary matriarchal factor. There is a connection between matriarchy and fraternity, even as there is an alliance between Mother Earth and the band of brothers led by Cronus to castrate Father sky. But Freud directs us to the idea that the true, the only contrary of patriarchy is not matriarchy but fraternity.[5]

---

[4] For further discussion, see "The Superman," chap. 10, in Arthur C. Nethercot's *Men and Supermen* (Cambridge: Harvard University Press, 1954); chap. 8 in Julian B. Kaye's *Bernard Shaw and the Nineteenth-Century Tradition* (Norman: University of Oklahoma Press 1958). Lest Shaw's internal development be given credit for too much mental originality, Kaye's view that "it is Ibsen's 'noble man' who becomes Shaw's superman, although it is Nietzsche who names him," is worth noting. My point is that Shaw's conversions disposed him to singular reception of the ideas in his intellectual milieu, and that the result is something more than the sum of influences.

[5] *Love's Body* (New York, 1966), p. 11.

Shaw discovered among his Fabian associates a model of this kind of alternative, because he once observed :

> There is no hope for civilization in government by idolized single individuals. Councils of tested qualified persons, subject to the sternest possible public criticism, and to periodical . . . removal and replacement, is our safest aim. (EP, p. 341)

Shaw was obsessed with government, but he did not covet power. He had his authoritarian side, but he did not worship authority. His Caesar was a pragmatist free from power drives —never hoping, therefore never despairing; and his best political play is about a peasant girl who hears voices. His Superman is at best an unspecified ideal, the next stage in man's evolutionary future. Leaping from biological sources into mystical idea, it is supported by his stalwart ego and confirmed by his vital genius, but it is never quite dressed up in the uniform of Fabian ideology. Nor did he ever consider the Fabian Society as his personal ramp to power. Although he believed that his "little stage army" by its bounce and cleverness could "conquer the country" (LS, p. 38), it remained for him a valuable role-identity, an organized outlet for his energies, and a counterforce to his feelings of superfluity.

> I am a politician because life only realizes itself by functioning energetically in all directions; and I find on the platform and in council opportunities for functioning away like mad with faculties that would otherwise be atrophied from disuse. (LS, p. 463)

The Shavian conversions, which had begun with mental energy's being channeled into oratory where it then connected up with revolutionary economic and political thought, culminated in the Fabian Society. It lent purpose to his asceticism as well as to his diabolism, and enabled him to reinforce the male components in his personality without submitting to the demands of a society against which he could constructively rebel and hope eventualy to supplant with his Socialism and Vitalism. In fact, the Fabians, with their blending of comradery and disciplined work, of intellectual stimulation and ascetism, and of sexual heterodoxy with revolutionary idealism, constituted for Shaw a kind of second family wherein he was warmly welcome, where his nonconformism was normalized, and within which he could put his executive ego to work on the executive board. Aiming to cure society, the Fabians were also therapy for Shaw.

Combining his Fabianism with his mastery over spoken language and his training from critical and pamphlet writing (SS, pp. 116–17), his discovery of positive uses for anticlimax, and his spritely sense of the "indescribable levity" of truth that comes immediately into the "head of the child or the fool" or of the thinker who "forces his way through many strata of sophistications" (SS, p. 27), we are reaching near the quintessential dramatist of the nineties.

Does the London outsider and social intruder that Shaw obsessively treats in his novels disappear when he turns to drama, dissolved in the onrush of renewed vigor and revolutionary goals? Not exactly. This basic disposition, whether in fantasy form or in his sober reflections thirty years later about being at ease only with the mighty dead, never left him; but it did undergo a sea change when the waves of energy were breaking over him in the 1880s. Bluntschli in *Arms and the Man* (1894) reenacts the transformations. In the beginning he is a social nobody who intrudes into the bedroom of a lady of the Bulgarian gentry. Fortified only with the chocolates in his cartridge belt, he is in fact armed with the genuine Shavian weapons of anticlimax, pragmatism, and Vitalism. Through these and along with clever turns of plot, he is soon master of the situation: he inherits a chain of hotels, announces himself a free Swiss citizen, which is his country's highest rank, and, having triumphed over his rival, he wins the hand of the lady. It is only at this point, when Shaw has fortified his ego with firm economic thought and turned to the stage, so much more closely associated with his mother than the novel, as well as where language is restored to its spoken, that is, oral, nature, that the family romance can act as a reunifying force and crystallize into art. Only then does the Life Force find its medium. Only then does the genius come into being.

In sum, the conversions of the 1880s encompass his whole being, leading to Vitalism as well as to Socialism. They take the form in drama of Bluntschli's mastery, Candida's pragmatism and natural history, Lady Cicely's quiet moral superiority, Ann Whitefield's quest for a father for the Superman, and the synthesis of *Major Barbara* as well as the conversions of Captain Brassbound, Dick Dudgeon, and Blanco Posnet.

Shaw's gravitational rise, as I have been reconstructing it, may be more like the firing in three successive phases of a space rocket than the ascent of a helium balloon, although the sensation from inside in either instance may be the same. I began with an account of early maternal gratification and deprivation that conditioned early identifications and narcissism. When Shaw was no more than three or four, his father's alcoholism encouraged a profound disillusionment that pervaded his conception of all systems of patriarchal authority and strengthened his alliance with his mother as the stronger. There is an interim of latency in which he is exposed to more of his father's and uncle's derisive debunking along with Lee's ingenuity and magnetism. After Shaw is ten, this period is also associated with pleasant summers spent at a country cottage in Dalkey, when he is overfed on honeydew daydreams of the Uranian Venus. Throughout, it is a time of exposure to heterodox attitudes and stimulating presences, of comic skepticism leading to jarring anticlimaxes, of prolonged reliance on fantasy leading to celestial voyages on the plains of heaven, and to hero-villains rescuing or being rescued by gracious, bountiful ladies. It is a time in which exposure to school induces boredom, and exposure to the fine arts stirs aesthetic feelings, but most of all it is a discordant time, aimless and uncertain. With puberty (around fourteen) come the "dawning of moral passion" and the formation of conscience; self-respect balances his "derisive incredulity" and regulates his fantasy life; he gives up religious practices and talks back to the school authorities. Soon he will become an efficient clerk and promising cashier. In other words, in this second phase of advance, he has begun to fulfill the conditions set down by the imagos of his infancy and to assert himself as a person.

Although Shaw's "moral passion" has particular relevance to a discussion of *Man and Superman,* its present importance is as an intermediate step toward integration, which precedes the adaptations and commitments discussed here as conversions. I have taken over and broadly applied Shaw's word *conversion* to describe changes within his personality that involve instinctual drives, mental organization, and ideological choices leading to his identity-in-the-world. At times one aspect of these processes may have prevailed over another, and because they were never purely psychological, intellectual, or political, I have intended the term to include all three major aspects of what were complex human changes. These conversions, constituting his third and final major phase of development, provide his transformations with purpose and endow him with a life mission. Henceforth, and for the next sixty-five years, his mind will be actively engaged in the world of art and politics, but always under the conditions and within the context of these conversions.

THE IDENTITY OF GENIUS

A few remarks on Erikson's remarks about Shaw's identity are in order.[6] He discerns a "crisis at the age of twenty" when Shaw, working as a cashier in a Dublin land estate office, comes to the realization that he must break away from the business world. "Breaking loose meant to leave family and friends, business and Ireland," interprets Erikson. This episode would better qualify as an "identity crisis" had Shaw become disillusioned with a career in business and then been forced to search his soul for some other vocation or path to success. But as it was, his "heart was not in the business" (SS, p. 55): "I was uncomfortable in an office because I was a round peg in a square hole" (SS, p. 100). And he has said he never questioned the presence of his genius any more than the taste of saliva in his mouth, or the inclination to write any more than the inclination to breathe (SS, p. 82). He was not breaking away from "family and friends": he was getting away from sharing a cramped apartment with his father, and McNulty, who alone knew of his lofty aspirations, was his only memorable friend. He was also getting away from Dublin, and he was content to stay away for thirty years before again visiting Ireland, which came about only at his wife's urging. In fact, by leaving home, he was traveling to the center of his emotional interest, which was his mother, and to the center of his cultural interest, which was London.[7]

[6] *Identity*, pp. 142f.
[7] While on the subject of what Shaw called "Biographers' Blunders Corrected," we might turn next to the question of Shaw's having an adolescent love affair before his departure from Dublin and whether the two are related, as Dan H. Lawrence speculates (LS, p. 5). Weissman also writes without supporting evidence that "occasionally he was overwhelmed by uncontrollable sexual urges. A love affair at fifteen" is one of the "outstanding moments." A Shelleyan poem evidently composed soon after Shaw arrived in London reveals three "blackeyed enslaver[s]": Queen Mab who has her home in the city, Yolanda who "has her foot on the

On safer ground, Erikson states that Shaw "granted himself a prolongation of the interval between youth and adulthood, which we call a 'psychosocial moratorium,' " in order to establish his identity. Elsewhere, Erikson quotes the following passage from Anna Freud:

> The abstract intellectual discussions and speculations in which young people delight are not genuine attempts at solving the task set by reality. Their mental activity is rather an indication of a tense alertness for the instinctual processes and the translation into abstract thought of that which they perceive,[8]

and he adds that "she presents the defensive half of the story of adolescent rumination, the other half being its adaptive function, and its function in the history of changing ideas."

It was in this period of extended adolescence that Shaw's conversions occurred, and it is clear that they were an adaptive response in which the ego mediated between instinctual urges and extrinsic possibilities. More difficult to assess is the value of this adaptive response in "the history of changing ideas." Partial answers are scattered piecemeal through this study. As a dramatist of ideas there is no doubt of Shaw's success, only of his influence; as a thinker he was provocative, though neither original, systematic, nor always very consistent; as a Fabian, he had to wait for sixty years before England came around to accepting his Socialist doctrine, and then it was for a host of

stage," and Calypso who "married forbidden Sorrento" in a "gaol by the sea" and whose "black tresses" have "smitten" the poet (*The Shaw Review* 105, no. 2). The three women are either objects of poetic fancy; derived from his mother and two sisters; or real. But who would dare to say? On such stuff are biographers' blunders made.

Nevertheless there was a romantic episode around the time in question, and he wrote of it to Mrs. Pat Campbell:

> Once, in my calfish teens, I fell wildly in love with a lady of your complexion; and she, good woman, having a sister to provide for, set to work to marry me to the sister. Whereupon I shot back into the skies from which I had decended, and never saw her again. Nor have I, until this day, ever mentioned that adventure to any mortal. (PC, p. 38)

[8] *Young Man Luther,* pp. 19–29.

reasons not directly related to his efforts. Not only does he deserve the ambiguous tribute of being an original person, but the import of his major endeavors remains problematic.

So far we can conclude that his conversions enabled him to create not so much a world of memorable characters and universal themes as Shakespeare had done, but to bring the world of ideas and issues into the theater as Chesterton long ago had realized. He legitimized economics and politics for the drama by seeing them creatively and integrally in somewhat the way that Joyce and Lawrence legitimized sex for the novel. With his great synthesizing intellect and through his humor he neutralized the negative charge of revolutionary ideas; through his Vitalism he thrust politics into the larger scheme of Creative Evolution.

Before closing this discussion of Shaw's developmental stages, I should note that a woman accompanies each one of them. The mother, of course, dominates the years of childhood and latency. Concurrent with his integration of intellect and moral passion, he records falling "wildly in love" during his "calfish teens." Then, on the heels of the conversions of his twenties, he lands in bed with his amorous widow. This affair turned out as frustrating as the earlier romance had ended abruptly. But given this pattern, we may be justified in wondering if there was not another purpose behind his reorganizations of mental processes, which was not so much the more realistic ones I have been emphasizing as attempts at procuring libidinal gratification. At such a juncture it may be advisable to invoke psychoanalytic theory's Catch-22, the principle of multiple function or overdetermination.

"AN ORIGINAL DIDACTIC REALISTIC" PLAY-WRIGHT

When Shaw's conversion to Fabianism delivered him in no small way from his family conflicts, it may have further predisposed him to conduct his romance with the world as an artist. In the novels, no peculiarly Shavian attitude toward society is discernible. His views are informed but conventional at heart. When he starts writing plays, however, he has his public firmly fixed in his mind, and we may speculate that he also had formed a new conception of his audience.

> It seems unlikely that the artistic performance or creative product is ever undertaken purely for the gratification of the self, but rather that there is always some fantasy of a collective audience or recipient. (PA, p. 58)

This assumption has an interesting application to playwrights. Certainly they must create their drama on an inner stage with ideal actors speaking their lines and an ideal audience responding to the action. What this implies is that the dramatist imagines a kind of living theater in which the audience shares in his creative energy. In receiving this overflow of energy, the ideal audience is elevated aesthetically to the higher realms of art. And this happens whether the real audience is going to be assaulted, insulted, or merely gratified; for the audience of the dramatist's imagination is ideal primarily in its responsiveness to drama. This may be why Brecht could conceive of a new kind of drama to be presented before an audience of intellectually engaged proletariat—an idealization that events never granted. It may also explain the intention behind Yeats's esoteric drama, which is meant to be performed before a cultural elite —another idealization that "dear, dirty Dublin" never lived up to. In America in the thirties there was much talk by Maxwell Anderson and others of the theater as the "temple of Democracy." In fact, the theater is rarely a mere auditorium, or the audience merely hetergeneous individuals on a night out. Shaw hardly ever missed an opportunity to harangue and abuse the English public, but I suspect that when he sat down to write a play he dispatched some of his narcissistic energy to equip an ideal audience for participation in his creative production. How could he expect the British people to listen to a brilliant disquisitory play unless they were to some extent Shavianized? In the Preface to what seems to me his most typical as well as his greatest play, *Man and Superman,* he acknowledges that "what I have always wanted is a pit of philosophers; and this is a play for such a pit." It is in other words a play for an ideally responsive audience. But it is also very possible that Shaw was encouraged to imagine such a audience after his associations with Fabian intellectuals.

Let us push these speculations a further step. A playwright may be thought of as "feeding lines" to actors who must in turn use them to fulfill the expectations of the audience. The audience has been described as a "unified, demanding force, entirely free of obligations to think or act—a kind of thoughtless hunger emanates from the auditorium." This state of "voracity" will soon be "shaped and regulated" from the stage by the "active exercise" of the actors' skills. The actors are "executive," the audience "visceral."[9] This primitive-sounding situation both distinguishes the two parts of the theater and defines the reciprocal relationship of the two groups—the audience being "anticipatory and appetitive," the actors being "consummatory." Such a situation psychologically reproduces the "primal dialogue" between the mother and the child in the first year of life in which the mother "speaks" to the child through nurturing, holding, fondling, and smiling, and the child, by utilizing the

9 Donald M. Kaplan "Theatre Architecture: A Derivation of the Primal Cavity," *The Drama Review* 12, no. 3 (Spring 1968): 105–16.

tongue, lips, cheeks, and throat (grouped together as the primal cavity), gratifies his appetite, begins perceiving, and in the process of regulating these organs, learns to respond to the mother as living reality. We seem always to be returning to this early stage (no pun intended), which psychoanalytically may have been where Shaw was most often at. Be that as it may, we need remain only long enough to observe that the playwright through his creative gifts enjoys fundamental control over this situation by becoming the dispenser of its life-energy in the form of words for the actors to deliver, which for Shaw would mean still another variant on the manic defense's "omnipotent manipulation," so characterized by Winnicott, and on the child-parent reversal. Certainly he was notorious for viewing actors as no more than vehicles for transmitting his ideas, and he necessarily gravitated toward executive functions. More to the point, a great deal of his brilliance consisted in the uncanny manner in which he carried on his "verbal dialogue" with audiences. The dexterity and empathy through which he could nudge them toward confrontations with their own suddenly untenable views, guide them along the steps of an argument they would never conceive, anticipate their objections, tantalize their wishes, and hint at new alternatives—all may very well proclaim the richness and tenacity of the "primal dalogue" between Shaw and his mother, the desire to continue it, and the need to master it by reversal, As a playwright of explosive ideas he could acquire the "executive power" sought by Cashel Byron in the boxing ring. Having earlier referred to the omnipotent properties with which Shaw endows language, I now have an important basis for this in the "action cycle" of "primal dialogue." For if the company of Fabians raised his expectations of an ideally responsive audience, and if he could assign starring parts to his actress-mothers, his evolving socialist and vitalist ideas also served to engage the interest of the audience as well as to keep it at a somewhat puzzled remove. But before saying that Shaw made himself into a writing machine from which he pumped the Life Force into the British public—I ought to stop.

Along with his exposure to the intelligentsia of the day, Shaw also had occasion to observe Ibsen's unprecedented impact on audiences. Shaw's interest in the revolutionary possibilities of the New Drama dates from 1885 when he met William Archer, the translator and leading English exponent of Ibsen. Their collaboration on adapting the Augier play *Ceinture Dorée* dates from that year, although their project was soon abandoned after Shaw complained of running out of plot about halfway along. When he got around to completing it in 1892, the influence of Ibsen was evident.

But Ibsen provoked no Shavian conversion; he was read with Fabian and feminist eyes and appropriated formally into the Socialist movement when Shaw delivered his Fabian lectures on Ibsen in 1890. Nevertheless, Ibsen must have played a decisive part in Shaw's development between 1885 and 1892, when his mind and voice were most active and his creative powers were lying dormant. "I wish I could write you a play myself," he wrote to an actress in February 1888, "but unfortunately I have not the faculty" (LS, p.188). In August 1889 he wrote, "Sometimes in spare moments I write dialogues; and these are all working up to a certain end (a sermon, of course) . . ." (LS, p. 222). Any number of significant events could have occurred during this eighteen-month interval, but the precipitating one undoubtedly was the Charrington-Achurch production in June 1889 of *A Doll's House*. In the spring of 1891 the Independent Theatre was inaugurated with a production of *Ghosts*; and when the demand arose for new native drama to match Ibsen's, Shaw unearthed his dramatic fragment in August 1892, completed it in five weeks, and saw its production in

December as *Widowers' Houses,* "an Original Didactic Realistic Play."

Short of conversion, the influence of Ibsen on Shaw was nonetheless important. It may have been just the thing to bring the simmering pot of Shavian energy to a creative boil. For this reason and because the two men are often associated without being clearly distinguished, a reconsideration of their relationship is next in order.

4

IBSENITE

ROSMER : I want to set democracy to its proper work . . . to
make all the people in the country into noblemen.
—*Rosmersholm*

LORD SUMMERHAYS : Democracy reads well; but it doesn't act
well, like some people's plays . . . to make Democracy
work, you need an aristocratic democracy. To make
Aristocracy work, you need a democratic aristocracy.
You've got neither; and there's an end of it.

TARLETON : Still, you know, the superman may come, the superman's an idea. I believe in ideas. Read whatshisname.
—*Misalliance*

INNOVATORS

Ibsen's contribution to Shaw's development as a dramatist
has been greatly discussed but scarcely clarified.[1] We should like
to know more about the manner in which Shaw used Ibsen's

---

[1] John Gassner, "Shaw on Ibsen and the Drama of Ideas," *English
Institute Essays* (New York, 1964), is one example. It would be exciting to
have a study undertaken similar to the imaginative investigation of influence that Harold Bloom, in *The Anxiety of Influence* (New York : Oxford
University Press, 1973), conducts on English poets.

material, ideas, and techniques; their differences in method; and their ultimate artistic visions.

When it came to borrowing from his English predecessors and contemporaries, Shaw was, as Martin Meisel has shown, the true aristocrat. He appropriated conventions of plot and character openly, and transmuted their base matter into true Shavian gold. T. W. Robertson, Dion Boucicault, even Pinero, Jones, and Gilbert may well enjoy a gratuitous immortality by having had Shaw dip into their works. One may think that the more formidable and individualistic Ibsen could not so readily be rifled.

But Shaw did appropriate Ibsen for his own purposes, and frequently in his early plays he did so deliberately and directly. *Mrs. Warren's Profession* employs Ibsenite means to make a point similar to the one in *Ghosts*. The potential evil in the deeds of one generation is manifested as it cripples the vitality of the next generation. Oswald, having discovered that his life has been blighted by his father's vices, turns to Regina only to learn that she is his father's bastard child. Similarly, the threat of sibling incest frustrates the affections of Frank and Vivie Warren. But whereas the guiltless Oswald goes down with the ship—disease and death being the inevitable end to the Manders system of values—Vivie is spared, and the cloud of incest is dispelled because Shaw concentrated his attack on the economic system. In *The Devil's Disciple* Shaw accounts for Mrs. Dudgeon's soured Christianity by a shorthand insertion of the Manders-Alvings triangle. Like Ibsen, Shaw employed fathers and daughters to symbolize either a confrontation between generations (*The Master Builder, Misalliance, Heartbreak House*), or to explore the relation of the artist to his work (*When We Dead Awaken, Pygmalion*). And in *Candida* (1895) the doll's-house situation is treated from the other side, with Morell as the doll.

Shaw used Ibsen's materials in ways similar to his exploitation of popular melodramas. He could pluck out of Ibsen a situation, theme, or set of characters as a basis for his own variations (*Widowers' Houses, Mrs. Warren's Profession*); or he could reverse Ibsen as he reversed melodrama, composing anti-Ibsen plays like *Candida* or *The Devil's Disciple* (which is also an anti-melodrama [MM, pp. 194f]). In fact, it may well be possible to discover in Shaw's use of preexisting dramatic materials a pattern that continues his early development: identification with the aggressor (Ibsen); chucking out (Shakespeare and Irving).

But in keeping with a method of examining drama as energy and structure, I find that the Ibsen play closest to *Candida* is the obscure *Love's Comedy* (1862). Both plays can be viewed as comedies of energy, or more precisely, of the liberation of energy. With minor differences they deal with a young man's early but nonetheless strong passion for a woman who is either worshiped as the Virgin Mother or idealized into the eternal feminine in a manner that renders her ultimately unattainable. Candida has already bound herself, irrevocably as it turns out, to a conventional husband. Swanhild ends betrothed to a vulgar but prosperous businessman who offers her a comfortable and dull, Candida type of marriage. Both women favor a plainly realistic life over their romantic lovers. Candida sends Marchbanks with a secret in his heart out into the night. Swanhild casts Falk's ring from a cliff into the fjord, signifying a lasting spiritual bond not to be tested by time or subjected to consummation. Both plays after a fashion are domestic comedies with the appealing wife (or wife-to-be), the dull husband (or husband-to-be), and the saving of the marriage by the expulsion of the poetic lover. But unlike the conventional models[2] of the time (Augier's *Gabriella*, 1849, is one), these plays are worked

2 *The Flower and the Castle*, pp. 83–84.

out from the lover's perspective. The happy ending does not result from the reunion of husband and wife, or from the anticipated marriage and preservation of social forms, but from innovations within the comic structure.

What the young lovers feel in the conventional loss of the desired object is more like exhilaration than disappointment. Marchbank's rejection by Candida is the discovery of his vocation. His "out, then, into the night with me," is his own rejection of bourgeois life in order to be under the stars, where he belongs as a poet. Nor does Falk, following his rejection, become dejected. He passes out of the play dressed in Alpine gear heading eagerly for the mountains to "scale the future's possibilities." C. L. Barber's formulation of Shakespearean comedy as moving from release of energy to clarification defines the movement in these modern works as well.[3] The secret in Marchbanks's heart is perhaps shared by Falk. Both have extricated themselves from the confinements of domestic existence in order to realize themselves and discover their vocations under the stars and on the peaks. More important, they have both turned away from defined objects and existing institutions in order to redirect their instinctual energies into other as yet undisclosed areas. Both plays come early in their authors' creative careers, and when read autobiographically suggest that the instincts are evidently preserved from immediate libidinal discharge and spared a fatal encounter with male rivals. If the women are to some degree oedipal creations by reason of their forbidden nature, libido has been liberated away from them with their blessing to be retained and used more in the freedom of art than in seeking other substitutes, which are unlikely to be found high in the Alps or among the stars of the heavens. The fact that Candida is clearly the older woman, while Swanhild is more the romantic sweetheart, may imply a psychological difference, with

[3] C. L. Barber, *Shakespeare's Festive Comedy* (Princeton, N.J., 1959).

Shaw's needs standing out as being earlier and more fixed. In any case, the escape from the impossible Candida-Swanhild type of love into an indeterminate reality opens new developmental phases for Marchbanks and Falk, and presumes a cognate advance in creativity for their authors. The liberation of libido and escape into reality can be viewed as the inner analogue of the capacity for major structural innovations in future plays.[4]

Although Shaw correctly traces the breakdown of teleological forms (tragedy and comedy)[5] in Ibsen's profoundly ambiguous tragicomedies as they more authentically come to express the open-ended conditions of modern life, he does not press this insight very far (BX). Rather, he insists elsewhere that "The Technical Novelty in Ibsen's Plays" is the discussion (QI). As we know, after a certain point when Shaw scrutinized Ibsen, he began to see what Narcissus saw in the pool; and whose quintessence Shaw is really discussing is a problem all readers have to contend with. We can grant that Candida's, "Let us sit and talk comfortably over it like three friends," has been cued by Nora's, "Sit down, Torvald, we have a lot to talk over." But what little discussion there is in *A Doll's House* is part of the play's iconoclastic structure; it is not intended to provoke thought and reform by educating the audience to social realities as Shaw's plays increasingly attempt to do. The liberated mental

4 While clearly differing in many respects, the lives of Ibsen and Shaw have surprising parallels. Both fathers were businessmen who married women socially their superiors. In both families there is the question of the woman's infidelity, although the rumors of Ibsen's mother having an affair concern the period around her engagement. But in each instance the possibility that the son is illegitimate is raised and never proved. Both fathers suffer disastrous bankruptcy while their children are small. However, Knud Ibsen withdraws from local society into the country, where he nurses his wounded pride, but continues to enjoy the loyalty of his wife. Neither son profits from formal education; both are shy or unusually extroverted in society. Ibsen was apprenticed to an apothecary at sixteen, saw little of his family thereafter, and had his first sexual affair at eighteen with his employer's twenty-eight-year-old maid.

5 In *The Modern Century,* Northrop Frye discusses the reluctance of modern literature to impart a sense of finality in traditional forms.

energy of Ibsen's creativity evidently rose up from pressures
deep in the psyche, with aggressive and anarchic sexual components. When this energy is molded into dramatic imagery
and archetypes of character, the action acquires a peculiar and
rigorous structure rendering the plays elusive and profound.
Speaking at the Norwegian League for Women's Rights, Ibsen
disclaimed his affiliation with feminism and maintained that
women belonged in the home, building character in their sons,
a view Shaw might privately have welcomed, but one that
baffled many of Ibsen's disciples. Shaw's liberated mental energy
flows more readily into accessible rhetorical modes, conventions,
and stereotypes of the established theater. Behind Ibsen's compressed and ambiguous symbolism and his rooting of character
in archetype is the force of primary process, more urgent and
more destructive; through much of Shaw the availability of the
family romance and its flowering into the undying Life Force
often conduces to optimism and compromise. And so despite
the apparent similarity in their initial creative displacements of
instinctual energy, the two playwrights disposed it in sharply
different ways, Shaw's early attempts to ally his practices and
purposes with Ibsen's notwithstanding.

Shaw's failure to penetrate the heart of Ibsen's work is but
another episode in the unwritten tragicomedy of the narcissist,
who tends to level differences rather than emphasize them. This
has been remarked upon, and it has been suggested that the
anxiety aroused from perceiving differences that are antithetical
to one's inner construction of the world could be overcome by a
denial of them, that is, regarding them in such a way that they
become congruent with the perceiver, which in effect is not to
perceive them at all. It is a common maneuver, but the narcissist overworks it until blindness and rigidity set in. For Shaw
to see Shaw when he should have been seeing Ibsen has inevit-

able consequences in his development as a playwright,[6] just as in later years his perception of the Shavian Life Force in Hitler, Mussolini, and Stalin affected his political views.

Thus, the price Ibsen paid for initiation into the Shavian brotherhood and to a large degree for his introduction into the English-speaking world was an emasculation of the most benign kind. The smiling Shavian sewing-machine removed some anarchy here, some idealism there, and obligingly stitched him together into a more socially conscious and more presentable composition. It was only many years later, when Shaw's dramatic reputation was firm, that he acknowledged the destructive forces in Ibsen's work and dissociated himself from his great model as less advanced than himself.

A DESCRIPTION OF HUMANITY

A great deal of confusion and difficulty in disentangling Shaw from Ibsen has centered on the two words *idealist* and *realist*. Shavian idealists were the good citizens of his day: the Morells and Ramsdens who, regardless of what they professed to believe in, actually upheld the status quo. Their principles were conventions; their morality was cowardly and inept; their social system artificial and ephemeral. The Bluntschlis, Candidas, and Dick Dudgeons were realists, like Ibsen and Shaw, who countered the status quo of the idealists. This has provoked Robert Brustein[7] into accusing Shaw of having a "whimsical

---

[6] The only other modern playwright to draw Shaw's energetic attention was Brieux, whom he ranks with Ibsen. In the Preface to an English translation of his plays (1911) Shaw represents Brieux as mistaken for a pamphleteer, a destroyer of taboos, a naturalist dealing with facts, and an interpreter of life. He may have been all those things, but he was a minor talent nonetheless. Shaw felt him to be a kindred spirit, and the Preface is as good a quintessence of Shaw's Unpleasant phase as could be desired.

[7] *The Theatre of Revolt*, p. 44.

approach to language" that "produces a semantic confusion as bewildering as the medieval boggle over the realist and nominalist." But if Shaw erred, it was less in "redefining words to suit his whims" than in defining reality as he perceived it through his singular formations of character. He never separated realism from Vitalism and always considered his realists as Vitalists. Moreover, in the following passage from *Ghosts,* the difference between Shaw and Ibsen is not apparent:

> *Manders*: Don't you, as a mother, hear a voice in your heart forbidding you to destroy your son's ideals?
> *Mrs. Alving*: But the truth . . .
> *Manders*: But his Ideals . . .
> *Mrs. Alving*: Oh, ideals . . . ideals![8]

Manders's error is to submit all moral principles to the acid test of respectability. Shaw's Morell is a far less harmful, comical Manders, who, while preaching Christian Socialism, foolishly clings to the outward forms of Victorian respectability, duty, and the sacredness of marriage, to the great neglect of inner reality. And as Mrs. Alving easily deflates Pastor Manders by telling him, "You're a great baby, Pastor, and always will be" (p. 69), so Candida one way and another infantilizes Morell.

The difficulty once again is not so much in a confusion of general terms as in keeping pace with the dynamics of these ideas as they inform the living substance of Ibsen's plays, and so we must consider Ibsen in some detail if we are to get clear his relation to Shaw.

It is my first contention that Ibsen's early play, *Brand* (1866), was a conscious attempt to write a play of pure idealism which, in being pushed to its extreme, was undercut by its own oppositions. In recent studies of Ibsen by Eric Bentley, Robert Brustein, Maurice Valency, and Michael Meyer, Brand emerges

[8] *Ghosts* (New York: Penguin ed., 1964), p. 59.

as a tragic failure on a heroic scale.[9] Yet Ibsen declared Brand to be himself in his best moments.[10] Moreover, he wrote *Brand* as an attack on his fainthearted countrymen who failed to rise to heroism in facing contemporary political issues. Brand scourged compromise by upholding principle and self-sacrifice even unto death. Only what resulted was that other people kept getting innocently sacrificed along the way. We begin to wonder whether he has been tested to the limits of human endurance or whether he is the victim of his own cruel ideals. In a symbolic and ambiguous finale, Brand on his snow-swept and austere heights sees the hawk of compromise—the last obstacle in his spiritual ascent—shot shown; but the shot also brings down an avalanche that says, "He is 'Deus caritatis'," before sweeping Brand to his death. Have we witnessed an act of Divine approbation, or an act of Divine wrath and the result of tragic error in Brand's forsaking love? Only Evert Sprinchorn among current critics has argued, in seminar if not yet in print, for the former view. The others, Shaw included, join with the mountains in stoning Brand.

The play was regarded by Shaw as the first of many attacks on false idealisms that were to become illusions in Ibsen's later realistic period. But the play's ambiguities have been hammered down and its ironies ironed out by Shaw. For Brand more likely represents Ibsen's attempt to deal with the archetypal male who sets out to purge his life of all feminine components as weakness and compromise. In the process he approaches identification with the stern ideal of the Old Testament God of Abraham; but he also deprives himself of the possibility of

[9] *The Playwright as Thinker*, p. 36; *The Theatre of Revolt*, pp. 51–59; *The Flower and the Castle*, pp. 123–35; Preface to Meyer's translation of *Brand*. Of these, Robert Brustein is most open to the ambiguities of Brand's character. Valency finds "something divine in Brand's mission" but concludes, he "is at bottom sentimental."

[10] *Letters and Speeches*, ed. Evert Sprinchorn, p. 102; also pp. 50, 59, 83–84.

human life, happiness, and instinctual gratifications. In the avalanche climax, an epiphany of the patriarchal Deity fuses with a triumph of the death instinct. It is this conjunction of conscious purpose (a play about the pure idealist) with unconscious and antithetical energies (aggression turned on the self for having given up instinctual pleasure) that rules out any one-sided verdict on the play.

Whatever else it may be, *Brand* is an account of that primary human struggle to renounce all instinctual satisfactions in order to placate and measure up to the demands of a primitive superego. Brand is purpose without pleasure. He ascends away from his mother and wife toward the eternal father and masculine ego-ideal. *Peer Gynt* (1867) is the other side of the Ibsen planet: an archetypal voyage conducted by the id to enjoy pleasure without purpose. When Peer's curve is complete, the "center of his orbit" is revealed as Solveig, his youthful sweetheart, whom he abandons and returns to in the end: the "eternal mother," according to Valency.[11]

In *Emperor and Galilean* (1870–73) Ibsen conceived a Third Empire, in which the ego could mediate between instinct and renunciation, ecstasy and asceticism, pleasure and reality. And in his final play, *When We Dead Awaken* (1900), the Brandian hero again ascends the mountain to disappear in an avalanche; but he has along with him the eternal feminine, and the last words of the play are *"Pax vobiscum."*

Even allowing for this final synthesis, the reader will find Ibsen a profound dualist in a sense that Shaw never was. Much of the antagonism between the pleasure principle and the reality principle for Shaw is resolved by the Life Force, which subordinates pleasure to reality while making reality the goal of an "evolutionary appetite."

In Ibsen's middle period the Brandian idealist is subjected

[11] *The Flower and the Castle,* p. 138.

to the conditions of real life, and is either relatively successful as Nora, chastised as Mrs. Alving, brutalized as Pastor Manders, or caricatured as Gregers Werle and Dr. Stockman. Similarly, the Gyntian principle is either driven into lecherous excess as Capt. Alving, or ridiculed as absurd compromise in Hjalmar Ekdal. Throughout, Ibsen was concerned with archetypes of human possibility, or as he put it, with a "description of humanity." As his creative energies acted on the materials of life around him, the idealist is subjected to a whole range of ambiguities, transformations, and nuances that Shaw's leveling mind skimmed over. It is clear today, if it was not then, that Ibsen was not a Shavian reformer, a Socialist, or an advanced thinker produced by the Life Force. Shaw once enlisted William Archer to clarify his position to the "terrible Norwegian," who was rumored to be infuriated by some apparently misleading report on the Fabian lectures. Had it not been for the language barrier, Shaw would have been happy "to explain his [Ibsen's] plays to him" (LS, pp. 257–58). For his part Ibsen explained that he was only surprised that in depicting "human character and human destinies" he had anticipated the "same conclusions as the social-democratic moral philosophers had arrived at by scientific processes" (*Letters and Speeches,* p. 292). Of course, the anticipations of Ibsen's art do not stop there.

WELL-MADE GENIUSES

Perhaps where Shaw differed most interestingly from Ibsen is in dramatic method. Both of these giants to some degree rode into prominence on the shoulders of Scribe and the well-made play, as did Chekhov, Wilde, and Strindberg. But certain obvious differences arise at once. Ibsen's early and late plays are poetic and episodic, and drawn from Scandinavian legend and folklore; Shaw's are in prose throughout and draw heavily on the popular modes of the English stage. Moreover, Shaw's plays, whether they are designated unpleasant, melodrama, disquisitory, or extravaganza, tend to remain in the great English and continental traditions of comedy. He identified his puppets with stock types of *commedia dell'arte* and himself with the comic line of Molière.

Traditionally, comic action alternates between two houses or at least admits an outside intruder, while tragedy is screwed tightly into one house. Comedy begins early with a few premises and moves resolutely forward without much backtracking, mainly because comic characters have no particular past or inevitable destiny. Classic tragedy tends to begin late and inch ahead, while its main business brings past events out into the open and places them in some critical alignment with the immediate present. Such, we are told, is the design of *Oedipus Rex* and *Ghosts*. With these plays everything important has already happened; it only remains to unlock the meaning of the past as present events take place. Exposition and revelation touch each other off with mounting explosions. It is as if every thing is concealed or repressed in these plays and must, through an arduous effort deftly handled, be rediscovered and brought into the open.

On the other hand, Shaw would seem to have little to hide in his plays, as he would seem to have had little to hide in life. Of Ibsen's "peculiar retrospective method," Shaw once observed, "there is not a trace in my work" (PWH). On his stage energy flows freely, granted it is largely verbal. There is little of the intricate structure required to unlock a buried or repressed past. There are no guilty secrets leading to devastating disclosures and tragic denouements because there may be less repressed aggression and guilt in the Shavian psyche. Shyness and shame, to which the early Shaw may have been prone, can be better relieved by physical action and the tonic of laughter. When one does encounter a Shavian play with a past, as in *Captain Brass-bound's Conversion* and *You Never Can Tell,* it is part of the time-honored machinery of comedy, cranking out scenes of recognition between long-lost relatives and correcting mistaken identities. *Mrs. Warren's Profession* stands out as a partial exception. Without the pressure of the repressed past, there is not likely to be any compelling sense of fate's inevitability. "The inevitable does not touch me; it is the non-avoidance of the evitable, the neglect of the possible . . . that set me raging" (LS, p. 58). Shaw was not directed toward the past, be it his own, his country's, or mankind's. Perhaps his leveling mind denied him a sense of history as the interplay of many complex and dynamic forces; in any event, he viewed history as the Life Force working through great men and gifted women, measured it on the scale of Creative Evolution, and valued it most when it offered parallels with the present and epiphanies of the Life Force. But the Life Force did not trade in ancestral curses and dark secrets.

Anthropology was not interesting enough for him to read far into *The Golden Bough,* and the fruits of this new field of investigation, which so profoundly conditioned Eliot, Lawrence, Joyce, and other moderns, were confined in Shaw to the dithyrambic drumming of Cusins in *Major Barbara.* He exploited myths for witty parallels, but he did not explore them for profound truths. His development was away from his past and not a struggle to bring it out into the open for reexamination and reiteration or rejection. He looked resolutely and often rigidly forward; behind lay confusion, despair, and desolation, but not meaning. "Our will to live depends on hope; for we die of despair" (BM, Postcript). Beyond Socialism, his solutions for human difficulties were further biological development and the prospect of longevity. "It's the time ahead of a man that controls him, not the time behind him" (TT, p. 5). This may be one reason why Freud was to Shaw merely a man of "vulgar indelicacy," and the very basis of psychoanalytic theory antithetical to his nature. Moreover, he displayed signs of his unconscious in his Mephistophelian features, and urged, if he wasn't always carrying out, antisocial impulses that would have been repressed beneath the tightly buttoned front of the Victorian gentleman Ibsen appeared to be in his photographs.

Ibsen's great plays, such as *Ghosts* and *The Wild Duck,* are deeply enmeshed in the tangled and subaqueous undergrowth the wild duck itself was mired in. Sins-of-the-fathers themes become as obsessive as in the guilt-infested Greek tragedies and invite analogies with them. Mrs. Alving, Gregers Werle, Rosmer, Brand, and many other characters suffer from irrational guilt. The present becomes an arena in which the repressed life of the past is made manifest. Guilt, repression, and rage are some of the dynamic factors that effect dramatic structure. To oversimplify, the intricate structure of an Ibsen play may spring from having faced oedipal conflicts head-on, whereas Shaw's simpler structure suggests earlier phases of character formation and subsequent oedipal evasions. Repression for Ibsen was perhaps a response to instinctual anxiety, which led to the return of the repressed in the sublimation of art and was elaborated through archetype, symbol, intricate structure, and emotionally complex characters. Externally his life was like the placid surface of a lake, serene and comparatively undisturbed, but below it was alive with the wild duck of primary process.

As Shaw's defensive strategies, such as flights of ideas and externalization of negative feelings onto society, minimized inner conflict and ambivalence, the same defence also fostered the creation of characters of emotionally simplicity, and left him free to play out in society much of what would ordinarily be prohibited, giving the impression of his being far less inhibited than he probably was.

The struggle with irreconcilable urges and values is behind Ibsen's dualism. The bi-parental puzzle for Shaw was such that, by the oedipal period, crucial decisions had apparently already been made, leading to irreversible formations. Although emotional autobiography may be embedded in both their works, the structural intricacy in Ibsen's plays bespeaks strong conscious resistance to equally strong ideas and impulses that threaten psychic autonomy and civilized order.

IBSEN'S CLASSIC: AN EXCURSUS

I can best illustrate these assertions and bring home the real contrast between Shaw and Ibsen by examining *Ghosts*. Of all the great plays in the history of the drama, this was surely one of the most shocking and vilified. What was it that contemporary audiences objected to most? Its content? The notion that venereal disease is a fact of life? Revive the play tomorrow and the critics will date it, as hysteria over VD is dated, and then sit back to congratulate themselves on their modernity, having patronized Ibsen for being only of his time. Surely before and since then more sensational things have occurred on the stage. Scenes of sadism, incest, rape, and madness, to name a few ancient and modern diversions, have always been with us. But content alone can leave us quite cool. "Art is shocking by reason of its form," says Susan Sontag, and others would concur.

But the form of *Ghosts* is classic Greek tragedy, according to Francis Fergusson, and to Robert Brustein in his elaboration of Fergusson's position.[12] Does classic form of itself produce shock? Hardly. "In its main aspects," it is "almost entirely static, con-

12 "The Plot of Ghosts: Thesis Thriller, and Tragedy," *The Idea of a Theatre* (Princeton, 1949); *The Theatre of Revolt,* pp. 67–70.

templative, and elegiacal, in the manner of the lyric tragedy of the Renaissance," contends Maurice Valency,[13] leaving us to wonder how that mold could suit Ibsen's sensational content and aggressive purpose so disturbing to his contemporaries. Fergusson makes a good case for *Ghosts'* being patterned on *Oedipus Rex* with a similar "tragic rhythm," but with Mrs. Alving's "tragic quest" being "brutally truncated" by Ibsen's shifting to Oswald's affliction in the final scene and thereby opting for the "requirements of the thesis and the thriller." The tragedy is thus aborted by the intrusion of Ibsen's anger, which he vented in proving the "hollowness" of his society. In effect, having found the play not measuring up to his classical apparatus, Fergusson declares the play and not his apparatus wanting. Such a victory of criticism over creative work seems suspect.

Perhaps it is impossible to oppose the unanimity of critics who structure their remarks around the conception of Mrs. Alving as the central figure, whether it is Shaw's paraphrase as the "story of a woman who has mistakenly faithfully acted as model wife and mother" (QI, p. 87) or subsequent attempts to reproduce a modern female Oedipus. But since the title is not *The Fall of Mrs. Alving* but *Ghosts,* some attempt should be made to free the play from the Procrustean bed of classical models and to rescue it from the burning issues of Victorian England.

No doubt Mrs. Alving is the central figure so long as we consider the play from the point of view of character, as even formalist and intellectualistic critics have done; but if *Ghosts* is truly a drama of ideas, then more account must be taken of its structure.

The play presents two sets of related actions: one in the past, the other in the present. The first is decisive for the characters involved; the second is a repetition of the earlier actions,

[13] *The Flower and the Castle,* p. 162.

a fuller realization of them, and a report on their meaning.

The critical events in the first set involved Mrs. Alving, her new husband, and her priest, Manders. We learn not only that Mrs. Alving has married a man of her family's and not of her own choosing, but that her heart's affections had strayed in Manders's direction. Moreover, before the end of the first year of her marriage she had fled to Manders out of a confusion based on repugnance for Alving's harmless, Gyntian inclination to pleasure, and in hope of some sympathetic human response from Manders. Instead, he sends her packing back to her husband with a few scraps of moral platitudes about duty to fling in her husbands's face and to make the best of her plight. If there is some original crime working its way through this tragedy, it is Manders's officious rejection of Mrs. Alving and the suppression of his humanity by substituting a life-denying morality built on the outward forms of respectability and not on the inward conditions of love. It is this authoritarianism that Mrs. Alving encounters, adapts to, and then inflicts on her husband in the name of devotion and self-sacrifice. Perhaps she is carrying out on her husband the revenge Manders provoked and deserved. Whether or not this is so, Manders is still the prime mover in the tragic sequence; Mrs. Alving is the instrument as well as the victim of his sinister will, and far less culpable for what happens than he is.

Manders's character is as fixed and rigid as the moral system that speaks through it. Hence in the second set of events he performs a similar action. Regina comes to him for help in escaping from the sailor's home that her step-father Engstrand (a figure in the Gyntian line but more depraved than Capt. Alving) has selected for her, because she recognizes that it is in fact a brothel. Manders's incorrigible purblindness is underscored, and his decisive part in the first set of events is made clear by analogy when he advises Regina to go with her father as he had earlier instruced Mrs. Alving to return to her husband, with the consequence of turning that home into a brothel.

Oswald reveals himself to be the captain's true heir by making a pass at Regina as his father had once done with her mother. The connection between the captain's passionate nature and Oswald's "joy of living" is made by Mrs. Alving, and the disclosure that Oswald's otherwise harmless instincts have been poisoned and perverted by his father's having had his way with the girl's mother is driven home when Oswald discovers that Regina is his half-sister. The curse of Manders's morality is passed on from Mrs. Alving to the Captain, and from them to Oswald. Like a tragic secret it stays buried in his bones, as Fergusson perceives, until it breaks out destructively like the fire in the orphanage.

And finally, as Mrs. Alving has been earlier instructed by Manders to cure her marriage with the poisonous doctrines of duty and self-sacrifice that conceal a rejection of humanity, to send her husband into lechery and her son away from her maternal love, she must in the final terrible scene literally give Oswald the deadening morphine : the cure that kills.

In all three instances the past is played over again during the course of the drama, and all that was implicitly promised and uncertainly enacted in the earlier sequence is explicitly fulfilled and boldly dramatized in the second. Together they constitute the dramatic structure. And throughout, the unmistakable movement is from Manders's morality to Oswald's disease. They are connected by the inexorable logic of cause and effect, for not only was Manders accessory after the fact when he presided over the marriage that the Captain had bribed Engstrand into making in order to take the maid Joanna (Regina's mother) off his hands, but also, when it is disclosed that Manders is blamed for carelessly setting the orphanage ablaze, that breaking out of natural energy is equivalent to the poisoned and destructive aspects of the Captain's passion's breaking out in Oswald. But since the Captain can thank Manders for his wife's behavior, and since his own descent into debauchery follows from Manders's moral premises, the whole action dealing with the destiny of the Alving family is the creation of Manders and can be viewed as a violently perverse return of his repressed instincts.

The story begins with Manders's rejection of Mrs. Alving, which is also a suppression of the natural energies of his life. Nature, passion, instinct—by whatever name we call this energy—driven underground thrives nonetheless in diseased, perverted, and destructive ways until it can out. From what ought to be the best in life comes the worst. Manders, instead of enlightening Oswald's mind and saving his soul, ultimately poisons his body. The stigma of moral degeneracy and even Divine vengeance result not so much from Oswald's lecherous father—that would tie the whole action in a symmetrical moral package of poetic justice with sins-of-the-fathers as a warning label—as from the moral pillar of the community and priest of God.

These repugnant and outrageous conclusions were forced on original audiences by the remorseless logic of the play's structure. The London reviews, which Shaw delighted in quoting, describing the play as "an open drain, a loathsome sore unbandaged; a dirty act done publicly," leave no doubt that it got through to its audiences and unlocked the vaults of Victorian reaction-formation, aversion, and denial. It left no one neutral, and if we agree today that what the critics described was not in the play, then there is only one other place to seek.

If this play has a classical form, it is not to be found in agons and tragic quests, but in the structure of Sophoclean irony, which confronts us with the truth that to be the most blessed and the most accursed of all living things is the human condition. There may be an "elegiacal" and "contemplative" note in all this, but Ibsen's ironic juxtapositions of the past and the present, of idealism and disease, form a biting commentary and bitter assault on his society. He has wired the highest (the Church) to the lowest (VD) with an invisible time fuse, which takes exactly as long to run its course as it takes the play to be acted. And while this play is similar to *Oedipus Rex* and *King Lear* in realizing the unforeseen and awesome consequences of human will, it is also in other ways closer to the repetition-compulsions that life has been reduced to in *Waiting for Godot* and *The Maids*. The fact that Manders is but a blind fool and not a blinded king only outrages us the more when we perceive that his cruel deeds do not recoil upon himself but strike the innocent Oswald, while Manders and his moral order blunder on to more crimes. And the ghosts can mean the persistent power of dead ideas and past actions to turn the lives of those in the present into a kind of living death where the only action is the past played out again.

Ibsen had written that if "I am not a builder, I am at least capable of destroying,"[14] and he is at his most destructive in *Ghosts*. This aggressive energy is set to work on creating a powerfully effective structure that serves to sustain this energy while letting the viewer experience it not directly but most unavoidably. When he let his countrymen know how he felt about society by offering to "torpedo the ark," he was also telling us that his plays are so potent precisely because he can set them off from below the ark of social structure, which he knew as intimately as the structure of his own personality.

The aggression of the play is directed toward Manders and the whole inhuman system of official patriarchal morality and religion he stood for, and not toward Mrs. Alving, who is one of its pathetic casualties along with Oswald. The system is

[14] *Letters and Speeches,* p. 68.

revealed as deceptively but quite terribly real in its powers of destruction, just as the father (taken either as Jehovah or as superego) is very real for Ibsen. Therefore a highly intricate, somewhat devious, but aggressively energetic structure is appropriate for his plays. His method of composition was first to write his play according to a conventional model (*A Doll's House* as domestic comedy), and then with the pretty portrait before him to realize the true struggle in his characters by twisting the lines and darkening the shadows according to the caricaturist's irony and the profounder vision of the realist. *Ghosts* is therefore the revenge of Dionysian energy on the structure of Olympian authority, for aggression aims only at society, and the inescapability of passion is celebrated even by its negation. The total impact is paradoxical instead of pessimistic. While Mrs. Alving is being torn asunder by the irreconcilable claims of the Gyntian and the Brandian, Regina quietly slips out of the hopeless world of the Alvings and the Manderses to seek her own Third Empire. And the play ends with a sunrise over the frozen peaks and glaciers of the North—surely one of the cruelest, most ironic sunrises in all literature.

Shaw dispatched his patriarchal examplars with great ease, and never lost his comic control or his temper. The patriarchal ideals he attacked were to him shallow illusions; their loss did not bring down the heavens. But then his father was no more threatening than a dancing skeleton. Ibsen wanted to send patriarchal society to the bottom of the ocean in the hope that a new order might arise. Shaw preferred to rescue the ship of state from drifting onto the rocks by replacing its incompetent pilots with Vitalist navigators, and only later did he consider exterminating some of the passengers. His anger stopped short of anarchy, and he did not turn it inward where it would affect his dramatic form and the depths of his characters.[15] He did not

15 *The Theatre of Revolt,* p. 193.

inwardly live through his plays as Ibsen once claimed he did. Shaw's most Ibsenite plays, *Widowers' Houses* and *Mrs. Warren's Profession,* are unpleasant and fairly straightforward, not ironic, somber, and ambiguous; they are intended to leave the audience "thoroughly uncomfortable," not profoundly outraged.

The applied Ibsenism in *Mrs. Warren's Profession* is instructive. Shaw demonstrates with unswerving logic that the free enterprise system leads to the prostitution of its women. But unwilling to go all the way, he curtails the destructive forces of the system under attack. The extent of potential damage hinges on the conditions of Oswald and Vivie, figures of the future, who have grown up at a seemingly safe distance from the carriers of the disease: the Alvings, Mrs. Warren, and Crofts. Here the difference between Shaw and Ibsen is striking. There is no social disease eating literally or figuratively into the bones of Vivie; she remains free to choose, and, by implication, so does the audience.

> VIVIE. . . . I am bidding you goodby now. I am right, am I not?
> MRS. WARREN. . . . (*Taken aback*) Right to throw away all my
>   money!
> VIVIE. . . . No: right to get rid of you? I should be a fool not
>   to? Isn't that so? (WP, p. 104)

The "you" that Vivie has decided to get rid of has expanded beyond her courtesan mother to include the whole Capitalist order because Shaw wanted to keep the characters individually blameless, the more effectively to indict the system. Moreover, Shaw's allegorizing treatment of character and his clearly designated target give his play a specificity that Ibsen would have transcended. Manders is undeniably the voice of middle-class hypocrisy and prejudice shared by the audience, but the present examination suggests that there is something basically anti-life in his behavior that goes beyond particular systems. If

Ibsen was more radical and even more modern in this regard, Shaw could at least be equally challenging when he addressed himself to the "dilemma that civilization means stabilization; and creative evolution means change" (PBM, p. 104).

For Ibsen, then, the past is dynamically and tragically real, while for Shaw rather unreal. What counts in Shavian drama is not what went before but what comes next. Present reality has been freed from the past, but at a certain price.[16] He "attaches little value to mere experience, holding that it is expectation of life and not recollection of it that determines conduct" (SS, p. 186). For Shaw the evolutionary process does not allow for a universal center in life; the myth is a point of departure or a rhetorical flower without racial or psychic roots. For Ibsen the myth is the "eternal in itself" created by the naive imagination and on which the mature imagination can build ("drag it up from its sea-depths, to study it on the plane of speculation").[17] Finally, Ibsen's high-pressured dramas require a tensile strength for mounting tensions, which end with the big bang; Shaw's low-pressured structure of wit, surprise, turnabout, and laughter allows his fireworks to pop off all along the way.

THREE IN ONE

But Ibsen, for all his anarchism, was a visionary no less than Shaw, for all his Socialism, was a mystic. And therefore, beyond their innovations in drama and their contributions to the thought

16 To some extent, Ibsen was a battering ram Shaw wielded in the 1890s to break down Victorian resistance to his own ideas. Once inside society and no longer needing the weapon, Shaw tended to separate himself from Iben's more anarchistic tendencies, especially since they conflicted with Shavian concepts of Will and Creative Evolution (BM, 1944 Postscript,, p. cvi).

17 From an 1851 article by Ibsen quoted in "The Mythic Foundation of Ibsen's Realism," by Brian Johnston, Comparative Drama 3 no. 1 (Spring 1969): 30.

of their times, their ultimate visions can be compared. From *Emperor and Galilean* on, Ibsen's plays give off glimmers of that new order, first called the Third Empire. It is "pan in logos logos in pan"; perfect freedom, and perfect self-control, a fusion of instinct and reason, of pleasure and purpose. Oswald has experienced it briefly as the unity of the joy of living and the joy of working. Rosmer can envision a democracy of true nobility. Ancient ecstasies and Christian asceticism harmonize when the past and present synthesize in a visionary future. Polarities fuse into a new whole, an unknown that contains both at the loss of neither. Psychoanalytically, it is the superego restrictions and the instinctual pursuits of the id integrated in and attuned to the ego.

Shaw's own vision is perhaps most cogently expressed by the defrocked priest and prophet of Vitalism, Keegan in *John Bull's Other Island* (1904), who dreams forward a vision of the Shavian earthly paradise:

> In my dreams it is a country where the State is the Church and the Church the people; three in one and one in three. It is a commonwealth in which work is play and play is life: three in one and one in three. It is a temple in which the priest is the worshipper and the worshipper the worshipped; three in one and one in three. It is a Godhead in which all life is human and all humanity divine: three in one and one in three. (JB, p. 611)

"It is, in short, the dream of a madman," Keegan, no more mad than Shaw, concludes.

At its best, the Shavian vision is a synthesis of the stability of civilization and the Life Force as the principle of change in the service of man's evolutionary possibilities helping him to realize the Divinity within. Unfortunately Keegan is not Shaw's ultimate mystic. In "As Far As Thought Can Reach," the last part of *Back to Methuselah* (1920), a mystic of the future and an image-breaker named Martellus informs the artist of the future :

> Your disillusion with your works of beauty is only the beginning of your disillusion with images of all sorts. As your hand became more skilful and your chisel cut deeper, you strove to get nearer and nearer to truth and reality, discarding the fleeting fleshly lure, and making images of the mind that fascinate to the end. But how can so noble an inspiration be satisfied with any image, even an image of the truth? In the end the intellectual conscience that tore you away from the fleeting in art to the eternal must tear you away from art altogether, because art is false and life alone is true. (BM, p. 225)

As man advances he can only evolve away from his animal origins toward that future state, regrettably treated in *Farfetched Fables,* in which the most advanced types of life are "thought vortexes." Shaw's image of himself in the 1890s as the advanced man of the day referred as much to his advanced thought as to his evolutionary advance over his biological origins by mastery over the body and freedom from instinctual claims. Orgasms are to be located in the brain, and the brain is finally etherealized into thought. This "peculiar doctrine" he once explained as follows :

> A point will be reached in human mental development when the pleasure taken in brain work by St. Thomas Aquinas and the Webbs (and saints and philosophers generally) will intensify to a chronic ecstasy surpassing that now induced momentarily by the sexual orgasm.[18]

Ibsen's synthesis would not exclude instinct but keep it at the vital center of life. His dualism would bring man back around to himself by the necessity to integrate his instinctual strivings into a meaningful value-system. His own personal synthesis and

[18] Ann Fremantle, *This Little Band of Prophets* (New York, 1960), p. 113.

triumph over conflicts between gratification and renunciation consisted in the freedom of the artist's imagination. His last hero is a sculptor; the woman he scales the heights with is his Muse.

Shaw accurately terms Ibsen's struggle to "build Brand's bridge between the flesh and the spirit, establishing this third empire in which the spirit shall not be unknown, nor the flesh starved, nor the will tortured and baffled" (QI, p. 73), but his own creative works swerved from such a task. And his Vitalism is somewhat undermined by a need to transport man away from personal instinctual objects toward ever "higher" transformations of libido into the avenues of culture. It is this secret in Keegan's vision that does not become apparent until the later works, and then removes Shaw from much of modern experience.

5

UNPLEASANT PLAYS
AND MELODRAMAS

I avoid plots like the plague. I have warned young playwrights again and again that a plot is like a jig-saw puzzle, enthralling to the man who is putting it together, but maddeningly dull to the looker-on. Stories are interesting, the exhibition of character in action is very much more interesting and, for the stage purposes, is the source of the story's interest; but the plots are the deadest of dead wood. My procedure is to imagine characters and let them rip, as you suggest; but I must warn you that the real process is very obscure; for the result always shows that there has been *something behind* all the time, of which I was not conscious, though it turns out to be the real motive of the whole creation. (TT, pp. 64–65)

Nothing that is admittedly and unmistakeably horrible matters very much, because it frightens people into seeking a remedy : the serious horrors are those which seem entirely respectable and normal to respectable and normal men. Now the formula of tragedy had come down to the nineteenth century from days in which this was not recognized, and when life was so thoroughly accepted as a divine institution that in order to make it seem tragic, something dreadful had to happen and somebody had to die. But the tragedy of modern life is that nothing happens, and that the resultant dullness does not kill. (BX, p. 199)

UNSHAVIAN PHASE

For research into the formation of Shaw's personality to be fruitful, it ought to bring us closer to the inner workings of his plays. My aim has not been to inflict a posthumous psychoanalysis on our subject, but to locate a unified personality with a center out of which it acted and created. This vital center, which is more of a great creating ego than a creative unconscious or some powerful, quasi-natural force, brought to life the variety of works we call Shavian. Although his plays resist definite grouping, the major ones fall into a sequence roughly as follows. The two Unpleasant Plays, *Widowers' Houses* and *Mrs. Warren's Profession,* aimed at conversions in the audience. *Candida* deals with the birth of the Vitalist; *The Devil's Disciple, Captain Brassbound's Conversion, The Shewing-up of Blanco Posnet,* and *Androcles and the Lion* are melodramas of conversion to Vitalism. *Man and Superman* presents the theory and system of Vitalism in terms of Creative Evolution, and *Major Barbara* illustrates this system operating in the socio-economic order. *Caesar and Cleopatra* and *St. Joan* depict visitations of the Life Force in history as *Getting Married* and *Misalliance* discover it in existing society. *Heartbreak House* is a vision of the breakdown of Vitalism; *Back to Methuselah* is a projection of it into the future.

The two Unpleasant Plays undertake the education of a group of socially representative characters to the harsh facts of life, which turn out to be essentially economic. They become implicated in the ugly dealings of slum landlordism and learn that the capitalism they support is a form of prostitution. The conditions of society revealed to them by irrefutable evidence and unswerving logic are intolerable and demand change. However, good intentions and individualistic gestures prove unavailing against a pervasively evil system. There is no Shavian blame or scapegoat for guilt. "I have allowed every person his or her own point of view" (PWH); therefore, there are only the few who resist and the rest who cooperate and have on their side the advantage of the system, which is presented as permanent.

In the audience's complacent acquiescence to the status quo is the thesis intended to be violently jolted by the antithetical presentation of their world, and they are disgorged from the theater with their consciences "smitten" and "thoroughly uncomfortable." In exposing the operations of the social organism, the plays are realistic and mimetic. In reworking the dramatic structure for themselves as they witness events on stage, the members of the audience experience these unpleasant social operations with results that must have amounted to a new experience in the theater. For the sources of evil are not in a remote Fate or in human nature, or in humours, eccentricities, or obstinate passions, or in someone's failing to measure up to social norms, or finally in *méprises* and other contrivances of plot to be unraveled at the end. Rather, the audience's own economic system is the evil, which comes loose in the process of reworking the play's structure and clings in unpleasant self-recognition.

Regardless of the unlikely ways they may have come about, Shaw's radical insights into the structure of society made it possible for him to create a new structure of drama. Traditionally comic playwrights collaborated with the defenses of the audience and provided it with Malvolios, Tartuffes, and Pinchwifes to project hostilities onto. Of course, they were also spokesmen[1] to balance the scales as there are no villains to

---

[1] "Precisely because each figure had to be so plausible, so convincing, and so free of guilt, none could know more than his own partial truth. Moreover, to make an audience uncomfortable, each has to justify himself in terms of existing society, not in terms of the author's heterodox opinions" (MM, p. 132). My debt to Martin Meisel in this section is so pervasive that I may in places appear merely to be paraphrasing what he has already discovered.

free to see themselves in the characters if they chose, but the hypocrites, misers, fops, and cuckolds exposed by comedy have not been more noted for their capacity for insight and self-awareness than their counterparts in the audience. Shaw reversed this mechanism of projection.

If there are no Shavian ideas in the dialogue, Shaw is nevertheless structurally felt in the drama, and there is a Shavian mind behind and beyond the play, with a Fabian synthesis that the newly aroused audience can advance toward as the third phase in the dialectic.[2] What bothered Archer and others who felt that they were not plays at all was that they were actually an incomplete dialectic, the completion of which, like the advancement of society, had been handed over to the audience. In reworking the structure, the audience is meant to liberate its vital energies and then to redirect them. This "advance" had already taken place in Shaw by means of his conversions, and he was figuratively up ahead, waiting for society to join him, while literally he was on the street or in the public hall spreading the word of Fabianism—all the while viewing the present as "artificial" and in a sense as already past.[3]

William Archer gives the following account of the genesis of *Widowers' Houses*:

[2] "Socialism is the almost unnamed alternative to the seemingly insoluble state of affairs" (MM, pp. 132–33). Meisel proceeds to discredit the Francis Fergusson view that Shaw's work is a kind of "romantic irony" because of the "unresolved paradox," by stating that "there is in fact generally an unstated resolution to the paradox," available to few or none of the characters themselves but available to the spectator."

[3] "They [the Unpleasant Plays] were pictures of middle class society from the point of view of a Socialist who regards the basis of that society as thoroughly rotten economically and morally" and "criticisms of a special phase, the Capitalist phase of modern organization" (LS, p. 632).

Partly because English society never really advanced to Shaw's position he continued to see himself as ahead of his time. When political upheavals occurred in Russia, Germany, and Italy, he assumed they were in his direction and went forth to welcome the leaders aboard, while Western culture generally was moving quite independently in a direction Shaw never really grasped.

I was to provide him with one of the numerous plots I kept in stock, and he was to write the dialogue. So said, so done. I drew out, scene by scene, the scheme of a twaddling cup-and-saucer comedy vaguely suggested by Augier's Ceinture Dorée. The details I forget, but I know it was to be called Rhinegold, was to open, as Widowers' Houses actually does, in a hotel-garden on the Rhine, and was to have two heroines, a senti-mental and a comic one, according to the accepted Robertson-Byron-Carton formula. I fancy the hero was to propose to the sentimental heroine, believing her to be the poor niece instead of the rich daughter of the sweater, or slum-landlord, or what-ever he may have been; and I know he was to carry on in the most heroic fashion, and was ultimately to succeed in throw-ing the tainted treasure of his father-in-law, metaphorically speaking, into the Rhine. (PWH, p. 699)

When Shaw went back for more plot six weeks later, Archer insisted on being let in on the play's progress only to conclude that "far from having used up my plot, he had not even touched it." Whereupon Shaw interjects his version :

The Rhine hotel garden, the hero proposing to the heroine in ignorance of the source of her father's wealth, the "tainted treasure of the father-in-law," the renunciation of it by the lover : all these will be found as prominently in the pages of the play as in Mr. Archer's description of the fable which he persists in saying that I did not even touch. As a matter of fact the dissolution of partnership between us came when I told him that I had finished up the renunciation and wanted some more story to go on with, as I was only in the middle of the second act. He said that according to his calculation the renunciation ought to have landed at the end of the play. I could only reply that his calculation did not work out, and that he must supply further material. This he most unreasonably refused to do; and I had eventually to fish up the tainted treasure out of the Rhine, so to speak, and make it last out another act and a half, which I had to invent all by myself.

Shaw is probably correct, but more important is the dis-tinction he makes : ". . . what I have called a story, Mr. Archer calls a plot. . . . I told the story but discarded the plot." By plot Shaw meant the arrangement of the story into a well-made play. This method of construction has been widely written about,[4] and can briefly be described as the contrived complications surrounding a given situation, usually a conflict of wills and a secondary love interest, with a suspenseful action seesawing toward a downturn in the hero's fortunes and his ultimate vindication by the timely revelation of some hitherto-withheld secret. Shaw's contempt for this method has been expressed by Meisel:

> Shaw's root objection to the "well-made" formula was that any serious play whose ultimate dramatic values lay in an intriguing situation and its circumstantial plausibility was likely to depend upon conventional moral and social values in its characters and in its audience. For example, Shaw wrote of *The Second Mrs. Tanqueray,* "I find little except a scaffold for the situation of a step-daughter and step-mother finding themselves in the positions respectively of affianced wife and discarded mistress to the same man. Obviously, the only necessary conditions of this situation are that the persons concerned shall be respectable enough to be shocked by it, and that the stepmother shall be an improper person" (OT, 1:46). Such a formula, Shaw felt, depended upon static attitudes and moral commonplaces. It was conventional in the deepest sense, "essentially mechanistic and therefore incapable of producing vital drama." (MM, p. 80)

Which is to say that, although Shaw would rarely discuss form (EB, p. 101), and would have the reader believe that "My natural way is to imagine characters and spin out a story about them" (WHP, p. 700), he was neither indifferent to form, negligent in handling it, nor innocent of its power. On the contrary he was on to its real nature. Form could be an accurate index of social attitudes and closer to philosophy than to stagecraft. Shaw's stagecraft employed devices of the well-

---

[4] John Russell Taylor, *The Rise and Fall of the Well-Made Play* (New York, 1967); Stephen Stanton, Introduction to *Camille and Other Plays* (New York, 1957); *The Flower and the Castle.*

made play and other perennial and popular formulas, as Meisel has demonstrated, but his philosophical point of view adapted them to entirely different purposes: "It is the philosophy, the outlook on life, that changes, not the craft of the playwright" (PU, pp. 56–57).

His first play is interesting because, in starting out with the cup-and-saucer realism of the 1860s, borrowing characters from Boucicault, plot from the French realists, adapting some of Ibsen's boldness, and finally making his own entrance at mid-point to invent the rest of the story from his recently gained knowledge of women and economics, *Widowers' Houses* spans about thirty years of theatrical development and anticipates much of the next thirty years. At that mid-point, which occurs about halfway into the second act, Trench has begun to realize that the income of his fiancée's father is tainted by his slum landlord profits. "I'd rather not take anything from you except Blanche herself," he says patronizingly to Sartorius (WH, pp. 532–35).

> SARTORIUS. Mr. Cokane : you will bear me out. I was explicit on the point. I said I was a self-made man; and I am not ashamed of it.

> TRENCH. You are nothing of the sort. I found out this morning from your man—Lickcheese, or whatever his confounded name is—that your fortune has been made out of a parcel of unfortunate creatures that have hardly enough to keep body and soul together—made by screwing, and bullying, and threatening, and all sorts of pettifogging tyranny.

Sartorius then proceeds to disillusion Trench of his "sentimental notions" by educating him to the economic facts of life :

> SARTORIUS *(pitying his innocence)*. My young friend : these poor people do not know how to live in proper dwellings : they would wreck them in a week. You doubt me : try it for yourself. You are welcome to replace all the missing banisters, hand-

rails, cistern lids and dusthole tops at your own expense; and you will find them missing again in less than three days : burnt, sir, every stick of them. I do not blame the poor creatures : they need fires, and often have no other way of getting them. . . . And now, Dr. Trench, may I ask what your income is derived from?

TRENCH *(defiantly)*. From interest : not from houses. My hands are clean as far as that goes. Interest on a mortgage.

SARTORIUS *(forcibly)*. Yes : a mortgage on my property. When I, to use your own words, screw, and bully, and drive these people to pay what they have freely undertaken to pay me, I cannot touch one penny of the money they give me until I have first paid you your seven hundred a year out of it. What Likecheese did for me, I do for you. He and I are alike inter-mediaries : you are the principal. It is because of the risks I run through the poverty of my tenants that you exact interest from me at the monstrous and exorbitant rate of seven percent, forcing me to exact the uttermost farthing in my turn from the tenants. And yet, Dr. Trench, you, who have never done a hand's turn of work in connection with the place, you have not hesitated to speak contemptuously of me because I have applied my industry and forethought to the management of our property, and am maintaining it by the same honorable means. . . .

TRENCH *(dazed)*. Do you mean to say that I am just as bad as you are?
SARTORIUS. . . . If, when you say you are just as bad as I am, you mean that you are just as powerless to alter the state of society, then you are unfortunately quite right.
(Trench does not at once reply. He stares at Sartorius, and then hangs his head and gazes stupidly at the floor, morally beggared, with his clasped knuckles between his knees, a living picture of disillusion.)

The lesson is concluded with Trench's "We're all in the same swim, it appears."

In the third act, Blanche reaches a similar conclusion when she learns that her father is "the worst slum landlord in London." "One would suppose," Sartorius apparently agrees, "that we are the most grasping, grinding, heartless pair in the world, you and I."

BLANCHE. Is it not true? About the state of the houses, I mean?

SARTORIUS *(calmly)*. Oh, quite true.

BLANCHE. Then it is not our fault?

SARTORIUS. My dear: if we made the houses any better, the rents would have to be raised so much that the poor people would be unable to pay, and would be thrown homeless on the streets.

BLANCHE. Well, turn them out and get in a respectable class of people. Why should we have the disgrace of harboring such wretches?

SARTORIUS. *(opening his eyes)*. That sounds a little hard on them, doesn't it, my child?

BLANCHE. Oh, I hate the poor. At least, I hate those dirty, drunken, disreputable people who live like pigs. If they must be provided for, let other people look after them. How can you expect anyone to think well of us when such things are written about us in that infamous book?

SARTORIUS *(coldly and a little wistfully)*. I see I have made a real lady of you, Blanche.

BLANCHE *(defiantly)*. Well? Are you sorry for that?

SARTORIUS. No, my dear: of course not. But do you know, Blanche, that my mother was a very poor woman, and that her poverty was not her fault?

BLANCHE. I suppose not; but the people we want to mix with now don't know that. And it was not my fault; so I don't see why *I* should be made to suffer for it.

SARTORIUS *(enraged)*. Who makes you suffer for it, miss? What would you be now but for what your grandmother did for me when she stood at her wash-tub for thirteen hours a day and thought herself rich when she made fifteen shillings a week?

BLANCHE *(angrily)*. I suppose I should have been down on her level instead of being raised above it, as I am now. Would you like us to go and live in that place in the book for the sake of grandmamma? I hate the idea of such things. I don't want to know about them. I love you because you brought me up to something better. *(Half aside, as she turns away from him)* I should hate you if you had not.

SARTORIUS *(giving in)*. Well, my child, I suppose it is natural for you to feel that way, after your bringing up. It is the lady-like view of the matter. (WH, pp. 548–49)

It is also society's view of the matter, and Blanche's momentary disillusion does not affect her training as a lady to marry into society. Trench, too has realized that everything comes down to a question of money, and "one has to live." Thus, when a Capitalist marriage of convenience is fittingly proposed by the blackmailing rent-collector Lickcheese ("Why not have a bit of romance in business when it costs nothing?"), the characters are all united finally, not in a bond of affection, but chained together by self-interest.

> *Exeunt omnes: Blanche on Cokane's arm; Lickcheese jocosely taking Sartorius on one arm, and Trench on the other.*

It is a closed society in which the Old Guard and the Capitalists, the aged and the young, the man and the woman are interlocked by power drives and mutual dependencies in an ending that unpleasantly mocks the anticipated happy one. It is as if the shell of comic wish fulfillment has been preserved while the core has been invaded by reality (as Shaw's unconscious had once been invaded by his ego?). And what made the audience so uncomfortable was having its passive enjoyment of fantasy invaded by reality. Deprived of its collective daydream, the audience can either manifest its collusion in a "thoroughly rotten" society by applauding, or it can acknowledge the need for change by action.

The economic barriers between Trench and Blanche are analogous to the incest taboos traditionally circumvented in comedy,[5] except that in this instance the economic taboos remain and the marriage is scheduled regardless of them. Thus, the final grouping suggests a morbid family picture of clandestine collaboration and culpability. Although we cannot conclusively demonstrate that life under Capitalism is constructed on the model of perverted family life, Shaw's remark that he became "an enemy . . . of perversions of mankind produced by private property plus the industrial revolution" speaks to the point. Clearly the two Unpleasant Plays deny the possibility of love under Capitalism, or in Freudian terms, of the formation of those sublimated libidinal bonds necessary for a healthy society. Shaw goes on to say that the "precept of 'Love one another' was impossible with human society divided into detestable unlovable classes" (EP, p. 78).

In addition, with the rent collector in the low comedy role suddenly raised to a leading position of power and prestige, with Blanche's shallow social prejudices and her irascible treatment of her maid, with Trench's lack of character and his friend Cokane calling him a damned fool, and with Sartorius's callousness all manifestly approved in the "happy" ending, this society is unmistakably modeled on the principles of random or circumstantial selection and survival of the fittest, that is, the

5 "New Comedy unfolds from what may be described as a comic Oedipus situation. Its main theme is the successful effort of a young man to outwit an opponent and possess the girl of his choice. . . . The girl is usually a slave or courtesan, and the plot turns on a *cognitio* or discovery of birth that makes her marriageable. Thus it turns out that she is not under an insuparable taboo after all, but is an accessible object of desire, so that the plot follows the regular wish fulfilment pattern." (Northrop Frye "The Argument of Comedy," *English Institute Essays*, 1948, 1949, pp. 58–73.)

most cunning beast—the side of Darwin rejected by Shaw as most repugnant to his Creative Evolution.

AUTHORIAL ECLIPSE

In *Mrs. Warren's Profession* the relationships are also tainted by the economic system, and there is an alternate ending when the characters disperse to face their respective conditions alone. Vivie Warren, whose education along the lines of Trench and Blanche is extended for the length of the play, tells her mother at the end that she is getting rid of her, and the audience senses that this is because Mrs. Warren's blameless profiteering from Capitalism has led directly to prostitution. But as to what is to replace Capitalism, the audience is not informed.

However, if the play is an indictment of the system served by Mrs. Warren's profession, it is also a defense of Mrs. Warren herself. Given her options of starving, dying of disease in a factory, or becoming a courtesan, she chose the least evil of these and succeeded by the Darwinian method of adapting to the changing conditions of life. She is individually as blameless as Mrs. Shaw in overcoming her marriage to a hopeless drunkard by taking up music and setting up what Shaw once called a "blameless *ménage à trois*" (AH, p. 37). This link is at best an indirect one and less important than the questions it raises. How could Shaw, who believed almost fanatically in the powers of will and self-determination over fatalism and in intelligence over chance, be so apparently deterministic about individuals under Capitalism? Allowing that he believed in the audience's capacity for change, how would he believe in characters who could not?

If we were to pull up these plays by their creative roots, we might find in them the results of a defense against their author's disagreeable experiences in Dublin's slums where his nursemaid took him out for exercise "just as she may have taken a dog," and against the perversions and confusions of his loveless family carried out by externalizing them out of his own past where they could not be altered, onto society where they could be. This transference of responsibility to the socioeconomic system left his mother like Mrs. Warren, less wrong than wronged, and many other characters-to-be more sinned against than sinning. It also freed his aggression to be discharged onto the social structure rather than against his family or onto himself in the self-hatred of the "disagreeable little beast" he was treated as. Along with prostitution, alcoholism was described by Shaw as less an individual illness than a symptom of a diseased society under Capitalism. Even his argument against vaccination is based on what he considered a false emphasis on the individual rather than on the conditions of dirt and disease created by poverty (IW, p. 399).

Similarly, the "clandestine sensuality" and the general sexual confusion in *The Philanderer* are attributed to the "passing phase of modern Capitalist organization." The connection between the promiscuity of the young and the corruption of the present system is tenuous enough to cloud the purpose of the play and caused Shaw to reject it later. This connection depends on the Capitalist tendency to make the woman an object of commercial and class interest and the private property of the man instead of extending the range of selection and more fairly distributing the wealth; the confusion comes from Shaw's drawing on materials from his recent philandering when he was trying to juggle a divided attraction for his amorous widow Jenny Patterson and the darkly beautiful Florence Farr. He was unsuccessful less because of economics, including his own impecuniosity, than because of his uncertainties over what to expect from women. And the play fails structurally because these conflicts and issues resisted projection, unlike those in the other

Unpleasant Plays. Eventually he disparaged the play as having "one or two good scenes in a framework of mechanical farce and trivial filth" (CR, p. 55). Finally we are left to puzzle over the paradox that while denial and externalization helped to free him from his humiliating past and cleared the way for releasing creative energies, those severe measures also contributed —in light of their desperate urgency and finality—to the impersonal and deterministic features in the works.[6]

Even allowing for the application of Ibsenite logic in drawing the extremes of society tightly together, the two other Unpleasant Plays are a brilliant *coup* of creative energy. The old problems of the novels are gone, along with the author's transparent personae. In finding a realistic purpose for his narcissism, he has to that extent transcended it. He is even at this point, like the dramatic artist in *A Portrait of the Artist*

[6] The way best to describe Shaw's aversions to enforced vaccination, to Capitalism as a source of perversion, to clandestine sensuality, alcoholism, disease, poverty, and crime is to say they are overdetermined. That is, his unbending belief that Socialism could cure all these problems, while it has some realistic grounds, was rooted in a defense mechanism in which he was so strongly invested as to reduce his effectiveness in dealing with other realistically pertinent factors.

In discussing the entrance of sex into modern literature, and indirectly the Freudian " 'Libido' school" of psychology, Shaw declared that far from having exhausted the subject of sex we were just beginning to open it up, but at present it was an impossible task.

The field of sexual selection is too narrowed by class and property divisions which forbid intermarriage to give anything like enough material for a genuine science of sex. I tell you you will never have a healthily sexed literature until you have a healthily sexed people; and that is impossible under Capitalism, which imposes commercial conditions on marriage as on everything else. (TT, pp. 101–2)

Although one may want to reply that Joyce, Lawrence, Freud, and others had overcome their Capitalistic handicaps remarkably well, in fairness to Shaw I must add that by a "science of sex" he meant eugenics, which would allow a free and purposeful process of sexual selection to operate. But this only raises more questions. Eugenics comes down to mere breeding and easily falls prey to racist theories. The one leads to better livestock, the other to Buchenwald. The step from economics to eugenics may have been a quick one in Shaw's mind; in reality he neglects the whole field in between of modern psychology and anthropology, the areas many feel most crucial for individual and cultural well-being, not to mention for the building of the Superman.

as a Young Man, nearly refined out of existence and outside, within, or above the work paring his nails, though more impatiently that indifferently. This apparent authorial eclipse is possible because the creative energies have broken free from preoccupations with character and produced a new antithetical structure. His presence is "derisive," mainly negative, and at best a nudge toward an unspecified, dialectical future. This structural originality sets him apart from his avowed rival, Shakespeare, and his model, Ibsen.

The three main components of Shaw's creative energy —Diabolonian, Vitalist, and Visionary—are really stages in a single progression. The Unpleasant Plays draw on the iconoclastic Diabolonian energy to strip the labels and disguises from society for a downright indictment of it. At the same time, because the conditions of society are revealed as both intolerable and unnecessary, the structure of the plays, by awakening a need for change in the audience, is open to comic shaping. The plays are dark comedies only because the artist is on the outside. Shaw's presence is felt more directly in the Vitalist plays in which a new point of view, still antithetical to present society, enters, but aims now at freeing and reorganizing the public's vital energies for real alternatives. And instead of a representation of the operations of society, there is a mimesis of the Life Force.

DISCIPLE OF VITALISM

The birth of the Shavian Vitalist occurs at the end of *Candida;* it is the secret in Marchbanks's heart, which has been awakened in him by Candida and which he takes with him into the night of the future. Thus, while the play, working on several levels, reverses Ibsen and resolves an oedipal situation through Marchbanks's departure, it also hints at the birth of something new in the transaction between him and Candida. This new element, Shaw declared, is the vocation of the poet freed from mother and wife as the Scylla and Charybdis of domesticity. Good enough; but we cannot overlook the impact on the poet of Candida's pragmatic and vital genius, which gives him the strength to make the separation. This variant on the oedipal crisis, which is accomplished by a transaction between "mother" and "son" that by-passes "father," means that instead of his identification with Morell, leading in time to sexual potency, there is the gift of Candida's vitality leading to social innovation and creative work.

Marchbanks departs before the results of his conversion have been made clear, but in three succeeding plays we find essentially the same situation with conversions duly occurring. In *Captain Brassbound's Conversion* (1899) the renegade hero of the title kidnaps his uncle and judge, Sir Howard Hallam, who is on a trip to Morocco with his sister-in-law Lady Cicely. The three of them form a triangle resembling the one in *Candida,* with Lady Cicely poised between an older and a younger man, each of whom appeals to her on ostensibly different grounds. The variation is that the presumed righteousness of the judge and the vengeance of the pirate (who has been nursing a grievance against Sir Howard for depriving him of his inheritance and for ruining his mother) are exposed as essentially interchangeable.

BRASSBOUND *(raging)*. He did not spare my mother—"that woman," he calls her—because of her sex. I will not spare him because of his age. . . . I shall do no more than justice.

SIR HOWARD *(recovering his voice and vigor)*. Justice, I think you mean vengeance, disguised as justice by your passions.

BRASSBOUND. To many and many a poor wretch in the dock you have brought vengeance in that disguise—the vengeance of society, disguised as justice by its passions. (CB, p. 640)

After Lady Cicely's disinterested prodding has compelled Brassbound to acknowledge the similarity of the two systems, both being built on "half-satisfied passions," he is converted to her civilized views. And since, unlike Candida, she is unmarried, Brassbound is bound to propose in the final moments of the play :

> When you came, I took your orders as naturally as I took Gordon's, though I little thought my next commander would be a woman. I want to take service under you. And there's no way in which it can be done except marrying you. Will you let me do it?

She is on the verge of accepting :

> LADY CICELY *(quite lost, slowly stretches out her hand to give it to him).* I—*(gunfire from the Thanksgiving. His eyes dilate. It wakes her from her trance).* What is that?

> BRASSBOUND. It is farewell. Rescue for you—safety, freedom! You were made to be something more than the wife of Black Paquito. *(He kneels and takes her hands.)* You can do no more for me now : I have blundered somehow on the secret of command at last.

Reminiscent of *Candida* and elaborating upon it, the secret in the poet's heart has become the secret of command in the captain's heart. The secret is derived from Brassbound's submission to Lady Cicely's persuasive selflessness, which is played off against the legalism in the judge and the primitivism in the code of the pirate. But loving persuasion is not all Lady Cicely has to offer. When she meets Brassbound he is at the head of a rowdy band of brigands who are shabbily clad, unwashed, and heavy drinkers; worse, they are given to sloppy speech and indulgence in romantic fiction. Like her escort, she insists that

> they must have good lungs and not be always catching cold. Above all, their clothes must be of good weaving material. Otherwise I shall be nursing and stitching and mending all the

way; and it will be trouble enough, I assure you, to keep them washed and fed without that.

When Brassbound protests that his men "are not children in the nursery," Lady Cicely reminds him that "all men are children in the nursery." Brassbound is "inwardly puzzled and rather daunted," because it soon becomes apparent that in taking the side of his wronged mother against Sir Howard, whom Lady Cicely incidentally calls the "most harmless of men," he is still reacting to the "Hell" that was his childhood. Brassbound's men are an extension of his personality: its primitive, unreconstructed components. And thus when Lady Cicely is occupied in finding shoelaces for one, getting another bathed, bandaging another's wound, and mending Brassbound's coat, she is physically performing what is actually an inner civilizing process on Brassbound. She is healing the wounds of his long-standing grievances, mending the torn fabric of his personality, making him whole, or, to be accurate, remaking him. In other words, there are psychological underpinnings to Shaw's allegorical imagination. In treating Brassbound's revenge obsession, Lady Cicely is also removing his "mother fixation."[7] She manages to make him confess that he never really got along well with his mother because of her "violent temper," much less loved her; and when Lady Cicely is repelled by the long-cherished mother's photograph, Brassbound tears it up and declares his allegiance to her. He would have her take charge of his life and fill his sudden emptiness with a reason for living. But her timely escape makes her a transitional figure whose function is to restore him to life—washed, healed, mended, and generally renewed.

Such a real-life transitional figure was Ellen Terry, for whom the part was written, as Candida's part was written for

[7] Shaw makes a belated and somewhat awkward bow to Freud by invoking this term in 1939, YA, p. 171, though not in the above context.

Janet Achurch, and Eliza Doolittle's for Mrs. Pat Campbell. "There was always somebody," he remarked ambiguously about his philandering years from twenty-one to forty-three.[8] Sexual escapades aside, one cannot help but feel that the real women in his life were those just mentioned, who successively sustained him, dressed and healed earlier wounds, and inspired his creative genius, because somehow he never seemed quite to complete the transition.[9]

In *The Devil's Disciple* (1897), a play in Revolutionary America, Dick Dudgeon, the outlaw-hero of the title, has turned his back on the puritan hypocrisy of his home only to turn the respectable marriage of the Rev. and Mrs. Anthony Anderson into a triangle. In the melodramatic action that follows, Dick realizes his true vocation in self-sacrifice for humanity, while Anderson discovers his as a man of military cloth. This is managed by converting a mechanical *méprise* of mistaken identity into a moment of human crisis. When the British come to arrest Anthony, they find Dick having tea with Judith Anderson and arrest him by mistake. In prison Dick is at a loss to account for why he permitted the arrest. Having discarded all values of home, religion, morality, romantic love, and gentility as inadequate values, he seems to have acted existentially:

> I had no motive and no interest: all I can tell you is that when
> it came to the point whether I would take my neck out of the

8 For Shaw, philandering was to adultery as a Preface is to a play, or as someone in Restoration comedy quipped about courtship and marriage, as a witty prologue is to a dull play. Shaw was accused on at least one occasion by a disappointed belle of writing the Preface but defaulting on the play (YA, p. 82).

9 Charlotte von Stein has been described as performing a similar therapeutic function for Goethe by K. R. Eissler in *Goethe: A Psychoanalytic Study*, 2: 1090f. The figure behind Ellen Terry and the inspiration for Lady Cicely is broadly suggested when Shaw claimed his mother was one of "those women who could act as matron of a cavalry barracks from eighteen to forty and emerge without a stain on her character" (RM, pp. 5–6).

noose and put another man's into it, I could not do it.
(DD, p. 332)

Having once chosen his vocation, he means to persevere in it.
When he cries out before the gallows, "Amen! my life for the
future!" he has become indeed a priest of the religion of the
future, facing martyrdom.[10]

The nature of this religion is made clear in another conversion play, *The Shewing-up of Blanco Posnet* (1909), described
as "A Sermon in Crude Melodrama." The situation is Blanco's
trial by a frontier court for horse stealing, and the catch is that
on the way out of town he meets a woman with a sick child
(that later dies).

> THE WOMAN. The man looked a bad man. He cursed me; and he
> cursed the child : God forgive him! But something came over
> him. I was desperate. I put the child in his arms; and it got
> its little fingers down his neck and called him Daddy and tried
> to kiss him; for it was not right in his head with the fever. He
> said it was a little Judas kid, and that it was betraying him with
> a kiss, and that he'd swing for it. And then he gave me the
> horse, and went crying and laughing and singing dreadful dirty
> wicked words to hymn tunes like as if he had seven devils in
> him. (BP, p. 269)

This is another existential moment of truth, and, like the devil's
disciple, Blanco acts not from any inherited system of values but
out of the depths of his being. From that moment he is a
changed man. After his acquittal he announces, "Boys, I'm going
to preach you a sermon on the moral of this day's proceedings."
He begins by denouncing the "rotten game" of a practical

---

[10] Similarly, Lavinia in *Androcles and the Lion* rejects the "artificial
system" of Christianity and offers to sacrifice herself for "something greater
than dreams or stories." She has found a new faith in an unknown but
immanent god. "When we know" who he is, she believes, "we shall be
gods ourselves."

For the similarity between the conversions of *Androcles and the Lion*
to *The Devil's Disciple,* see MM, 347–48.

Christianity that is based on human sinfulness and yet fails to explain the riddle of a benevolent God and the existence of evil.

> Why did the child die? Tell me that if you can. He cant have wanted to kill the child. Why did he make me go soft on the child if He was going hard on it Himself? Why should He go hard on the innocent kid and go soft on a rotten thing like me? Why did I go soft myself? . . . Whats this game that upsets our game? For me theres two games being played. Our game is a rotten game that makes me feel I'm dirt and that your all as rotten dirty as me. T'other game may be a silly game but it aint rotten . . . theres a great game. I played the rotten game; but the great game was played on me; and now I'm for the great game every time. Amen. (BP, pp. 274–75)

Having followed the birth of the Vitalist in Marchbanks, its value as a source of command over oneself in Brassbound, and its development into an alternate religion in Dick Dudgeon, we now have the first Vitalist sermon. As Blanco speaks, we learn that the God of Christianity has not so much been rejected as adapted to the god of Creative Evolution.

> What about the croup? It was in His early days when He made the croup, I guess. It was the best He could think of then; but when it turned out wrong on His hands He made you and me to fight the croup for Him. You bet He didn't make us for nothing; and He wouldn't have made us at all if He could have done His work without us. (BP, p. 274)

The God of Christianity made Blanco feel like a miserable sinner, useless as dirt, and abjectly dependent on Him for salvation; the Life Force is dependent on Blanco and needs him to carry out the work of salvation through evolutionary development. This rearrangement has come about through the by now familiar process of reversal (disagreeable little beast into universal genius), and it leads to the synthesis of an immanent deity, a "godhead," as another Vitalist preacher put it, "in which all life is human and all humanity divine."

THE STRUCTURE OF VITALISM

As the Vitalist hero with his Creative Evolution doctrine has come into his own, his vital origins have receded proportionately into the background. At the early stages Candida and Lady Cicely are prominent figures, but Judith Anderson is never much more than a romantic heroine, and the anonymous woman in Blanco's life appears only long enough to precipitate his conversion. Brassbound, Dick Dudgeon, and Blanco have their immediate origins in nineteenth-century melodrama. Meisel calls attention to the "broad strokes and strong coloring" of this genre, its perils, sudden reversals, and conversions; and quotes Shaw as saying, "you have to go to the core of humanity to get it. . . ."

> The whole character of the piece must be allegorical, idealistic, full of generalizations and moral lessons; and it must represent conduct as producing swiftly and certainly on the individual the results which in actual life it only produces on the race in the course of many centuries. (MM, pp. 184–85)

Meisel notices that for Shaw this meant transforming the workings of Providence into Creative Evolution, which is certainly the way to approach these plays. In relating Shaw to the popular stage, Meisel provides us with an intermediate link between his life and work. These Vitalists are drawn on the model of the "heavy" in melodrama, hero-villains who with their great energies occupy an ambiguous relation to society and often end converted to virtue or shamed into reform. They have a standard appearance or mask, which Shaw also used. Brassbound has "dark southern eyes and hair," "dark eyebrows drawn towards one another; mouth set grimly; nostrils large and strained." Dick Dudgeon's "expression is reckless and sardonic, his manner defiant and satirical, his dress picturesquely careless. Only, his forehead and mouth betray an extraordinary steadiness; and his eyes are the eyes of a fanatic." Less Byronic is the "Scape grace ne'er do well" Blanco, "evidently a blackguard," with an "upturned red moustache," a "fairly resolute mouth," and the "fire of incipient delirium tremens is in his eye." Besides the sign of alcoholism, Blanco believes he has stolen a horse from his brother, presently a pillar of the community, but also a drunkard who once deprived Blanco of his share of their deceased mother's possessions. Dick Dudgeon once stole some sherry from his mother, but has been a teetotaler ever since, although he is alleged to be a smuggler living among gypsies. He returns home to claim his rightful family inheritance. Brassbound, known as Black Paquito (little pirate), heads a band of desperadoes who engage in smuggling while smashing the slave trade on the side. He has also been cheated by society of his inheritance.

The crimes of theft, smuggling, and piracy appear to be acts of retaliation and compensation for certain deprivations and injustices. Taking by force what one feels a right to but is prohibited from, can be thought of in psychoanalytical terms as an oral crime : acting out unmet oral wishes which are socially forbidden. Addiction to alcohol, when it is believed to be a magical, potent fluid, becomes an oral crime in the unconscious mind of the alcoholic. And it is away from this mode of behavior that the Shavian heavies are converted or weaned. From an aimless life of taking and demanding, they acquire a capacity for doing and giving as a mastery over their oral cravings, and this advance is typically accomplished through the agency of a woman.

As a child, before his defenses were well formed, Shaw must have conceived of himself as a bandit of the oral phase seeking and possessing in fantasy what was denied him in reality. "Just as I cannot remember any time when I could not read and write, I cannot remember any time when I did not exercise my imagination in daydreams about women. . . . I was overfed on honey dew. The Uranian Venus was bountiful" if the earthly mother was not (SS, pp. 176–77). If Shaw was reminded of Coleridge's "milk of paradise," he was not referring to a "pleasure-dome" in Xanadu, but rather to his childhood days spent at a cottage in Dalkey, overlooking an "enchanting panorama of sea, sky, and mountains," which Lee had shared with the Shaws. On another occasion (IM, p. 666), Shaw remembered his "taste running so strongly on stage villains and stage demons," that he "painted the whitewashed wall in my bedroom in Dalkey with watercolor frescoes of Mephistopheles." And at about thirteen, he produced his "first serious literary effort," a no-longer-extant comic melodrama whose hero had a "series of breathless adventures which were constantly anticlimaxed by the arts of a sardonic demon" (EM, p. 9). These early self-projections soon changed when "intellectual integrity synchronized with that dawning of moral passion" to form a more capable ego ready for the conversions of the 1880s.

But the stage villain and operatic demon do not disappear. "When nature completed my countenance in 1880 or thereabouts . . . I found myself equipped with the upgrowing moustaches and eyebrows, and the sarcastic nostrils of the operatic fiend whose airs (by Gounod) I had sung as a child, and whose attitudes I had affected in my boyhood" (IM, p. 667). Camus once remarked that a man's responsibility extends even to his face, and we have been dwelling on the coincidence between the origins of an early self-image and its eventual visible form because they are related to each other and to the shape of these plays. It was earlier suggested how forces in the Shavian personality came to be expressed in the features of the Shavian face. Likewise, the oral bandit's impulses do not disappear; they are repressed insofar as they are converted into an opposite, which is not that of the English gentleman or the

Christian saint, but of the Vitalist hero, who, with his Nietz-schean adherence to the laws of his own nature rather than to conventional morals, and with his "evolutionary appetite" rather than the "honey dew" of the Romantics, adapts without entirely abandoning the original thrust of the instinct, for by his act of self-sacrifice he achieves fusion with the Life Force. The emergence of the Vitalist hero highlights a paradox running through Shaw's life and works, for the implication of his instinctual transformations is that they were accomplished at the price of neutralizing sexual components, along with reducing and displacing aggressive drives. This connotes a diminished potency of functioning in some areas and a gain in other areas, notably culture and creativity. What drives home this double-ness is the Shavian Vitalist. He is the creation and very emblem of socially transformed instincts, and yet he stands over his contemporaries and opposes the present system of civilization, itself the product of instinctual transformations.

It is a tribute to Shaw's adaptive powers as well as to his artistic originality that convenient categories of self-against-society, or primitive-versus-civilized, or even classic, romantic, and modern, do not contain him and even though a new word—Shavian—has been minted to satisfy the need, it has been employed in altogether too narrow a sense.

Although the conversion plays have a great deal in common, *The Devil's Disciple* differs from the other two in having no Candidalike figure behind the hero. This is because there are two branches of fantasies growing out of the family romance that Shaw employed in organizing his dramatic materials, and particularly these Vitalist plays, with either fantasy shaping a given play differently. In one fantasy a character like March-banks, Brassbound, or Blanco escapes from a family situation by means of a liberating maternal figure. In the other, a variant on the reversal fantasy is worked out. The son, released by the mother, is complemented by the man who creates, restores, converts, or rescues a young woman. *Arms and the Man, Caesar and Cleopatra, Major Barbara, Pygmalion,* and *The Devil's Disciple* reflect this shaping. Both types of hero retain a special affinity with the woman, especially as mother.

Dick Dudgeon returns home to a group of people including his mother, who is an "elderly matron," her face "firmly trenched by the channels into which the barren forms and observances of a dead Puritanism can pen a bitter temper and a fierce pride," and who will soon burst into "angry, dry tears" at the news of her husband's death; a senior uncle, "large, shapeless . . . bottle-nosed and evidently no ascetic at table"; a junior uncle, who is a "reformed drunkard," otherwise useless; and a "fattish, stupid, fair-haired, round-faced" younger brother dominated by his mother. Although none of these can be traced directly back to the parents, uncles, aunts, and cousins of Shaw's Dublin, they are a fair approximation of some of them.

Dick Dudgeon's entrance represents the Diabolonian son revisiting his youthful environment and finding there disordered appetites, vices, and wasted lives. His first request is for a glass of water, and an "irregular child" of a late uncle, at present a servant and the object of Mrs. Dudgeon's moral aggression, who "has been hanging on his every word," goes out for the water. And at the end of the first act after the others in their hasty departures have forgotten this waif, Dick is left alone with her.

ESSIE *(anxiously).* Mayn't I stay?
RICHARD *(turning to her).* What! Have they forgotten to save your soul in their anxiety about their own bodies? Oh yes : you may stay. *(He turns excitedly away again and shakes his fist after them. His left fist, also clenched, hangs down. Essie seizes it and kisses it, her tears falling on it. He starts and looks at it.)* Tears! The devil's baptism! *(She falls on her knees, sobbing. He stoops good naturedly to raise her, saying)* Oh yes, you may cry that way, Essie, if you like. (DD, p. 295)

This is less a conversion of any kind than an epiphany of Dick's natural virtue, which has the dual purpose of starting him on the road of Vitalist progress and of rescuing the girl.

In the second act Dick is having tea with Judith Anderson, the romantic heroine and minister's wife, when he is mistaken by British soldiers for the minister and allows himself to be arrested. In so doing he chooses almost inadvertently a heroic course of action, and incidentally circumvents an incipient flirtation with Judith, conventionally compelled by his heroism to fall in love with him. The melodramatic concoctions and the Shavian inversions of them that ensue lead to Dick's last-minute release, the Andersons' being reunited, and the loyal Essie's rushing to Dick's side.

The play recapitulates a series of emotional events in Shaw's development up to 1897, the year before his marriage. The first act is really the first act of Shaw's life revisited. All the adult figures of his childhood are there, except himself. He is transformed into the dashing Diabolonian, and in his place is the ill-clad, scorned, and superfluous child, Essie, whom he takes with him when she almost magically reappears at the end of the play. The second act draws on Shaw's early London years during which, like his hero, he intruded into respectable society and upset the lives of several married couples. Dick is saved from adultery by a conversion of energy, turning him away from the woman as love-object to the cause of Life itself, and culminating in his becoming a disciple of the Life Force. All of these have analogues in Shaw's life.

But at the end of the play, as Dick is carried off on the shoulders of the cheering crowd (as Shaw would soon be), Essie is still at his side. Who is she? Dick almost gives the game away when he first addresses her as "Bessie," placing her in the company of Eliza Doolittle (*Pygmalion*) and Ellie Dunn (*Heartbreak House*). Both of these names are diminutives of Elizabeth, which Philip Weissman would trace back to Elizabeth Gurly Shaw, and probably rightly so. While Essie-Eliza-Ellie is the early mother as she is re-created in a fantasy of reversal, in this play some of the original features of the superfluous child Sonny —the one who really needed to be rescued—have also been displaced onto her. In rescuing her he is also rescuing himself, betraying an underlying passive wish, and incidentally illustrating the symbolic or narcissistic blurring of self and object. Furthermore, by her bringing water to Dick, she is associated with the mother in birth dreams (OC, p. 202), and in particular with the mother who has served as model for the Life Force, for it is Dick's *acte gratuite* that has won him over to her service. Saving a life, his own or another's, is as close as Shaw's creative imagination has come so far to approximating woman's power of reproducing life. A persistent fantasy, it will stay with him as Essie stays with Dick Dudgeon at the end of the play.

The Devil's Disciple, then, has an underlying structure of dream with its components of wish fulfillment, displacement, and the splitting of real-life figures into separate characters (Mrs. Dudgeon the "sinning" side of the mother,[11] Essie the "sinned

---

[11] If the unloving Mrs. Dudgeon is the real mother, Mrs. Shaw, she also has qualities borrowed from her upbringing in the aunt with the will of iron against whom Mrs. Shaw rebelled. And like Mrs. Warren, another unpleasant mother, Mrs. Dudgeon makes it clear that she is not entirely to blame for her present condition:

We are told that the heart of man is deceitful above all things, and desperately wicked. My heart belonged, not to Timothy, but to that poor wretched brother of his . . . Rev. Eli Hawkins . . . warned me and strengthened me against my heart, and made me marry a God fearing man . . . as he thought. What else but his discipline has made me the woman I am? (DD, p. 278)

This is straight out of the Alvings-Manders relationship in *Ghosts,* making *The Devil's Disciple* an anti-Ibsen play in the *Candida* sense, with Dick Dudgeon the Shavian alternative to Oswald.

Whether this rationalization of Mrs. Dudgeon's character is dramatically justified or whether her Puritanism was not already a dead issue by then can be argued; but there seems little doubt that in attacking Mrs. Dudgeon, Shaw was compelled to defend her even if it meant interrupting the play to do so.

against" side, Judith the forbidden oedipal object), and the dream material blending autobiography with family romance and molding them according to the secondary elaboration available in the conventions of popular theater.

ALLEGORICAL DREAMER

Although art has always given to airy nothings a local habitation and a name, and energy surges through the great works of literature, no one before Shaw or since has ever tried to dramatize the Life Force itself. And it would not be surprising if the reader has begun to feel that this noble enterprise has been so qualified by some all-too-human fantasies as to seriously compromise it. It is true that the presence of Essie does not contribute very much to the play. She brings out the hypocrisy of the family and the inherent kindness of the hero, which could have been handled more economically; and the contrast of her real tears of gratitude with Mrs. Dudgeon's dry, angry ones is lost without reference to the text or to the level of fantasy. Lady Cicely's wishful psychology is similarly lost :

> I have never been in love with any real person; and I never shall. How could I manage people if I had that mad little bit of self left in me?

And while the conversion dramas depend either on the liberating or on the reversal fantasy for their construction, the fantasy itself has not always been completely absorbed into the drama. Critics may feel inclined to overlook the operation of fantasy in art, but to do so would be as reprehensible as not noticing intrusive or undigested ideas, because both fantasy and discursive thought can effect artistic structure. The oft-used analogy of dramatic structure and living organism is apt because in both cases excrescences and oddities may persist.

Shaw's avowed model in English literature was the seventeenth-century Protestant, John Bunyan. Christianity had been susceptible to allegorizing by medieval writers and later by Bunyan because it had become pretty well defined and specified, and because Divine Providence was believed to be conveniently and precisely located in the heavens overhead. But the Life Force was a principle hidden in the cosmos and latent in man; and when Shaw set out to externalize and define it, much more came out than he could have been expected to bargain on. Like primitive man's birth mimicry, Shaw revealed more about the rituals of life than about the facts of life. If the ideas in his plays have been given too much attention, and if he has finally been given credit for mastery of theatrical conventions, clearly the subjectivity in his work has been neglected. No one would have associated his plays with Strindberg's dream plays, and yet at least in some instances, Shavian drama resembles the construction of dreams, which may only be the universal substratum of all drama. It is one Nietzschean idea that Shaw may have unconsciouly implemented.

Obviously Shaw does not let the dream take over the plays, as it seems to with Strindberg and Tennessee Williams. Primary process cannot be measured for purposes of comparison, and like every other artist Shaw drew on its capital. But he would set the dream to work for some extrinsic purpose rather than explore its inner dynamics, found a new dramatic form on it, or test its power for a deeper rapport with the audience. If "every dream is a prophecy" of the future for Shaw, it should not also offer itself as a prism of the past. Perhaps for these reasons we find either reality invading dream-wishes or two versions of a basic fantasy in play after play. This restriction affected the treatment of the Life Force at times by diluting the otherwise original content and by deflecting the attention of the audience away from the central business of the works. The fact that they were not free from sentimental gestures by Lady Cicely and from other intrusive libidinal components may merely mean that Shaw was not wholly converted to the new religion he was so busily founding. However, he had also begun instigating a new basis for sexual relations. In *Man and Superman,* where this, along with the paradoxes of Vitalism, is most fully explored, he is a great deal more successful.

6

MAN AND SUPERMAN

Discouragement does in fact mean death; and it is better to cling to the hoariest of the savage old creator-idols, however diabolically vindictive, than to abandon all hope in a world of "angry apes," and perish in despair like Shakespeare's Timon. Goethe rescued us from this horror with his "Eternal Feminine that draws us forward and upward" which was the first modern manifesto of the mysterious force in creative evolution. (BM, Postscript, p. 106)

I think it well to affirm plainly that the third act, however fantastic its legendary framework may appear, is a careful attempt to write a new Book of Genesis for the Bible of the Evolutionists. (MS, Foreword to the Popular Edition of *Man and Superman,* p. 748)

SHAW RESHAVIANIZED

In *Man and Superman* (1901–3) Shaw's most challenging theories energize his characters and create situations that weld idea and part into a synthesis that is both philosophical and comic. It is his most original and convincing treatment of the sexes; a piece of genuine myth-making; a solution to difficulties raised in earlier plays, and the most profoundly optimistic play

237

of our century. It is also an attempt on a nearly heroic scale to rationalize sexuality and to control the sexual experience.

It begins with a situation reminiscent of the one in *Candida*. Roebuck Ramsden prides himself on being a liberal democrat and an advanced man of his day, now thirty years past, which means that at bottom his ideas are as conventional as Morell's Christian Socialism and Sir Howard's jurisprudence. All three accept implicitly the existing patriarchal social structure; they depend on it and advance their ideals within it. Ramsden is the fatherly guardian of Ann Whitefield, who, like Candida, will play the *eiron* to his *alazon*.[1] Suitor to Ann is the passive and poetic Octavius, who idolizes her as Marchbanks worshiped Candida. But hardly an outsider, Octavius is a longstanding and trusted friend of Ann's family and of Ramsden, who is happy to turn Ann over to him. We have, then, apparent character types from *Candida* and a situation superficially like it, but one that does not develop into a triangle for another domestic comedy.

In the first place, while Ann resembles Candida and Lady Cicely, she is a notable advance over them. Candida is described as a woman of thirty-three "now quite at her best, with the double charm of youth and motherhood. Her ways are those of a woman who has found she can always manage people by engaging their affection, and who does so frankly and instinctively without the smallest scruple." Her "serene brow, courageous eyes, and well set mouth and chin signify largeness of mind and dignity of character to ennoble her cunning in the affections." The "Virgin of the Assumption over the hearth" suggests "some spiritual resemblance" (CA, p. 293). "Candida, between you and me, is the Virgin Mother and nobody else," Shaw wrote Ellen Terry who was to have her own Virgin-

[1] Perhaps these technical terms from the Greek should be explained. The *eiron* is the self-deprecator, who conceals his (her) identity to achieve some future end; the *alazon* is usually the impostor, who is unmasked or exposed.

Mother part in Lady Cicely (LS, pp. 623, 641–42). She is "between thirty and forty, tall, very good-looking, sympathetic, tender and humorous . . . a woman of great vitality and humanity" (CB, p. 601). She too is fond of people, her favorite word being *nice*, and in her quiet way manages to get others to do her will even when it means making a fool of Sir Howard and turning inside out the character of Brassbound. Candida has managed Morell and Marchbanks no less efficiently, evidently in everyone's own best interest, as the happy endings testify.

But with Candida as managerial a Virgin Mother as Lady Cicely was a manipulating angel of mercy, they were formidable women; and it is no wonder Marchbanks goes off into the night and Brassbound back to his crew. True, they had their respective secrets, but had they stayed around, they might have lost a good deal more than secrets.

Ann is similarly described as a

> perfectly respectable, perfectly self-controlled woman and looks it; though her pose is fashionably frank and impulsive. She inspires confidence as a person who will do nothing she does not intend to do; also some fear, perhaps, as a woman who will probably do everything she means to do without taking more account of other people than may be necessary and what she calls right.

But beyond this, views differ widely :

> To Octavius she is an enchantingly beautiful woman, in whose presence the world becomes transfigured, and the puny limits of individual consciousness are suddenly made infinite by a mystic memory of the whole life of the race to its beginnings in the east, or even back to the paradise from which it fell. She is to him the reality of romance, the inner good sense of nonsense, the unveiling of his eyes, the freeing of his soul, the abolition of time, place, and circumstance, the etherealization of his blood into rapturous rivers of the very water of life itself,

the revelation of all the mysteries and the sanctification of all the dogmas. (MS, pp. 530–31)

To her mother she is "nothing of the sort," and may be "what the weaker of her own sex sometimes call a cat." But that is mild compared to the veritable Darwinian jungle of cruel and comic terrors she arouses in Octavius's friend, Jack Tanner. He sees her as a prowling tigress, a boa constrictor, and a black widow. *Formidable* hardly does her justice; she is a predator.

The woman as devouring predator may not have been the secret in the poet's and pirate's hearts, nor entirely explain their willingness to escape, but in this play in which all secrets are let loose, a latent dimension in the Shavian woman has opened up, and former defenses along with previous styles and forms can no longer contain her.

The energies of the Vitalist plays arose out of fantasy and relied on conventions of melodrama as the vehicle for unconventional ideas. Fantasies of rescue and reversal coincided with heroic actions and Vitalist conversions. But these fantasies also fostered a simplistic denial of the complexities of experience that the plays often reflected. Although all fantasies are, in a formal sense, defenses against reality, they are also the raw stuff of drama and so cannot be altogether eliminated, any more than dramatic conventions can be. But in *Man and Superman* Shaw seemed boldly willing to lessen the controlling power of fantasy and allow more reality to enter, greatly enriching the content, extending the range of ideas, and forging a more suitable structure for them.

The first significant inclusion is the hitherto-suppressed predatory nature of woman. And while views of Ann differ greatly, Tanner's quickly lending itself to comic exaggeration, Shaw adds that Octavius's admiration is not in "any way ridiculous or discreditable" but "beside the point as an explana-

tion of Ann's charm." Even as a flower girl Ann "would make
men dream." Yet it would not be any ordinary dream.

> Vitality is as common as humanity; but, like humanity, it
> sometimes rises to genius; and Ann is one of the vital geniuses.
> Not at all, if you please, an oversexed person : that is a vital
> defect, not a true excess. (MS, p. 530)

There is a sort of anthropology of character-drawing in Ann.
Like the evolution of Greek divinities, who retain the marks of
primitive eras while advancing with the values of society—as
matriarchy and owl are gradually transformed into the wisdom
of grey-eyed Athena—the Virgin Mother of earlier plays and
the "devouring" mother of early experience are still present in
the evolution of Ann into vital genius.

No longer controlled or confined by fantasy, her potent
presence and ambiguous appeal could engulf the other characters were it not matched by an equally formidable philosophy
and a character who is nearly her equal and the play's second
major innovation. Encountering Jack Tanner in the first act
is like looking out of the window one morning into your back-
yard and discovering a full-grown oak among the shrubs, or
if you live in New York, a skyscraper among the brownstones.
Whether Shaw never dared to include so much of himself
before, preferring to operate behind the scenes of social realism
and the masks of melodrama, or whether he never had so much
available to draw on, Tanner is a towering presence in the play.

He too is a composite, and the culmination of an evolutionary
process reaching back to those early fragmentary heroes of the
novels. He is as "prodigiously fluent of speech, restless, excit-
able" as Owen Jack; as pugnacious in words as Cashel Byron
in the ring; and like Sidney Trefusis, he is a doctrinaire opponent
of the established order, having recently written "Down with
Government by the Greyhaired." The "imposing brow," "snort-

ing nostril and the restless blue eye, just the thirty-secondth of an inch too wide open" keep alive the hero-villain of Vitalist plays, and his unconventional approach to society had been sketched earlier in Bluntschli. Tanner is an advanced thinker, author of "The Revolutionist's Handbook" and philosopher of Creative Evolution. In addition, he is a "sensitive, susceptible, exaggerative, earnest man : a megalomaniac who would be lost without a sense of humor." And having burst angrily into the Ramsden study, he is finally identified as the perennial intruder now sufficiently evolved to have a decisive effect on society. Moreover, in light of his "Olympian majesty," the "lofty pose of the head," and his "frock coat" that would "befit a prime minister," he already has arrived (p. 523). As in other plays where there is a question of the hero's inheritance, Tanner has just found out that he has inherited Ann as her co-guardian with Ramsden. This rivalry establishes the triangle.[2]

[2] Having located Tanner as the apogee of Shaw's personal and creative development, I anticipate an objection that Tanner is after all not Shaw but a fictional character supposedly drawn after Shaw's acquaintance, the wealthy Socialist, H. M. Hyndman, who was also a big, red-bearded man. It is true that Tanner superficially, in the ways noted, is drawn after Hyndman. It is also true that Tanner is a fictional character and not Shaw, but only because, once life is interrupted and fixed in a form, it is no longer life, but art or fiction. Hyndman may have sat for the drawing, but Shaw drew himself, and the portrait is called Tanner. "Tanner, with all his extravagances, is first hand," and his vain struggle against marriage is a "poignantly sincere utterance which must have come from personal experience" (SS, p. 200).

As in his Unpleasant Plays, Shaw states that all the characters are "right from their several points of view; and their points of view are, for the dramatic moment, mine also" (PMS. p. 505). This is too modestly and even a little equivocatingly stated. It is misleading for Shaw to pass off his Don Juan as a "political pamphleteer" with "his pamphlet in full by way of appendix" (p. 505) when the proper place to find a clear exposition of Don Juan's views is in Shaw's own Preface (The Epistle Dedicatory). And although he maintains that as a dramatist he has no more of a conscience than Shakespeare, he has already pointed to his conscience as the "genuine pulpit article" (p. 486); and after he states that "I plank down my view of the existing relations of men to women in the most highly civilized society for what it is worth" (p. 506), he plumps squarely for didactic art (p. 515).

For these reasons I find it hard to agree with those who would make

Candida as bourgeois wife had been forced to choose between the rival claims of husband and lover; now Ann as vital genius must decide whether her interests can best be served by Ramsden's dependence on the status quo or by Tanner's allegiance to the future. But even while they battle it out dialectically, Ann has already made her choice. And far from having it forced on her as Candida's was, Ann had previously manipulated her father into making Tanner her co-guardian, while Tanner mistakenly attributes his appointment to the impact of his vigorous ideas on her father. But if Ann in the comedy has selected Tanner unmindful of his ideas, in the philosophical sequence in Hell she is inspired by them to find a father for the Superman.

Octavius functions as a decoy to keep Tanner off his guard until Ann can dispatch her admirer as coolly as, and a good deal more ruthlessly than Candida dispatched Marchbanks.

ANN *(looking at him with a faint impulse of pity)*. Tavy, my dear, you are a nice creature—a good boy.

OCTAVIUS *(humiliated)*. Is that all?

ANN *(mischievously in spite of her pity)*. That's a great deal, I assure you. You would always worship the ground I trod on, wouldn't you?

Tanner the comic butt of the play. He is often the object of laughter, but that is something different; so is his early ancestor, the Restoration Rake. Shaw recognized the humor in his own affairs, public and private, but he was no fool. Tanner *is* comical, though for several reasons. When he misjudges Violet's unexplained pregnancy as a sign of the new woman, he momentarily joins the foolish company of Ramsden and Octavius, but for a different reason. As a zealot of reform he reads his vision of the future into what is happening before his eyes. It is an important qualification that is imposed on the figure who must utter Shaw's most advanced ideas and at the same time be subjected to the oldest of female traps. For what Tanner overlooks is the normal erotic motive in life. He also embodies a host of hypomanic traits, such as buoyancy, impatience, restless energy, and the inclination to flight. Like Leonard Charteris in *The Philanderer*, Tanner's philandering consists mainly in running from women; only as his historic prototype, Don Juan, can he call on sexual experience.

OCTAVIUS. I do. It sounds ridiculous; but it's no exaggeration. I do; and I always shall.

ANN. Always is a long word, Tavy. You see, I shall have to live up always to your idea of my divinity; and I dont think I could do that if we were married. But if I marry Jack, you'll never be disillusioned—at least not until I grow too old.

OCTAVIUS. I too shall grow old, Ann. And when I am eighty, one white hair of the woman I love will make me tremble more than the thickest gold tress from the most beautiful young head.

ANN *(quite touched)*. Oh, thats poetry, Tavy, real poetry. It gives me that strange sudden sense of an echo from a former existence which always seems to me such a striking proof that we have immortal souls. (p. 670–71)

Although the former existence literally refers to Ann's prototype, Doña Ana, this scene clearly echoes the last scene of *Candida*. But this time the young lover is not going to be sent into the night with his secrets intact.

ANN . . . you know you are really getting a sort of satisfaction already in being out of danger yourself.

OCTAVIUS *(startled)*. Satisfaction! *(Reproachfully)* You say that to me!

Ann had begun by saying, "I wouldn't for worlds destroy your illusions . . . you must be a sentimental old bachelor for my sake," and she is soon informing him, "You are very foolish about women . . . you must keep away from them, and only dream about them. I wouldn't marry you for worlds, Tavy" (p. 672). So much for the reworking of *Candida*.

STRINDBERG IMPROVED

Octavius begins as *jeune premier* and ends as scapegoat

because his worship of the Uranian Venus in Ann paralyzes his powers to respond to her as a real woman and leaves him in a state of pathetic fixation. That Shaw could dramatize this dilemma as clear-sightedly as he does indicates he had some distance from it as well as insight into it. But that Octavius is linked with Tanner as his "inseparable friend" when the ineffectual poet and the vigorous thinker have little in common suggests that Shaw never completely left behind his Octavius side but developed another personality alongside or grew one over it comparable to the publicly dazzling G.B.S. of the nineties, who left behind the shy youth of the seventies by a series of conversions.[3]

Although it may be dangerously reductionist to assert that Octavius is inseparable from Tanner as instinct is inextricably bound up with defense in personality, it does make a more coherent reading of the play possible. It helps explain why Ann can be scarcely aware of the would-be poet, who idealizes her, and be subtly ingratiating to Tanner, who considers her a predator. She passes over the romantic sexual instincts of Octavius in favor of the converted energies of Tanner, who by reason of his converted instincts sees himself safe. "The question is, which of us will she eat? My opinion is that she means to eat you,"

[3] The genesis of Tanner and the vitality of the play as a whole, as well as Shaw's recent marriage, combine to confirm the impression that his energies were increasingly freed in the years following his conversions. This can be attributed in some degree to his relationship with Ellen Terry which thrived from 1896. His deep attachment to her, which gave many early feelings a definite focus, may have enabled him to realize a corrective emotional experience by reliving more critcally hs early experiences as a patient will do in a transference relationship with a therapist when there is very little interpreting. Discovering the Great Mother or the Uranian Venus in Ellen Terry would then lead to self-discoveries, and the gratification of possession even in its token form would help make up for early deprivations, enabling him eventually to give up the mother in the actress and go on to others, or to get married as he did in 1898. It is at least plausible, and Eissler's study of Goethe offers instructive parallels. But that the results were only partially successful is borne out in the restrictions of his marriage and the subsequent correspondence with Mrs. Pat Campbell, which in many ways was similar to her predecessor's.

he warns Octavius, whose "I do so want her to eat me" makes Tanner a sort of danger signal for the blatantly oral-passive wishes of Octavius:

TANNER. Tavy: thats the devilish side of a woman's fascination: she makes you will your own destruction.

OCTAVIUS. But it's no destruction: it's fulfilment.

TANNER. Yes, of her purpose; and that purpose is neither her happiness nor yours, but Nature's. Vitality in a woman is a blind fury of creation. She sacrifices herself to it: do you think she will hesitate to sacrifice you?

OCTAVIUS. Why, it is just because she is self-sacrificing that she will not sacrifice those she loves.

TANNER. That is the profoundest of mistakes, Tavy. It is the self-sacrificing women that sacrifice others most recklessly. Because they are unselfish, they are kind in little things. Because they have a purpose which is not their own purpose, but that of the whole universe, a man is nothing to them but an instrument of that purpose.

OCTAVIUS. Dont be ungenerous, Jack. They take the tenderest care of us.

TANNER. Yes, as a soldier takes care of his rifle or a musician of his violin. (p. 537)

Tanner goes on to describe for his friend's benefit the relationship between the "artist man and the mother woman."

To women he is half vivisector, half vampire. He gets into intimate relations with them to study them, to strip the mask of convention from them, to surprise their inmost secrets, knowing that they have the power to rouse his deepest creative energies, to rescue him from his cold reason, to make him see visions and dream dreams, to inspire him, as he calls it. He persuades women that they may do this for their own purpose whilst he really means them to do it for his. He steals the mother's milk and blackens it to make printer's ink to scoff at her and glorify ideal women with. He pretends to spare her the pangs of child-bearing so that he may have for himself the tenderness and fostering that belong of right to her children. Since marriage began, the great artist has been known as a bad husband. But he is worse : he is a child-robber, a blood-sucker, a hypocrite, and a cheat. Perish the race and wither a thousand women if only the sacrifice of them enable him to act Hamlet better, to paint a finer picture, to write a deeper poem, a greater play, a profounder philosophy! For mark you, Tavy, the artist's work is to shew us ourselves as we really are. Our minds are nothing but this knowledge of ourselves; and he who adds a jot to such knowledge creates new mind as surely as any woman creates new men. In the rage of that creation he is as ruthless as the woman, as dangerous to her as she to him, and as horribly fascinating. Of all human struggles there is none so treacherous and remorseless as the struggle between the artist man and the mother woman. Which shall use up the other? That is the issue between them. And it is all the deadlier because, in your romanticist cant, they love one another. (p. 538)

On the face of it this imposing speech appears to be irrelevant; it would make a great play by Strindberg, but Shaw never tackled it : there is little of the artist man visible[4] in Octavius,

---

[4] If we take the concept of the "artist man" not as Octavius is but as Tanner describes him, then it could be the oral aggressive side of Octavius's passive wishes. The two characters then may represent the two sides in Shaw's divided attitude toward women : Octavius, the wish to worship; Tanner, the fear of being devoured. As spokesman for the aggressive instincts Tanner may have taken it over and converted it to the evolutionary appetite. Regardless, Tanner and Octavius form a kind of whole; and in Hell Octavius is not needed because the Devil has taken over as advocate of the romantic sex instincts. Moreover, if Octavius were capable of what Tanner ascribes to the artist man, namely of converting "mother's milk" into "printer's ink," Octavius would not be at the mercy of his needs.

In the preface Shaw elaborates on the struggle between woman and the "men of genius" who are "selected by Nature to carry on the work of building up an intellectual consciousness of her own instinctive purpose" (pp. 498–99). In adding that the man of genius may be the artist as "poet or philosopher, moralist or founder of a religion," Shaw further blurs the distinction between Octavius and Tanner.

If we consider Octavius's idealization of woman, Tanner's defense, and Don Juan's adaptation, we have Shaw's own threefold attitude toward woman. In writing to Mrs. Pat Campbell a decade after *Man and Superman,* Shaw once launched a Tannerlike tirade : "cruel stony hearted wretch, snatcher of bread from a starving child," only to have him upstaged by the voice of Octavius :

and there is no titanic struggle between him and Ann. Then why include it if a head-on combat is not in Shaw's intention or within his range?

It becomes integral when Tanner makes it his reason for rescuing his defenseless friend by entering the lion's cage himself, as eventually happens. But perhaps the best reason for Tanner's not simply taking flight is that both he and Octavius glorify the woman in Ann in their respective ways. Octavius bases his worship on romantic fantasy, and it eventually collapses as illusion. Tanner bases his on a philosophical system that converts and ennobles the predatory, devouring instincts of the Darwinian woman into the creative Life Force of Nature, which may be his illusion or Achilles heel, but it does hold up. The real struggle that emerges in the comedy is between Ann and Tanner and what they come to represent.

Left together for a while, they begin conversing as old friends and more than individuals. "I always attend to you, somehow," Tanner concedes, momentarily lowering his defenses. "I should miss you if I lost you." They have grown up together from childhood, and like the eternal feminine, Ann has always been there, as we learn when they review the stages of their relationship.

> I wanted to brag to you, to make myself interesting. And I found myself doing all sorts of mischevous things simply to have some-

> I want my plaything that I am to throw away. I want my Virgin Mother enthroned in heaven. I want my Italian peasant woman. I want my rapscallionly fellow vagabond. I want my dark lady. I want my angel—I want my tempter, I want my Freia with her apples. I want the lighter of my seven lamps of beauty, honor, laughter, music, love, life and immortality. I want my inspiration, my folly, my happiness, my divinity, my madness, my selfishness, my final sanity and sanctification, my transfiguration, my purification, my light across the sea, my palm across the desert, my garden of lovely flowers, my million nameless joys, my day's wage, my night's dream, my darling and my star. (PC, pp. 96–97)

And a little later the woman has become the "anticipation of the fulfilment of the destiny of the race which is thousands of years off" (PC, p. 131). Don Juan would approve.

thing to tell you about. I fought with boys I didn't hate; I lied about things I might just as well have told the truth about; I stole things I didn't want; I kissed little girls I didn't care for. It was all bravado : passionless and therefore unreal. (pp. 547f)

Once she rescued him from wasting his energies on a trivial romance, but he reversed the results of her intervention.

TANNER *(enigmatically)*. It happened just then that I got something that I wanted to keep all to myself instead of sharing it with you . . . It was something youd never have let me call my own.

ANN *(incredulously)*. What?

TANNER. My soul. . . . Up to that time I had played the boy buccaneer with no more conscience than a fox in a poultry farm. But now I began to have scruples, to feel obligations, to find that veracity and honor were no longer goody-goody expressions in the mouths of grown-up people but compelling principle in myself. . . . It is the birth of passion that turns a child into a man.

ANN. There are other passions, Jack. Very strong ones.

TANNER. All the other passions were in me before; but they were idle and aimless—mere childish greedinesses and cruelties, curiosities and fancies, habits and superstitions, grotesque and ridiculous to the mature intelligence. When they suddenly began to shine like newly lit flames it was by no light of their own, but by the radiance of the dawning moral passion. That passion dignified them, gave them conscience and meaning, found them a mob of appetites and organized them into an army of purposes and principles. My soul was born of that passion.

ANN. I noticed that you got more sense. You were a dreadfully destructive boy before that.

TANNER. Destructive ! Stuff ! I was only mischievous.

ANN. Oh, Jack, you were very destructive. . . .

TANNER. Pooh ! pooh ! pooh !.... I am ten times more destructive now than I was then. The moral passion has taken my destructiveness in hand and directed it to moral ends. I have become a reformer, and, like all reformers, an iconoclast. I no longer break cucumber frames and burn gorse bushes : I shatter creeds and demolish idols.

ANN *(bored)*. I am afraid that I am too feminine to see any sense in destruction. Destruction can only destroy.

TANNER. Yes. That is why it is so useful. Construction cumbers the ground with institutions made by busybodies. Destruction clears is and gives us breathing space and liberty.

ANN. It's no use, Jack. No woman will agree with you there.

TANNER. That's because you confuse construction and destruction with creation and murder. They're quite different. . . . It was the creative instinct that led you to attach me to you by bonds that have left their mark on me to this day. Yes, Ann : the old childish compact between us was an unconscious love compact—

ANN. Jack ! . . . .

TANNER. You must take me quite seriously. I am your guardian; and it is my duty to improve your mind.

ANN. The love compact is over, then, is it? I suppose you grew tired of me?

The evolution of their relationship recapitulates the evolution of the sexes generally as Shaw has come to view them; their discussion is broken off until it can be resumed in the more intellectually expansive setting of Hell and from Don Juan's perspective of sexual experience. Their conversation also recapitulates Shaw's own development, which is later described in the Preface to *Immaturity*. There he recalls that as a child he used to recite the Lord's Prayer as a "protective spell" against thunderstorms, but forced himself to stop when he no longer believed in the Christian Deity :

this sacrifice of the grace of God, as I had been taught it, to intellectual integrity synchronized with that dawning of moral pasion in me which I have described in the first act of Man and Superman. Up to that time I had not experienced the slightest remorse in telling lies whenever they seemed likely to help me out of a difficulty : rather did I revel in the exercise of dramatic invention involved. (IM, pp. 665–66)

After Shaw ceased believing in God the Father, the onset of moral passion at puberty eventually led him to the "eternal womanly principle in the universe" (PMS, p. 491), and to the somewhat more impersonal Life Force. But this shift entailed relinquishing direct libidinal claims on any woman. "The moral passion," Tanner tells Ann, "made our childish relations impossible." The surplus energy and its later conversion to civilizing causes made for Tanner's "jealous sense of my new individuality." And he can conclude, "I had become a new person" (MS, p. 551).[5]

The male therefore acquires his identity by retaining the energy he might otherwise release sexually; and he maintains his autonomy by displacing it into the building of civilization, which becomes his protection from the female. Her claim on his sexual energy would fulfill her destiny but be destructive of his. To be taken over sexually by the woman in such a contest can only mean regression to helpless infancy and leave the man prey to fears of being devoured.[6] "Life seized" Don Juan and threw him

[5] "The natural growth which I have described in my play, Man and Superman as the birth of moral passion had taken place in me," Shaw wrote of his school days, when he was fourteen. Puberty then is the period for Shaw when a resurgence of infantile urges is transformed into moral passion. Elsewhere he is more explicit :
  if you read the first act of Man and Superman you will be reminded that boys' consciences do not develop until their sex develops. A boy who will tell you bushels of lies without the slightest remorse at 12½ may be fiercely truthful at 15. (YA, p. 161)
[6] The Continental influence on Shaw has shifted from Ibsen to the Strindberg of *The Father*, about which Maurice Valency (*The Flower and the Castle*, p. 270) has written as follows :
  It could hardly have been shocking in the late 1880's to have it demon-

into the woman's arms "as a sailor throws a scrap of fish into the mouth of a seabird." And what was happening to Shaw was that having converted his moral passion into Socialism for the betterment of civilization, and in order to acquire an identity in the world, he finds defense, ideal, and identity in jeopardy in his new attraction for Charlotte.

This is the root cause of the warfare between the sexes. Woman must win man over to the Life Force to continue the species; man must direct the Life Force toward Creative Evolution in order to preserve his fragile hold on civilization. So they become antagonists that sorely need each other. "You seem to understand all the things I don't understand," Ann remarks, summing up one phase of their dialectic, "but you are a perfect baby in the things I do understand" (MS, p. 554). And Don

strated in the theatre that the female of the species is more deadly than the male; the whole current of European thought at the time led in that direction. The suggestion, however, was startling that a woman could love a man truly only as a mother, and that therefore the sexual relationship involved for her the shame of incest. . . .

In this situation, Strindberg saw the root of the sexual conflict. In *The Father* the woman is strong; the man is weak. They are in the relation of mother and son. Yet in order to propagate the race, it is necessary for a time that their roles be reversed—the man must dominate; the woman, submit. The conflict is therefore inevitable.

Strindberg realizes a paranoid potential in the battle of the sexes that Shaw with his comic sense and Vitalism moderates. Moreover, a deeper probing of Strindberg's plays may disclose the paranoia to be a defense against homosexual fears, whereas the antagonism underlying Shaw's view of genital sexuality is based on the oral model of reciprocal depletion, and is transformed by his Vitalism.

Tanner is aggressive mentally and vocally but passive sexually, while the opposite is true of Ann, whose triumph does not make this "the most tragic of his comedies," as Valency holds (p. 269), but rather ends the play on a note of compromise and complement. It places a comic perspective on Tanner's ideas because Life necessarily qualifies Thought. The irony is comic, and the bestial imagery, whether Darwinian or Strindbergian, is exploited for a comic catharsis (cf. Norman Holland, *The Dynamics of Literary Response*, pp. 249f; and above, for the "primal dialogue" as model for Ann and Tanner's reciprocity).

Moreover, considering the witty sex duels, the animal imagery, the condition scene, and the comic fall of the hero into marriage, *Man and Superman* can take its place in the mainstream of English comedies of manners from the Restoration.

Juan enlarges the subject by creating a myth of the origin of the sexes:

Sexually, Woman is Nature's contrivance for perpetuating its highest achievement. Sexually, Man is Woman's contrivance for fulfilling Nature's behest in the most economical way. She knows by instinct that far back in the evolutional process she invented him, differentiated him, created him in order to produce something better than the single-sexed process can produce. Whilst he fulfils the purpose for which she made him, he is welcome to his dreams, his follies, his ideals, his heroisms, provided that the keystone of them all is the worship of woman, of motherhood, of the family, of the hearth. But how rash and dangerous it was to invent a separate creature whose sole function was her own impregnation! For mark what has happened. First, man was multiplied on her hands until there are as many men as women; so that she has been unable to employ for her purposes more than a fraction of the immense energy she has left at his disposal by saving him the exhausting labor of gestation. This superfluous energy has gone to his brain and to his muscle. He has become too strong to be controlled by her bodily, and too imaginative and mentally vigorous to be content with mere self-reproduction. He has created civilization without consulting her, taking her domestic labor for granted as the foundation of it. (pp. 624–25)

The two patriarchal myths of Eve made from Adam's rib and of Athena springing from the head of Zeus at the headwaters of Western civilization are replaced by matriarchal parthenogenesis. In *Back to Methuselah* the preexisting Life Force is named Lilith, who recalls "that day when I sundered myself in twain and launched Man and Woman on the earth . . . (p. 262). Originally brought into existence to serve woman, man constructs with his surplus energy a civilization that he uses to free himself in much the same way that psychological defenses separate him from the object of his original instinctual aims. This biological dialectic can be resolved if man uses his intelligence to free institutions and open structures to serve the Life Force. In so doing he acquires a new vocation as the brains of the Life Force, which has been stumbling rather blindly along the path of Creative Evolution by a process of trial and error. In the Preface it is the man of genius who has been "selected by Nature to carry on the work of building up an intellectual consciousness of her own instinctive purpose." He "incarnates the philosophical consciousness of Life," and woman "incarnates its fecundity" (p. 499).

The theories of sexual antagonism and the construction of civilization from the surplus sexual energy are familiar to us today from another source.

> Women represent the interests of the family and sexual life; the work of civilization has become more and more men's business; it confronts them with ever harder tasks, compels them to sublimations of instinct which women are not easily able to achieve. Since man has not an unlimited amount of mental energy at his disposal, he must accomplish his tasks by distributing his libido to the best advantage. What he employs for cultural purposes he withdraws to a great extent from women and his sexual life; his constant association with men and his dependence on his relations with them even estrange him from his duties as husband and father. Woman finds herself thus forced into the background by the claims of culture and she adopts an inimical attitude toward it.[7] (CD, p. 73)

Shaw's comic masterpiece, therefore, has biological origins, philosophical dimensions, and a great deal of psychological insight. And if he did not pursue these insights far enough to found a revolutionary modern psychology, neither did Freud write *Man and Superman*.

MASTER OF REALITY

Before leaving the Shavian underworld of metaphysics for

[7] The Joan Riviere translation of *Civilization and its Discontents* (London, 1930) has been substituted here.

the terra firma of the English drawing-room, we must question the reading of the "Don Juan in Hell" sequence as a rhetorical tour de force or a "philosophical interlude" detachable from the rest of the play (AH, p. 578), for it is indeed a metaphysical setting where universal truths of which the comedy is but a single instance can be explored and worked out to their fullest implications. For instance, it doesn't take long for Don Juan to discover that he does not belong in Hell, but in Heaven among the masters of reality. But what, precisely, is a master of reality? This indeterminate phrase is concretely rendered in the comedy, where there is a question of who is master of the situation involving Ann. Of the three men, Tanner is clearly the master of that reality because he is aware of Ann's true nature if not of her particular designs on him. Ramsden sees her as a dutiful and loving daughter; Octavius at this early point regards her as a helpless orphan in need of their protection. At which Tanner exclaims:

> TANNER. Stand by her! What danger is she in? She has the law on her side; she has popular sentiment on her side; she has plenty of money and no conscience. All she wants with me is to load up all her moral responsibilities on me, and do as she likes. I might as well be her husband.

> RAMSDEN. You can refuse to accept the guardianship. *I* shall certainly refuse to hold it jointly with you.

> TANNER. Yes; and what will she say to that? what does she say to it? Just that her father's wishes are sacred to her, and that she shall always look up to me as her guardian whether I care to face the responsibility or not. Refuse! You might as well refuse to accept the embrances of a boa constrictor when once it gets round your neck.

Momentarily crushed, Octavius is soon defending his friend as a man of honor against Ramsden.

TANNER. Dont, Tavy : you'll make me ill. I am not a man of
honor : I am a man struck down by a dead hand. Tavy : you
must marry her after all and take her off my hands. And I had
my heart set on saving you from her !

OCTAVIUS. Oh, Jack, you talk of saving me from my highest
happiness.

TANNER. Yes, a lifetime of happiness. If it were only the first
hour's happiness, Tavy, I would buy it for you with my last
penny. But a lifetime of happiness ! No man alive could bear it :
it would be hell on earth. (pp. 525–27)

And in fact the pursuers of happiness on earth become the
inhabitants of Hell, which Tanner must desert for reality.

The irony is in Tanner's being so much more the master of
the situation, having struck down Ramsden with his rapier wit
no less than his predecessor ran his sword through Doña Ana's
father, that, as the symbol of his victory, he is awarded the
woman, want her or not. For so loudly and so often does he
protest in protecting Octavius that he protests too much, and he
cannot deny that there is a "sort of fascination" in her. Both
dramatic situations spring from an earlier psychological one.

Shaw has defended himself vigorously against typical infantile
wishes to devour and fears of being devoured by means of
protective reaction-formations that enabled him to champion
the cause of womanhood and be the emissary of the Life Force.
But as often happens in life, one of the best ways to draw the
grateful regard of women is to identify with their cause and
eloquently attack the system of male oppression of which one
may accidentally be a part. The eager throng of women drawn
to Shaw in effect act as the revival of repressed wishes returned
in a different capacity, insofar as the women are associated with
the generating source of the defense. It is this deeper dilemma
without the magic of fantasy to transform it that Shaw represents when Tanner finds he is compelled to contend with Ann's

designs on him. In attacking society he has freed the prisoner of society : Ann, the female Prometheus, the eternal feminine, the Life Force.

As Tanner attempts simply to deny everything, Ann sets about using his reforming zeal to further her own ends.

> TANNER. Do! Break your chains. Go your way according to your own conscience and not according to your mother's. Get your mind clean and vigorous; and learn to enjoy a fast ride in a motor car instead of seeing nothing in it but an excuse for a detestable intrigue. Come with me to Marseilles and across to Algiers and to Biskra, at sixty miles an hour. Come right down to the Cape if you like. That will be a Declaration of Independence with a vengeance. You can write a book about it afterwards. That will finish your mother and make a woman of you.
>
> ANN *(thoughtfully)*. I dont think there would be any harm in that, Jack. You are my guardian? you stand in my father's place, by his own wish. Nobody could say a word against our travelling together. It would be delightful : thank you a thousand times, Jack. I'll come.
>
> TANNER *(aghast)*. You'll come! ! ! (pp. 514–15)

There is little more on the surface of the comedy to support this deeper psychological coherence; it is simply presented with historical parallels adding to it and philosophical ideas deepening it later on. But since the Ramsdens of society obstruct progress, Tanner's iconoclastic pamphlet, "Down with Government by the Greyhaired," which he feels (erroneously) contributed to Ann's father's making him her guardian, could be interpreted as a thrust in behalf of the Life Force at removing some of the dead wood from its path. Ann knowingly refers to Jack as the Giant Killer. And the overall movement of the action makes it fitting that Tanner, the evident master of reality and philosopher of the future, should suffer the comic fate of having to grapple with Ann, who becomes in reality the Life Force and object of the philosopher's quest.[8]

While Tanner is worrying about Octavius's cheeks looking to Ann like a nice undertone chop, Ann is patting Tanner's, and flirtatiously wrapping her arms around him in the boa constrictor embrace; and while Tanner is preparing for a motor trip to Spain, Ann is quietly at work behind the scenes turning every situation, like Tanner's advice, to her advantage. Tanner at last wildly realizes that, like a modern, comic Oedipus, instead of escaping from his fate he has been backing into it. "Then—*I am the bee, the spider, the marked down victim, the destined prey*," he cries, and the love-chase is on as Act Two ends.[9]

[8] "Miss Townshend was puzzled at first by my ideas on the subject of marriage. My personal horror of it seemed quite in the line of the 'advanced ideas' she was interested in; but she was surprised to find that my advice to women was always to insist on marriage, and refuse to compromise themselves with any man on any cheaper terms, and that I considered the status of a married woman as almost as indispensable under existing circumstances to a woman's fullest possible freedom. In short I prescribed marriage for women, and refused it for myself" (OB, 1961). But when Miss Townshend went to have her prescription filled, it was Shaw who signed on the dotted line of the marriage contract.

[9] The predatory metaphor is slightly changed in the Preface: it is assumed that the woman must wait, motionless, until she is wooed. Nay, she often does wait motionless. That is how the spider waits for the fly. But the spider spins her web. And if the fly, like my hero, shews a strength that promises to extricate him, how swiftly does she abandon her pretence of passiveness, and openly fling coil after coil about him until he is secured forever! (p. 498)

And a few years earlier (1897), Shaw had tried out the metaphor on Charlotte after they had quarreled.

You count that I have lost only one Charlotte; but I have lost two, and one of the losses is a prodigious relief. I may miss 'die schone grunen Augen' [sic] occasionally, though the very privation throws me back, brutally great, to my natural dreamland; but then think of the other Charlotte, the terrible Charlotte, the lier-in-wait the soul hypochondriac, always watching and dragging me into bondage, always planning nice sensible, comfortable, selfish destruction for me, wincing at every accent of freedom in my face, so that at last I get the trick of hiding myself from her, hating me and longing for me with the absorbing passion of the spider for the fly. Now that she is gone, I realize for the first time the infernal tyranny of the past year, which left me the licence of the rebel, not the freedom of the man who stands alone. I will have no more of it: if you hate women who pull flowers, what do you think of women who cut down trees? *That's*

TO STEER OR TO DRIFT

The scene in Act Three shifts to the Spanish countryside and a band of comic brigands led by Mendoza. We seem to have stepped momentarily back into the world of adventure melodramas and Diabolonian heroes. Mendoza is a "tall strong man, with a striking cockatoo nose, glossy black hair, pointed beard, upturned moustache, and a Mephistophelean affectation" (p. 587). In between raids he conducts discussions of "political economy" to maintain self-respect, and he dines on "prickly pears and broiled rabbit."

These qualities connect Mendoza with Tanner as a grotesque caricature to a photograph, or as a bad dream to waking reality. He is Tanner's Diabolonian double, an inversion of his revolutionary ideals; in developmental terms, he is the Shavian personality before reaction-formations and conversions have organized the "mob of appetites" into "moral pasion." In the immediate context of the play, he symbolizes the dire prospect of regression from the dilemmas posed by Ann. For Mendoza has been made a "brigand and an outcast" by his frustrated love for Louisa, who is the untransformed *femme fatale* side of the eternal feminine. He spends his leisure gazing off at the mountains, dreaming of women and writing poems to Louisa. Tanner consciously resists Mendoza's potential threat by insisting that the mountains "will not make me dream of women, my friend : I am heart-whole." He composes himself for sleep as Mendoza warns him, "Do not boast until morning, sir. This is a strange country for dreams." And with that he proceeds to recite his love poetry to his drowsy guests :

the Charlotte I want to see married. The Charlotte of Iken Heath is another matter, yet I have her in my dreamland, and sometimes doubt whether the other devil ever had anything to do with her. (JD, p. 119) There was no unusual pursuit—Strindbergian or otherwise—of Shaw by Charlotte, except in Shaw's imagination (JD, p. 149).

Louisa, I love thee.
I love thee, Louisa.
Louisa, Louisa, Louisa, I love thee.
One name and one phrase make my music, Louisa.
Louisa, Louisa, Louisa, I love thee.

Mendoza thy lover,
Thy lover, Mendoza,
Mendoza adoringly lives for Louisa.
Theres nothing but that in the world for Mendoza
Louisa, Louisa, Mendoza adores thee . . .

O wert thou, Louisa,
The wife of Mendoza,
Mendoza's Louisa, Louisa Mendoza,
How blest were the life of Louisa's Mendoza!
How painless his longing of love for Louisa!

This state of virtual symbiosis leads logically to the prison of fixations and oral crimes, filled with the happiness seekers and presided over by Mendoza as the Devil. In short, to Shavian Hell. "Here we worship Love and Beauty. Our souls being entirely damned, we cultivate our hearts." Doña Ana may belong there, because, as Don Juan explains,

wherever ladies are is hell. Do not be surprised or terrified: you will find everything here that a lady can desire, including devils who will serve from sheer love of servitude, and magnify your importance for the sake of dignifying their service—the best of servants. (p. 604)

If Hell is the destination of regression, where forbidden pleasures are enacted and antisocial pursuits punished, as both literature and our imaginations suggest to us, why should Tanner as the Libertine Don Juan find himself there when Mendoza is the real oral criminal? Ostensibly the cause is murder: "I ran my sword through an old man who was trying to run his through me."

THE OLD WOMAN [Doña Ana]. If you were a gentleman, that was not a murder.

DON JUAN. The old man called it murder, because he was, he said, defending his daughter's honor. By this he meant that because I foolishly fell in love with her and told her so, she screamed; and he tried to assassinate me after calling me insulting names.

He further explains:

Hell is the home of honor, duty, justice, and the rest of the seven deadly virtues. All the wickedness on earth is done in their name : where else but in hell should they have their reward? Have I not told you that the truly damned are those who are happy in hell?

So it appears that he has landed in Hell for his iconoclasm, which is really a superior moral passion, just as Tanner's assaults on Ramsden's society are based on his more advanced ideas. The two offenses are related because they are symbolic oedipal crimes directed against the father-rival or patriarchal society as a barrier to freedom; and this, far from carrying a damning burden of guilt, is easily forgiven and even applauded in light of Shaw's development and unconventional views. But the more immediate and dramatically more compelling reason is that this subterranean sequence represents as Tanner's dream the effects of Ann's invasion of his life, which has disrupted his system of defenses; and he must again prove himself master of his instinctual life by triumphing over its advocate and spokesman, the Devil.

Thus the immediate task of Don Juan is to establish the reality of his defenses and the superiority of his ideals by winning out over the Devil and by demonstrating to Doña Ana that her father (the Statue, played by Ramsden) is really in the Devil's camp. The effect of this will be to woo her away from the woman-worshipping devils to the cause of reality and the embodiment of the Life Force. Once freed from infantile associations of symbiosis, oral fixations, incest, and from romanticized sex, she can escape from the pleasure-mongering that makes life Hell and collaborate with the philosopher in making the Superman, the next advance in life's struggle toward perfection; and in the mundane world of the comedy the marriage between Ann and Tanner will be sanctioned.

Not only must taboos be lifted and abysses be avoided, the sex relation itself must be transformed from something trivial and unworthy of men and women to something serious and greater than individuals. They can then fulfill the "purpose that transcends their mortal personal purposes" (PMS, p. 497). And we find a continuation between Don Juan and Doña Ana of the ongoing dialectic between man and woman that began with Tanner and Ann in the Ramsden study. Don Juan is useful precisely because he can speak from experience of the genital phase of sexuality, and the nominal setting of Hell enables him to speak beyond the confines of theatrical and historical time :

> I turned my back on the romantic man with the artist nature, as he called his infatuation. I thanked him for teaching me to use my eyes and ears; but I told him that his beauty worshipping and happiness hunting and woman idealizing was not worth a dump as a philosophy of life; so he called me Philistine and went his way.

> ANA. It seems that Woman taught you something, too, with all her defects.

> DON JUAN. She did more : she interpreted all the other teaching for me. Ah, my friends, when the barriers were down for the first time, what an astounding illumination ! ! I had been prepared for infatuation, for intoxication, for all the illusions of love's young dream; and lo! never was my perception clearer, nor my criticism more ruthless. The most jealous rival of my mistress never saw every blemish in her more keenly than I. I was not duped : I took her without chloroform.

ANA. But you did take her.

DON JUAN. That was the revelation. Up to that moment I had never lost the sense of being my own master; never consciously taken a single step until my reason has examined and approved it. I had come to believe that I was a purely rational creature : a thinker! I said, with the foolish philosopher, "I think; therefore I am." It was Woman who taught me to say, "I am; therefore I think." And also "I would think more; therefore I must be more." (pp. 630–31)

Octavius, "the romantic man with the artistic nature," represents the past historically and psychologically. Tanner, the Vitalist philosopher, represents the future and consequently the appropriate mate for the eternal feminine and collaborator with the Life Force. And when Doña Ana affirms that sex is not only personal and friendly but holy and sacred as well, Tanner redefines her terms to bring her in contact with her future destiny :

In the sex relation the universal creative energy, of which the parties are both the helpless agents, overrides and sweeps away all personal considerations, and dispenses with all personal relations. The pair may be utter strangers to one another, speaking different languages, differing in race and color, in age and disposition, with no bond between them but a possibility of that fecundity for the sake of which the Life Force throws them into one another's arms at the exchange of a glance. (p. 637)

Shaw had made it plain that the traditional "libertine" concept of Don Juan was not to be his. He conceived his Don Juan in the "philosophic sense" as the man who, "though gifted enough to be exceptionally capable of distinguishing between good and evil, follows his own instincts without regard to the common, statute, or canon law" (PMS, p. 488). But philosophically the sexual iconoclasm is converted into social and political iconoclasm. And Shaw's advance over society is reflected in Don

Juan's evolutionary appetite as his decisive advantage over the Devil's mundane appetites. There may be the usual comic conventions of wish-fulfillment as well as other concealed wishes being worked out in the play, but far more engaging is the fulfillment of evolutionary wishes. It is as if the ego, quite independent of the id, is granted its own distinctive pleasures of growth, continued development, and concern for the future of the species.

> I tell you that as long as I can conceive something better than myself I cannot be easy unless I am striving to bring it into existence or clearing the way for it. That is the law of my life. That is the working with me of Life's incessant aspiration to higher organization, understanding. It was the supremacy of this purpose that reduced love for me to the mere pleasure of a moment, art for me to the mere schooling of my faculties, religion for me to a mere excuse for laziness, since it had set up a God who looked at the world and saw that it was good, against the instinct in me that looked through my eyes at the world and saw that it could be improved. I tell you that in the pursuit of my own pleasure, my own health, my own fortune, I have never known happiness. It was not love for Woman that delivered me into her hands : it was fatigue, exhaustion. When I was a child, and bruised my head against a stone, I ran to the nearest woman and cried away my pain against her apron. When I grew up, and bruised my soul against the brutalities and stupidities with which I had to strive, I did again just what I had done as a child. I have enjoyed, too, my rests, my recuperations, my breathing times, my very prostrations after strife; but rather would I be dragged through all the circles of the foolish Italian's Inferno than through the pleasures of Europe. That is what has made this place of eternal pleasures so deadly to me. It is the absence of this instinct in you that makes you that strange monster called a Devil. It is the success with which you have diverted the attention of men from their real purpose, which in one degree or another is the same as mine, to yours, that has earned you the name of The Tempter. It is the fact that they are doing your will, or rather drifting with your want of will, instead of doing their own, that makes them the uncomfortable, false, restless, artificial, petulant, wretched creatures they are. (pp. 641–42)

The Devil's unconverted instincts, eternally seeking happiness, are shown to lead to boredom and idleness because they are not conducive to evolutionary growth; they are instead bound by the repetition-compulsion of fixation that ends in despair and death.

> THE DEVIL. . . . men get tired of everything, of heaven no less than of hell; . . . all history is nothing but a record of the oscillations of the world between these two extremes. An epoch is but a swing of the pendulum. . . .
>
> DON JUAN (*out of all patience*). By heaven, this is worse than your cant about love and beauty. Clever dolt that you are, is a man no better than a worm, or a dog than a wolf, because he gets tired of everything? Shall he give up eating because he destroys his appetite in the act of gratifying it? Is a field idle when it is fallow? . . . .
>
> THE DEVIL. . . . You think, because you have a purpose, Nature must have one. You might as well expect it to have fingers and toes because you have them.
>
> DON JUAN. But I should not have them if they served no purpose. And I, my friend, am as much a part of Nature as my own finger is a part of me. . . . Were I not possessed with a purpose beyond my own I had better be a ploughman than a philosopher; for the ploughman lives as long as the philosopher, eats more, sleeps better, and rejoices in the wife of his bosom with less misgiving. This is because the philosopher is in the grip of the Life Force. This Life Force says to him "I have done a thousand wonderful things unconsciously by merely willing to live and following the line of least resistance : now I want to know myself and my destination, and choose my path; so I have made a special brain—a philosopher's brain—to grasp this knowledge for me. (pp. 644–46)

Finally the Devil warns, "The end will be despair and decrepitude, broken nerve and shattered hopes, vain regrets for that worst and silliest of wastes and sacrifices, the waste and sacrifice of the power of enjoyment. . . ." "But at least I shall not be bored," Don Juan retorts, illustrating what he has been doing all along, which is not denying the Devil's case but either turning it inside out or building his own on it.[10] The Devil has not been merely repudiated or struck down in a duel of wills but has had his position taken over and used against him, demonstrating again that Diabolonian energy may be used when converted to a higher purpose. And perhaps Shaw was not equivocating after all when he said all "points of view are, for the moment, mine also." In getting the Devil to engage in a civilized debate, Don Juan assured himself of victory. Even though the Devil was eloquently given his due, he could not put his rhetoric, wit, or conviction in the service of a cause of the same magnitude as Don Juan's. The Devil did not have the Life Force behind him.

If the Devil is outmatched in the oratorical contest, Don Juan's mastery over him is principally verbal. He can talk the Devil down, but when it comes to Ana, his mastery is paradoxically the submission necessary for cooperation in Creative Evolution. His verbal virtuosity is just so much sound to her. "Go on talking," Anne says to Tanner, firmly caught in grip of the Life Force. "You really talk so well."

[10] Tanner's talent reflects Shaw's ability to deal intellectually and on a verbal level with what he had to deny on an emotional level. At the suggestion that the world may be only a joke, he replied, "Would you work any the less to make it a good joke instead of a bad one?" But when it came to dealing with pain of loss, as when his mother, sister, and wife died, he had to deny his feelings, make a joke, and affirm his own good health. And when the Devil says, "Beware of the pursuit of the Superman: it leads to an indiscriminate contempt for the Human," Tanner cannot reply because he has already departed.

Perhaps most deeply rooted in the drama is Lewin's (*Elation,* 1951) famous oral triad: the threefold wish of the nursing infant to eat, to be eaten, to sleep. Octavius proclaims a wish to be eaten by his omnivorous beloved, and it falls Tanner's lot to protect his friend from being devoured in the comedy sequences, just as Don Juan defends against the fatal wish to sleep by keeping everyone awake during the dream sequence. Most undreamlike, this Act bares Shaw's manic compromise between succumbing to sleep as reabsorption into the mother and the anxiety of full consciousness. These concerns are expressed not only in the highly intellectualized dialogues, but also in the growing compulsion to keep the audience awake through increasingly long and discursive plays. The enemy is the archaic death-threat of sleep, here represented by the Devil. The conflict is fundamental to life.

7

DISCUSSION PLAYS

Creative Evolution is already a religion, and is indeed now unmistakably the religion of the twentieth century, newly arisen from the ashes of pseudo-Christianity, of mere scepticism, and of soulless affirmations and blind negations of the Mechanists and Neo-Darwinians. But it cannot become a popular religion until it has its legends, its parables, its miracles. (PBM, p. 80)

THE MIRACLE WORKER

After the dramas of Vitalist conversions which seem to spring from the timeless theater of mind and melodrama, and after the synthesis of *Man and Superman* achieved by mingling past and present, drama and debate, comedy and philosophy, Shaw once again directs his energies to the recognizably real world of his Unpleasant Plays. The nine full-length and ten short plays between *Man and Superman* and World War I mark this decade as his most productive and most performed period. Having climbed onto a high plateau in *Man and Superman,* he showered great works from on high until with the war the slopes began to crumble beneath him.

In most of these plays certain sectors of society are singled out as targets for Shavian lightning bolts. Bentley and Meisel have demonstrated that in these plays Shaw has developed discussion into a new dramatic genre.[1] In the Discussion Plays as in the Unpleasant Plays, "society is shown to be all of a piece," and "without the great transformation there is no local remedy, merely local alleviation" (MM, p. 305). And since "no single character is possessed of more than a corner of the whole truth," there are no Shavian spokesmen, although one may feel that the talk is lively and entertaining because each of the characters embodies a bit of the Shavian ego. And if, as Meisel has further pointed out, "the dialectical results are not even stated," and the discussion is not "driven to a prearranged conclusion," the plays are nonetheless far from unpleasant. More than discussions based structurally on comic conventions and inversions, they are religious works in the sense that *Man and Superman* was intended as a "New Book of Genesis for the Bible of the Evolutionists." The most representative of the Discussion Plays, *Getting Married* and *Misalliance,* are no less than *exempla* of the Life Force.

In *Getting Married* at least a dozen attitudes toward marriage are explored; and if the characters propounding these views do not reach any firm conclusions, the audience has been made newly aware that a single institution can hardly be expected to support the infinite variety of human yearnings and impulses. This conclusion the play accomplishes by pursuing a verbal mode along a plane of consciousness as required by the drama of ideas. But there is movement in another direction as well.

Among his socially representative figures Shaw has inserted

---

[1] Meisel traces the origin of the Discussion Play from the third act of *Man and Superman,* its development in *John Bull's Other Island* and *Major Barbara,* its maturity in *Getting Married* and *Misalliance,* and culmination in *Heartbreak House.*

a pair who have little in common with his, or for that matter, with any society. They are Mrs. George (Collins) and the Bishop. The action, or rather the discussion, is set in the kitchen of the Bishop's remodeled Norman castle. Preparations for a marriage that is about to take place that morning are under way, and Collins the greengrocer is gossiping with the Bishop's wife about his sister-in-law, Mrs. George. When she married her coal merchant, she was a "fine figure of a woman," but "changeable and what you might call susceptible."

> She didn't seem to have any control over herself when she fell in love. She would mope for a couple of days, crying about nothing; and then she would up and say—no matter who was there to hear her—"I must go to him, George"; and away she would go from her home and her husband without with-your-leave or by-your-leave. (GM, p. 398)

Her supposed promiscuity did not lead her anywhere in particular. The men would bring her home or manage to escape from her. Finally she took George's advice and let the men call on her at home. Collins, no longer disapproving of her conduct, has come to value her "variety of experience" and seeks out her advice. The clue to her special knowledge is in her bisexual name and is made explicit in her encounter with the misanthropic Lesbia.

> MRS. GEORGE. When I was annoyed *I* didn't control myself : I scratched and called names. Did you ever after you were grown up, pull a grown-up woman's hair? Did you ever bite a grown-up man? Did you ever call both of them every name you could lay your tongue to?
>
> LESBIA *(Shivery with disgust)*. No.
>
> MRS. GEORGE. Well, I did. I know what a woman is like when her hair is pulled. I know what a man is like when he's bit. I know what they're both like when you tell them what you really feel about them. And that's how I know more of the world than you. (p. 467)

A Shavian Tiresias with symbiotic overlaps, Mrs. George is "clairvoyant." "She goes into a trance and says the most wonderful things!" the greengrocer exclaims, ". . . as if it was the whole human race giving you a bit of its mind" (p. 400).

She is also mayoress of the Borough and its symbol of secular authority, as the Bishop represents the interests of the Divine. They form the bulwark of the play and oversee the action something like Titania and Oberon ruling Fairyland—except the Shavian figures are not seen exercising the magic implicit in the larger dimensions of their relationship. But they can be heard, as befits this genre, discussing it. "It was from you," she informs the Bishop, "that I first learned to respect myself."

> It was through you that I came to be able to walk safely through many wild and wilful paths. Dont go back on your own teaching. (p. 473)

More recently she has been writing "love" letters with an "intensity of passion in them that fascinates" the Bishop, and signing them "Incognita Appassionata." According to the Bishop's wife :

> She says she is happily married, and that love is a necessary of life to her, but that she must have, high above all her lovers . . . some great man who will never know her, never touch her, as she is on earth, but whom she can meet in heaven when she has risen above all the everyday vulgarities of earthly love. (p. 420)

The Bishop may be that great man; he clearly is not an orthodox Anglican or any other variety of Christian. He is a "slim active man, spare of flesh. . . ."

> He has a delicate skin, fine hands, a salient nose with chin to match, a short beard which accentuates his sharp chin by bristling forward, clever humorous eyes, not without a glint of mischief in them, ready bright speech, and the ways of a successful man who is always interested in himself and generally rather well pleased with himself. (p. 415)

His first contribution to the dispute over marriage is to offer to give the devil fair play.

> We always assume the devil is guilty : and we wont allow him to prove his innocence, because it would be against public morals if he succeeded. (p. 416)

At some time earlier he had decided that because bishops become too caught up in the business affairs of the diocese and that the Church's "influence on the souls and imaginations of the people, very soon begins to go rapidly to the devil," he ordained a young solicitor as his chaplain. Soames "is a celibate; fasts strictly on Fridays and throughout Lent," and sets the Bishop free for "spiritual and scholarly pursuits" (pp. 445–46), which are not made any more explicit than his orthodoxy. He is his own man, and replies to Mrs. George :

> I'm not a teacher : only a fellow-traveller of whom you asked the way. I pointed ahead—ahead of myself as well as of you. (GM, p. 473)

She threatens to kill him and herself if he proves a fraud. On asking why, the Bishop is told, "So that we might keep our assignation in Heaven." And he draws the intended conclusion, "You are Incognita Appassionata!" With that much of their relationship known by the audience, Mrs. George goes into a trance.

> MRS. GEORGE. Put your hand on my forehead : the hand with the ring. *(He does so. Her eyes close.)*
>
> SOAMES *(inspired to prophesy)*. There was a certain woman, the wife of a coal merchant, which had been a great sinner—
>
> *(The Bishop, startled, takes his hand away. Mrs. George's eyes open vividly as she interrupts Soames.)*
>
> MRS. GEORGE. You prophesy falsely, Anthony : never in all my life have I done anything that was not ordained for me. *(More*

quietly) I've been myself. I've not been afraid of myself. And at last I have escaped from myself, and am become a voice for them that are afraid to speak, and a cry for the hearts that break in silence.

SOAMES *(whispering)*. Is she inspired?

THE BISHOP. Marvellous. Hush.

MRS. GEORGE. I have earned the right to speak. I have dared : I have gone through : I have not fallen withered in the fire : I have come at last out beyond, to the back of Godspeed.

THE BISHOP. And what do you see there, at the back of Godspeed?

SOAMES *(hungrily)*. Give us your message.

MRS. GEORGE *(with intensely sad reproach)*. When you loved me I gave you the whole sun and stars to play with, I gave you eternity in a single moment, strength of the mountains in one clasp of your arms, and the volume of all the seas in one impulse of your souls. A moment only; but was it not enough? Were you not paid then for all the rest of your struggle on earth? Must I mend your clothes and sweep your floors as well? Was it not enough? I paid the price without bargaining : I bore the children without flinching : was that a reason for heaping fresh burdens on me? I carried the child in my arms : must I carry the father too? When I opened the gates of paradise, were you blind? Was it nothing to you? When all the stars sang in your ears and all the winds swept you into the heart of heaven, were you deaf? were you dull? was I no more to you than a bone to a dog? Was it not enough? We spent eternity together; and you ask me for a little lifetime more. We possessed all the universe together; and you ask me to give you my scanty wages as well. I have given you the greatest of all things; and you ask me to give you little things. I gave you your own soul : you ask me for my body as a plaything. Was it not enough? Was it not enough?[2] (pp. 476–77)

---

[2] This celestial imagery will be identified with the images noted in Shaw's correspondence with Mrs. Pat Campbell, which was going on at the same time as the play was being written. Mrs. Pat stimulated Shaw to reproduce her as the Great Mother and convert her into the Life Force

The Incognita Appassionata that speaks through Mrs. George can only be the Life Force itself, which has learned to advance with the intellectual consciousness of the Bishop who, rather than relying on the authority of the past, points ahead toward Creative Evolution. Together the Bishop of the religion of the future and the Cybele of the Life Force play their part in human destiny; for while the trance was taking place, the young couple, hurled together no doubt by the same Life Force, had taken matters into their own hands and gone off and gotten married. But it is the onstage "miracle" that consumes our attention.

SOAMES. My lord : is this possession by the devil?

THE BISHOP. Or the ecstasy of a saint?

HOTCHKISS. Or the convulsion of the pythoness on the tripod?

THE BISHOP. May not the three be one? (p. 478)

A kind of Life Force Trinity, Mrs. George reveals her serpentine and seductive appeal to the philanderer Hotchkiss and arouses fear of the devil in the ascetic Soames. Neither the

as Mrs. George. As in *Man and Superman,* woman elicits a threefold attitude : ascetic idealism (Octavius-Soames), fruitless romance (Mendoza-Hotchkiss), and Vitalism (Don Juan-The Bishop).
Mrs. George is described as "every inch a mayoress . . . not afraid of colours . . . intensely alive. . . . But her beauty is wretched, like an age-less landscape ravaged by long and fierce war," suggesting her history as woman of passion and force of life. To Hotchkiss she wonders:
Do you see this face, once fresh and rosy like your own, now scarred and riven by a hundred burnt-out fires? Hotchkiss. . . . Fires that shoot out destructive meteors, blinding and burning, sending men into the streets to make fools of themselves. (p. 462)
The planetary imagery, rightly associated with the coal merchant's wife, suggests the energy in matter, while architectural descriptions of the Bishop's castle as it has survived and been added to during the centuries suggest a development of mental structure. The kitchen as the setting links matter and mind with male and female. These metaphorical dimensions, although rare in Shavian drama, indicate that he could be his own kind of symbolist.

sensual man who falls in love with her nor the celibate who has "sung the Magnificat to the Queen of Heaven" has so far been converted to her religion, although they are singled out for it. Only the Bishop is moved to canonize her as a saint of Vitalism, since of the prescribed Christian virtues she has none.

In *Misalliance* the intrusion of the Life Force in human affairs is much more simply accomplished. While the characters are talking about "parents and children," the topic up for discussion, and generally laughing at one another while the audience is laughing at them, Shaw is having a laugh on all of us. The Life Force merely drops out of the sky onto the stage in the person of the mysterious Polish acrobat and aviator Lina Szczepanowska;[3] and while mundane alliances are broken and new ones formed, she swoops up Bentley, whose only saving grace is his brain, and flies off with him to work for her purposes as the play ends.

SHAVIAN EROS

Along with their religious aims the Discussion Plays have the more earthly purpose of establishing new and exemplary combinations of forces within society. And in this regard the Discussion Plays are counterparts of the Unpleasant Plays. What had earlier been represented as a hopelessly fragmented society or a morbid society hypocritically bound together is revisited as it were on the wings of the integrative Life Force. Eric Bentley and K. H. Gatch[4] have capably covered this stretch of

---

[3] Like Mrs. George's careless disregard for the rules of conventional morality in pursuing a greater purpose, Lina continually dares the laws of nature on the high ropes and in the skies. Lina is also attractive to different types of men. Her mystical power is symbolized by her ability to juggle oranges while reading the Bible, and her capture of Bentley is nothing more than a turnabout of the rescue fantasy.

[4] Katherine H. Gatch, "The Last Plays of Bernard Shaw: Dialectics and Despair," *English Institute Studies* (1954).

Shavian terrain, and their ideas will serve as starting points for further analysis.

Dialectically *John Bull's Other Island* (1904) moves toward a fusion of the Englishman's genius for getting things done, the Irishman's moral passion, and the defrocked priest's Utopian vision. *Major Barbara* (1905) combines the power and "practical genius" of the munitions maker, the scholar's humanism and historical awareness, and Barbara's "love and faith" as she is converted from Christianity to the Life Force.[5] Barbara is in fact the historical shift of the Life Force from an obsolete form of religion to the new one heralded by Shaw. And similarly Lavinia in *Androcles and the Lion* (1912) is converted from the "stories and dreams" of Christianity to the unknown religion of the future.

Barbara, Lavinia, and later on Joan are in the line of composed, idealistic, and strong-willed heroines whose original in the plays was Vivie Warren. But because the center of Vivie's Capitalistic society cannot hold, lacking the cohesion of Vitalism, the characters are scattered at the end of *Mrs. Warren's Profession*. The movement in the Vitalist and Discusion Plays, however, is centripetal: new combinations form new wholes. And this operation of energy binding together ever larger units of society, this *élan vital*, is similar to Freud's object-libido which, when it is aim-inhibited as Shaw's mainly was, goes out to the world forming bonds with its sublimated energy. The object-instincts along with the self-preservative ego-instincts comprise the great creative and civilizing force in life that Freud later came to call Eros.

In tracing social combinations back to their sources in libidinal energies, we find ourselves in a better position to examine certain other implications of these plays. In *Major Barbara* there is a correlation between the three main characters

5 *Ibid*, pp. 132–34.

and the instincts referred to above. Although Andrew Under-shaft has been identified as a maker of money and gunpowder, the forces of death and destruction, it is not in that dimension alone which Shaw treats him:

> I was an east ender. I moralized and starved until one day I swore that I would be a full-fed man at all costs—that nothing should stop me except a bullet, neither reason nor morals nor the lives of other men. I said "Thou shalt starve ere I starve"; and with that word I became free and great. I was a dangerous man until I had my will: now I am a useful, beneficent, kindly person. (MB, p. 435)

He has survived and thrived because of his will to self-preservation and because of his capacity to deal with aggression, both of which are functions of the ego-instincts. But his great personal success, while paradoxically a potential boon for mankind, has left him impoverished in other ways. A foundling and a self-made man (another instance of gravitational rise), he has only a nominal wife and family, and no sustaining personal relationships. His life is his work. He is living self-preservation, industry, and externalized aggression, but not fully human; and therefore it becomes essential that he be united with the two libidinal object-instinct characters, Barbara and Cusins, in order to channel the power for evil into power for good and to form an integrated entity. This might be called the underlying Freudian synthesis toward which the play moves.

But the nature of the object-instincts is far from simple. There is little of romantic attraction between Barbara and Cusins. "By the operation of some instinct which is not merciful enough to blind him with the illusions of love, he is obstinately bent on marying Barbara" (p. 352). And he informs Undershaft:

> I am in many ways a weak, timid, ineffectual person; and my health is far from satisfactory. But whenever I feel that I must have anything, I get it, sooner or later. I feel that way about

Barbara. I dont like marriage : I feel intensely afraid of it;
and I dont know what I shall do with Barbara or what she
will do with me. But I feel that I and nobody else must marry
her. Please regard that as settled. (p. 387)

He is more determined will than flesh and blood virility. And
Barbara, with her generalized "larger loves and diviner dreams
than the fireside ones," is willing to include Cusins among them
as her spouse. Cusins is a "collector of religions" and sees
Barbara's Salvation Army as the "army of joy, of love, of
courage . . . with music and dancing." It "reveals the true
worship of Dionysos to him; sends him down the public street
drumming dithyrambs . . ." (p. 385). And when he proves
himself an exception to the Shavian rule of abstinence by getting
happily intoxicated on Spanish burgundy, he attributes it to
Dionysian possession.

In a sense then Cusins is a Dionysian figure wedded to
Barbara's self-sacrificing faith. These are more authentically
Ibsenite opposites ("pan in logos, logos in pan") than Shavian
components, but nonetheless they have been appropriated to the
Third Empire of Andrew Undershaft's regulated economy.
True, they will transform it, but they also are absorbed into it
as Cusins takes Barbara in marriage, and as Undershaft takes
Cusins into the business. In Barbara's struggle to make the
brutal, worldly power of Undershaft "spiritual," along with
Cusins's to make it "intellectual" and "imaginative," they must
transcend their own immediate instinctual goals by desexualizing
their libidinal energies and extending them into the world. For
the play is fundamentally about the uses of energy.

This combining of energies signifies the workings of a powerful ego; and Freud's contention that the ego has its own energy
system applies many times over to the great Shavian ego. In
addition, Freud came to believe that the energy system of the
ego had its own goals and its own unconscious apart from the id.

Of Shaw it may safely be said that his ego extended deep into the unconscious id, and at the base of his personality are inchoate cravings going back to his earliest experiences at the dawn of life, which somehow he managed to articulate and put to use. But for access to this powerhouse of energy the ego must pay the price of aim- and object-inhibition. Undershaft can enable others to have the kind of happy marriage that for himself he was unable to have. And just as he incarnates Shaw's obsessional narcissism, the genius of his Capitalism, which prepares the way for a better society, is cognate with the genius of Shaw's plays, which aims at joining forces for a new social order. Finally, Undershaft's indirect gratification in seeing his goals realized through others, corresponds to the fulfillment of Shaw's dreams through his characters.

8

HEARTBREAK HOUSE AND AFTER

All the great artists who have lived long enough have had a juvenile phase, a middle phase, and a Third Manner, as we say when we are talking about Beethoven. (HP, p.218)

ADAM. I can make nothing of it, neither head nor tail. What is it all for? Why? Whither? Whence? We were well enough in the garden. And now the fools have killed all the animals; and they are dissatisfied because they cannot be bothered with their bodies! Foolishness, I call it.

LILITH . . . They have redeemed themselves from their vileness, and turned away from their sins. Best of all, they are still not satisfied: the impulse I gave them in that day when I sundered myself in twain and launched Man and Woman on the earth still urges them; after passing a million goals they press on to the goal of redemption from the flesh, to the vortex freed from matter, to the whirlpool in pure intelligence that, when the world began, was a whirlpool in pure force. And though all that they have done seems but the first hour of the infinite work of creation, yet I will not supersede them until they have forded this last stream that lies between flesh and spirit, and disentangled their life from the matter that has always mocked it. (BM, pp. 260–61)

THE GREAT CURVE

Can a developmental reading open up Shavian drama in some new way? Granted it may open up Shaw, but apart from passing insights, can we now discern anything more than was already possible through existing studies?

That we can may not be apparent from whatever headway we have made so far. Perhaps it might help to step back and view Shavian drama as a whole and against the backdrop of other major dramatists' works. In the plays of Shakespeare, Ibsen, Strindberg, and to some degree of Brecht, a great curve of development can be made out. Most simply, it consists in a building-up period of expansion and initial grappling with major themes, followed by an opening-out of great complexity and full dramatic range, and a final rounding-off into synthesis and unitive vision. Take Shakespeare as an exemplar. In his comedies, country and court, youth and age, and all the vicissitudes and varieties of romantic passion are harmonized to satisfy erotic drives and social forms; in the cycle of histories, rebellion and civil disorder are ultimately resolved in accord with Elizabethan manifest destiny, a quasi-biblical design of fall and redemption, and Christian Humanism. In the great tragedies of the middle period there is an expansion of creative vision to include the most devastating effects of human passion, the relentless power of evil, the discovery of the abyss. As the vision becomes more complex it also darkens. The comic-villain Malvolio and the tragic-villain Richard are more easily conceived than the villain-hero Macbeth. The structural safety of relying on social types, historical guidelines, and dramatic conventions seems pretty well abandoned in order to expose the totality of human nature. In the third phase, the turbulence of the tragedies is contained within the larger vision of the late romances: Othello's raging jealousy is compressed into the first act of *The Winter's Tale* and is followed by Leontes' recovery and reconciliation with his family; Lear's madness and estrangement from his daughters receive an ultimate and posthumous reconciliation in the sinning or sinned-against fathers: Pericles, Leontes, Cymbeline, and Prospero. Lear's impotent curses confound with the ambiguous thunder during the storm on the heath to split asunder the idea of human integrity and the belief in Divine solicitude, whereas in *The Tempest* the storm at sea is quickly over and leads to fortunate reunions, the music of cosmic harmony, and a masque of fertility and seasonal order.

We thus make out a movement in three stages, which are roughly constructive, destructive, and transcendent; green, brazen, golden; or thesis, antithesis, synthesis, encompassing —regardless of how we try to state it—the whole of human experience. Ibsen's early Viking plays and especially *Love's Comedy, Brand, Peer Gynt, Emperor and Galilean,* construct archetypal human alternatives which, in their remoteness and sketchiness, are closer to universal types than to individuals. There follows a descent into the fallen world of Shakespeare's tragedies, in which realism subjects the characters to the acutely painful and ludicrous conditions of observed life. His last plays increasingly break free from those limitations which he imposed in his middle period; and by the time we come to *When We Dead Awaken,* we have climbed out of the abyss and mounted the heights for a virtually pure fusion of the oppositions of human nature. Strindberg's early plays (*Lucky Per's Journey, Sir Bengt's Wife, Comrades*) are mild and sanguine in comparison to the devastating realism of *Miss Julie, The Father, Creditors,* and the Inferno period of *To Damascus* and *The Dance of Death.* And finally he breaks more completely than Ibsen with realistic conditions in the summing-up of *Easter, The Ghost Sonata,* and *The Great Highway.*

Brecht began after World War I flush in the middle period

with the savage nihilism of *Baal,* the incomprehensible cruelty of *In the Jungle of Cities,* and the slashing exposure of bourgeois civilization in *The Three-penny Opera.* In the 1930s he worked up the ladder of Marxism in such works as *The Measures Taken* and *The Exception and the Rule.* And with his great parabolic plays, dating from *Galileo* in 1938, he entered his final period of synthesis.

Thus the late romances, *When We Dead Awaken, Ghost Sonata,* and *The Caucasian Chalk Circle,* acquire interesting relationships with one another. Just as the last reverberations of the storm on the heath are pounded into a finale in *The Tempest,* so the failures and guilt-feelings of Ibsen's Rubek are summarily recalled as he hastens toward his apocalyptic rendez-vous with Irene, the goddess of art. *The Ghost Sonata* opens when the Student, who has just survived the conflagration and implied misery of one human dwelling, is symbolically reborn and newly befriended only to enter another house, the ultimate dwelling of human illusion. And as *The Winter's Tale* concentrates on the recovery of Leontes from his insane jealousy (with its suggestion of paranoia masking homosexual feeling) instead of documenting and dwelling on its etiology, the sado-masochism rampant in early Brecht is locked within the scene of Azdak's interrupted trial in *The Caucasian Chalk Circle.*

These plays are examples of art after it has passed through earlier phases; they accept suffering and tragic conflict as a given, and represent it not as pervasive but as prelude. The favoring of characters of archetypal simplicity, the use of symbolism and other concentrated effects, and the episodic action transport the spectator beyond tragedy and comedy, leaving him closer to dream and vision than to traditional forms, or styles of realism.

AND THE PSYCHIC CURVE

This great curve of creative energy suggests certain psychological analogies which, if they are not taken too strictly, can be useful. The early phase is similar to instituting defenses aimed at psychic equilibrium and control over impulse and reality by circumscribing or externalizing aggression and by channeling sexual drives. The dramatist is exercising a high degree of conscious control over his material. Let us next suppose that this mastery by means of defenses increases the dramatist's perception and insight, setting up conditions conducive to a greater release of creative energies. He is then fortified and encouraged to take his work into the middle period. Reality at this stage either invades him in its most horrifying dimensions, or the primary processes of the unconscious are released and turned against the earlier network of constructive defenses; or both may occur. The resultant tearing down of defenses has its dramatic parallels in Lear's stripping himself of all royal and paternal and finally even human garments to discover "the thing itself," the bare forked animal of unaccommodated man and the primitive unconscious; in Ibsen's stripping the moral illusions from his society to lay bare its diseased core; in Strindberg's denuding his characters of any innocent neutrality or humane conjugal sentiments to get at paranoid sources; and in Brecht's viciously sado-masochistic characters. All of these processes are tantamount to a directing inward of aggression and the subsequent destruction of psychologically internalized objects, which are the raw material of the imagination and the very fabric of personality. Consider the course of Tennessee Williams's drama. In his first major play, *The Glass Menagerie* (1944), the son escapes from the neurotic conflicts in which his family are embroiled. In succeeding plays a hero (or heroine) encounters clusters of characters drawn from underlying features in the

members of the original family, and the results are rape
A Streetcar Named Desire, 1947), dismemberment (*Orpheus
Descending,* 1957), cannibalism (*Suddenly Last Summer,* 1958),
and castration (*Sweet Bird of Youth,* 1959).

The ravages of this unflinching encounter in the middle
phase with the anarchy within or the chaos without result
initially in emptiness. It is as if the dramatist's created edifice
is consumed in the holocaust of his own tragic realism. After
Hamlet's tragic tale of "woe and wonder," "the rest is silence."
But the example *par excellence* is George Buechner's *Woyceck*
(1837). Its realism is matched only by its horror. The frenzied,
illogical episodes convey the hero's dehumanization and disintegration into paranoia as the plot enacts his descent into
madness and murder. In the midst of this objective nightmare,
a grandmother tells some children a story :

> Once upon a time there was a poor little girl who had no
> father and no mother. Everyone was dead, and there was no
> one left in the whole wide world. Everyone was dead. And the
> little girl went out and looked for someone night and day. And
> because there was no one left on the earth, she wanted to go to
> Heaven. And the moon looked down so friendly at her. And
> when she finally got to the moon, it was a piece of rotten wood.
> And so she went to the sun, and it was a faded sunflower. And
> when she got to the stars, they were little golden flies, stuck up
> there as if they were caught in a spider's web. And when she
> wanted to go back to earth, the earth was an upside-down pot.

What follows psychologically in the third phase are
attempts at reconstituting the devastated psyche, at repairing
the damage brought on by energies and impulses released in
the interest of absolute realism of vision—in short, a healing
and restoring process. And it is at this point that "regression
in the service of the ego" may be particularly useful to explain
the tendency in these late works toward the simplification
of dreams.

Shakespeare succeeds because he manages to remain in touch with "great creating nature." The discovery of Perdita is more than the rebirth of Cordelia: it is the rejuvenation of the life principle. The vigor and resiliency of Shakespeare's imagination and the resources of his formal mastery enable his romances to restore the destruction of internal components with new or revitalized creations. The late romances are like the buildings and gardens of a village that have grown up on or been rebuilt over an area that had been destroyed by warfare. At the other extreme, Strindberg appears to end destitute of everything except the power of his personal imagination, and the final vision of *The Ghost Sonata* only reaffirms the futility of striving for happiness in an essentially illusory world. There is no pure flame burning through the rubble of tragic ruin, but rather a pure gaze penetrating the void. In this regard Ibsen seems to be closer to Shakespeare than to Strindberg. And once Brecht's communism fills the emptiness seared by his nihilism, his vision of reality acquires a firm structure from which no amount of political contradiction from the West could distract him as he increasingly succeeded in universalizing his drama. Tennessee Williams almost made it in *Camino Real* (1952), and is still struggling to transcend the "family romance" of Big Daddy, Bad Mama, Sick Sister, and the hapless son, fatally transfixed between incest and castration.

SHAW'S MIDDLE PHASE

Where, if at all, does Shaw belong in the pattern? His works up to World War I move consistently along the constructive slope. Socialism, pragmatism, Vitalism, and Creative Evolution are the forces behind the plays; and throughout all of them Shaw's stance against society stays as certain as his control over his material remains firm.

With the outbreak of World War I his society is thrown into a crisis. The writing of *Heartbreak House* spans the war years, and it was eventually published with its abrasive Preface in 1919.

It reproduces not only the social crisis of "cultured, leisured Europe before the war," but an artistic crisis and almost necessarily some sort of personal crisis as well. "The nightmare of a Fabian" is Bentley's description of it, and the play truly seems to advance Shaw's art into the middle phase. The abrupt entrances and exits, the nonsequiturs, and the memory lapses make the action angular and jagged; the juxtaposing of patterns and characters from other plays—*King Lear, The Way of the World, The Master Builder,* and *The Cherry Orchard*—combines to give the piece a modern, cubistic glitter. And the peculiar schizophrenia of the characters beneath the formal design is described in the Preface. The "Heartbreak people" went to church but were not religious, electioneered but were not political; they "rhapsodized about love" but "believed in cruelty"; they drifted with their culture and leisure while others with economic power did the steering; and if they "did not know how to live," they boasted that "they knew how to die: a melancholy accomplishment which the outbreak of war presently gave practically unlimited opportunities of displaying."

But while the Shavian lens is focusing on the social picture, the eye of the artist is also turned inward: Heartbreak has a double reference. The characters are also shattered fragments of previous Shavian constructions. The senile genius of Shotover is splintered from Caesar, Higgins, and Undershaft, as Ellie Dunn is an unhappy continuation of Vivie Warren, Cleopatra, Eliza Doolittle, and Barbara. Boss Mangan has usurped practical power, entitling him to Ellie Dunn and a meaningless synthesis with the future. What drops out of the skies is not the Life Force but the Death Force in the shape of a German bomb. It destroys Mangan's capitalism and the Church of England with perhaps more Shavian precision than natural selection, while the fate of those spared remains problematic. Shotover has been struggling toward evolutionary advance in his quest for the "seventh degree of concentration," but the "evolutionary appetite" is being deflected by a fondness for rum, which is veering his ship toward the rocks. Ellie Dunn, who ordinarily would occupy the Vitalist role, seeking to organize her energy around new combinations in society, encounters only fragments in Mangan's vulgarity, Hector's random romancing, and Shotover's drunken dotage. And she draws down the curtain hoping aloud that the thrilling bombers will return soon. It is as if Shaw had endowed Major Barbara with a death wish.

For the first time Shaw has allowed aggression to be turned inward against his own created world. His construction of reality has at least temporarily been shattered, and a new and destructive capacity in the Shavian psyche has opened up. If it were 1919 now, we would be justified in asking whether he would next enter fully into a tragic phase and explore the modern experience of fragmentation and alienation—look into the eyes of that "rough beast" slouching "toward Bethlehem to be born." Or was that climatic explosion not apocalyptic, but just more Shavian ground-clearing? And was Ellie's final wish only expressing the need for a little more of the same?

Shaw did not go on to confront modern experience as we would perhaps have liked him to, but his later plays retain marks of the shattered vision, the fragmented characters, and the ravaged structure of *Heartbreak House,* without, however, giving the plays the seal of modernity. And although we can safely affirm that *Heartbreak House* reveals cultural and artistic crises, we can only suppose they were accompanied by a personal crisis from the way he went about organizing his next play.

THE THIRD MANNER

Back to Methuselah (1919–20) is a characteristic Shavian response to all three presumed crises. It is as philosophically constructive a work as one might imagine. Instead of plunging into the existential abyss, Shaw climbs into the thin atmosphere of philosophical speculation; instead of penetrating more deeply into modern chaos, he offers an alternative to it.[1] And no mere political extravaganza is called for: nothing less than a "metabiological pentateuch" will do. It is a whale of a play with a whale's body and a whale's brain. If it overwhelms the imagination, it is from physical magnitude rather than by vital energies. The concentrated energy that he brought to the subjects of other works is dissipated in its vacuous structure; its content sprawls across three nights of viewing, a profusion of scenes, and countless periods of history and projected futures, all more or less related. To get at its few ideas, the only solution is to boil down the blubber. And what remains is little more than naked will and a cry for longevity. In failing to shape the roomy emptiness, the ideas stand exposed more as an enormous evasion of the modern world than an evolutionary incentive to surpass it.

It may always be a mistake to take Shaw too literally, but there is a desperate literal-mindedness beneath all the invention of the play that is hard to overlook. If a giraffe can survive by growing a longer neck, man must learn to survive by growing a longer life. This analogy is the very kernel of the play inside all the metabiological, Platonic, and Swiftian trimmings. If a tail is "a habit of which your ancestors managed to cure themselves," then why not proceed to cure ourselves of our heads and other bodily encumbrances, and become immortal thought vortexes?

[1] *The Struggle of the Modern*, pp. 72f. "His messianic rebellion is his last refuge, his Utopian idealism, his last escape, from the tragic impasse of modern existence," *The Theatre of Revolt*, p. 205.

The artist, whose statues of today are models for the future to follow, has turned his interest away from the rag dolls and the "pretty children" of ordinary humanity to the "intensity of mind" in the ancients who have mastered longevity (the problem is, they have mastered nothing else). "Art is the magic mirror you make to reflect your invisible dreams in visible pictures." But the dreams are evolutionary ones, and art is subservient to the evolutionary appetite. For Yeats the tempting illusion of Platonism is discredited, because "All dreams of the soul / End in a beautiful man's or woman's body." For Shaw it is the reverse. "The body always ends by being a bore. Nothing remains beautiful and interesting except the thought, because the thought is the life" (BM, p. 255). "Thought" is a dangerous basket for the artist to put all his creative eggs into (even when lovely people break out of them), for thought freed from material limitation can produce a play like *Back to Methuselah*.

And so we are left wondering whether the play is not in large part a personal response to larger crises. If Shaw experienced disintegration of Europe as his own world falling apart, his energies may have been summoned to strengthen the defenses used in analogous early personal crises. Certainly he was deeply involved with his world and depended on it as a doctor depends on disease. It had become his *raison d'être*. As a sort of denial and reaction-formation of monstrous proportions against this threefold crisis, *Back to Methuselah* stands as a defense against chaos and disintegration that reveals, in spite of all intentions, its own kind of hopelessness.

Man and Superman dramatized a working model of Shaw's energy system. *Heartbreak House* dramatized the process of energies breaking loose from structure. And now *Back to Methuselah*, in attempting to dramatize ideas, continues the disintegrative process as the "center cannot hold," and content sprawls over structure like lava over a city.

THE FATE OF NARCISSISM

The plays that follow, with the possible exception of *Saint Joan*, are interesting for their ideas, which are no longer new; for their topicality, which has passed; and because they are from the hand of a genius, which makes them valuable chiefly in relation to the whole of Shavian drama. But they are not arresting in their structure, and for this reason the quality of his Prefaces begins to gain on his dramas and even pass them up in such virtuoso pieces as the Preface to *The Apple Cart* (1929). What it comes down to is that the plays become an increasingly drawn-out and cumbersome technique for illustrating ideas. They wear the hand-me-down structure of the earlier plays; they have no perceptions powerful enough to inspire a restructuring of society, no insights that could lead to new adaptive strategies, and consequently not enough dramatic tension and pressure to excite and engage an audience. Some of them are amusing, but mostly they test the reader's loyalty and endurance, while remaining unknown to most spectators.

In *Geneva* (1938) the ideas that briefly flame up are quickly drenched in a verbal downpour. And in plays like *The Simpleton of the Unexpected Isles* (1934), the destructive vigor of the Recording Angel seems to spring willfully from its creator's head. Ill temper and bickering too often mute the Promethean rage that the issues demand. The allegorizing becomes attenuated and insubstantial instead of extended and parabolic. Or else there is the gratuitous intrusion of straight autobiography as in the "Interlude" in *The Apple Cart*. Nowhere is there the bite and ambiguity of Brecht's last plays. The movement of *Too True To Be Good* is too wayward and uncertain to have the coherence of dream or the solidity to objectify modern experience. Robert Brustein seems justified in detecting an "autobiographical note" in the final speech of the play, despite Shaw's vehement disclaimer:[2]

> my gift has possession of me : I must preach and preach and preach no matter how late the hour and how short the day, no matter whether I have nothing to say—

Even *Saint Joan,* with its rightly praised dialectic and brilliant epilogue, must depend on historical records for structural support, a practice too common to be faulted in this instance; but it is mainly in the slackness of the scenes more completely invented by Shaw that one can see how indispensable the historical superstructure was. Some of the early scenes exist solely to make a single point, or to provide miracles and further edifying illustrations for Shaw's Bible of Vitalism; and the Epilogue, Shaw's justification for writing the three-and-one-half-hour play (HP, p. 367), can be reduced to a statement about society's treatment of its heroes, even though it does happen to be a profound one.

To be an unproduced playwright in the nineteenth century was bad enough, but to be an unheeded prophet in the twentieth was worse. Prometheus did not belong atop Mount Olympus; but the Shavian Titan, who began rising gravitationally, not content with the high human plateau of *Man and Superman,* climbed the rest of the way up by will; and once on top there was no other part to play except Zeus. The only trouble was that from so remote a spot the lightning bolts can at best irritate; they cannot strike shattering illuminations.

And so instead of coming full circle in what Shaw himself conceived as the Third Manner, the curve of his creativity swells into a huge bubble of mere longevity, and progress toward a synthesis in drama is blocked. Or, we should say, an ultimate

[2] *The Theatre of Revolt,* pp. 205.

synthesis is not achieved. For Creative Evolution is the central and perennial synthesis of all Shaw's work. But not only was it possibly formed too early and closed too tightly, thereby excluding much of the world, but Shaw is not so content with it that he can keep from tinkering around. What we can expect to find from a closer scrutiny of Shaw's late period is a groping toward a synthesis that is more nearly realized in narrative than in drama. After having examined how his narcissism was formed, and having followed the manifold routes along which it was transformed, we must now consider whether some disastrous detours made it in some ways malformed.

9
CONCLUSION

". . . we are still savages at heart and wear our thin uniform of civilization very awkwardly."

"Because we destroy illusions we will be accused of endangering ideals."

SHAW AND FREUD

One of the quotations is from Shaw and one is from Freud. Since it is the prerogative of human beings, if not of stage characters, to speak out of character at times, and before I am accused of imitating Shaw by scoring points through inversions of the expected, let me quickly admit that Shaw spoke the first (RS, p. 97) and Freud the second. Their ideas, seldom associated, play off one another in illuminating ways and often overlap even as their lives.[1]

[1] Arthur H. Nethercot ("Shaw and Psychoanalysis," *Modern Drama*, 11, no. 4 (Feb. 1969): 356–75) has traced the evolution, such as it was, of Shaw's awareness of Freud and the psychoanalytic movement. Although Shaw seems to come around to a nominal acceptance of psychoanalysis as a *fait accompli*, there is no evidence that he ever really grasped what it was all about. Freud is rarely mentioned by name and then slightingly; none of his works, or his colleagues and disciples, or their work is even

They were born the same year in provincial capitals on the fringes of European culture and grew up in a Victorian society that was neither of their making nor to their liking. They rejected the omnipotence and fatherhood of the Christian God (Freud[2]; EP, pp. 232f), and dismissed prayer as a means of magical control (p. 164; IM, p. 633). They were influenced by some of the same leading minds of the nineteenth century—Goethe, Darwin, Nietzsche. They accepted a form of cultural evolution (Freud: magic, religion, science; Shaw: Jehovahism, Christianity, Creative Evolution). They drew their metaphors of man from Plato: Freud used the man on horseback for the ego and id; Shaw used the enlightened pilot steering the ship of state. But whereas Shaw warned of the danger of complacent drifting, Freud reminded us of the force of the primitive energy that man sought to direct. They allowed that children were cruel and selfish (PMI, pp. 16, 78), but they also recognized that the child is father to the man and pleaded the child's case as a developing person. They came to view art as a kind of illusion (PMI, p. 160; BM, pp. 251f.), although Freud would add "harmless" and Shaw, "useful." They spurned the liberal virtues of tolerance, broadmindedness, and compromise in favor of their respective doctrines (PMI, p. 160), although each in his own life was continually adapting to the exigencies of new situations and tolerating difficult friendships.

When Shaw pronounced that "every dream is a prophecy: every jest an earnest in the womb of time" (JB, p. 611), his link between jest and dream was reciprocated by Freud's discovery of the similarities between the processes of dream-work and joke-work (*Jokes,* pp. 159f.). However, for Freud the dream is a

referred to. Thus Dr. Nethercot is justified in raising the question of whether Shaw had in fact read Freud. For more, see Sidney P. Albert, "Refllections on Shaw and Psychoanalysis," *Modern Drama* 14, no. 2 (Sept 1971).
    [2] "The Question of a *Weltanschauung,*" *New Introductory Lectures on Psychoanalysis* 35 (New York, 1964): 162.

"completely asocial mental product," containing an unacknowledged or unrecognizable wish, and relating chiefly to the dreamer; whereas the joke is the "most social of all mental functions that aim at a yield of pleasure," and, more than wish, it is "developed play." But Shaw, who was more jester than jokester, in advising us that "when a thing is funny, search it for a hidden truth," places the jest with its latent content and prophetic bent closer to dream, without sacrificing social function or pleasurable yield, than does Freud, who was neither jokester nor jester, and concluded that "jokes and dreams have grown up in quite different regions of mental life" (*Jokes,* p. 179).

In their own fashions, they adopted a hard line on the instincts. If Freud did not exactly discover them, he did develop a theory of their dynamics, their influence on human behavior, and their role in history. He articulated their importance for modern man, but sided with traditional humanism and the primacy of reason when he affirmed that "where id was there ego shall be." Shaw came to view life as the struggle of energy to become conscious of itself through intelligence and will. Both recognized the dichotomy between pleasure and reality, and in their respective styles opted for reality.

In analyzing the repetition-compulsion in neurosis and in observing the tendency in organic life generally to repeat patterns of behavior, Freud assigned a conservative role to the instincts. He observed that if the sexual instincts should be fully satisfying, there would be no cultural progress. Similarly, Shaw observed the tyranny of the pleasure principle in his father's alcoholism and the repetition in his Victorian countrymen's woman-worshiping fixations. He boasted of never being "duped by sex as a basis for permanent relations, nor dreamt of marriage in connection with it" (SS, p. 178). Freud developed a system of therapy to intervene in the repetition-compulsion, which was aided and abetted by inadequate or excessive defenses, cutting off the individual from his own vital being and from the world. Shaw observed that men live by a system of arbitrary and meaningless conventions no less inhibiting and disabling (PMI, p. 68), and dramatized the intervention of the Life Force. They both saw man's salvation—either as a process of psychosexual or biological development—accomplished through the higher faculties. The Freudian ego and the Shavian will aimed at liberating man from his conservative sources. Each recognized the need for nurture and education of the sex instincts (BX, p. 216), the one for the sake of the psychic well-being of man now, the other for the Superman to come. They valued civilized goals along with individual development and were thrown into conflict with society (and particularly with the medical establishment) for their uncompromising convictions.

It may be regrettable that these contemporaneous geniuses were scarcely aware of each other. But it is a more disturbing irony that Shaw, who claimed to be searching for a true science of sex, resisted Freud's doctrines and dismissed Freud himself as a man of "vulgar indelicacy." It may have been that Freud was too foreign and threatening to Shaw's narcissistic *modus operandi*, while Bergson's more limited and benign *élan vital* fitted in perfectly. It may have been that Shaw deceived himself when he praised Ibsen and Brieux for violating taboos and insisted that unmentionable things must be "mentioned again and yet again, until they are set right" (BX, p. 214), when his own defenses were set irrevocably against what Freud was mentioning. How much a recognition of Freud's theories could have affected the relative sterility of Shaw's later plays is a question perhaps too tantalizing even to pose.

Shaw's reluctance to entertain Freud's ideas and his failure to comprehend them point to their deeper differences. Shaw was a Vitalist. He saw the sources of human energy as one with the great energy that turns the universe and called this the Life

Force. Freud was a dualist. He recognized the Life Force in man and named it Eros. But he also recognized the equally powerful force of aggression in shaping life and threatening civilization. Shaw admitted a Darwinian carry-over from man's savage past into his present life, but his own past, along with his evolutionary appetite, drew him away from a deeper consideration of it. He did not "overlook the facts that war depends on the rousing of all the murderous blackguardism still latent in mankind" (PMI, p. 105), but he blamed the "romancers" who perpetuate this archaic activity by reworking its raw facts into "military glory." In *Arms and the Man,* war is not so much attributable to the aggression as to the folly of men who are goaded by their novel-reading, opera-going women to live up to the "heroic ideas" of Pushkin and Byron. And waging war, like promoting the "higher love" that Sergius complains to the maid about, gets to be a "very fatiguing thing to keep up for any length of time." Romantic love and war belong to the "artificial system" of conventions that have outlasted their utility. Like mosquitoes, the whooping-cough, Jehovah, and other nuisances, they are acidental by-products of the trial-and-error method of the Life Force as it tries to create more perfect forms of organization. The solution to aggression is evolution. What Freud elevated to equal instinctual rank with Eros and the Life Force was for Shaw a derivative and not worth troubling over, while in psychoanalytic terms Shaw's conception of the Life Force would be a derivative.

In the Freudian dispensation aggression follows three routes: it is taken over by the superego to use against the ego for failing to live up to its demands, resulting in guilt; it is externalized by the ego; and, finally, it dwells intrapsychically as the Death Instinct, whose conservative aim is to return the organism to its original state of inorganic matter. The reason this Instinct appears to be inoperative in most human beings, and unreasonable to almost all, is that in the struggle with the forces of life, conducted by the ego-instincts, it is taken over by the ego, which regulates and delays it sufficiently for the organism to return *naturally* to its original state. In this paradoxical scheme, wherein man is capable of tragic conflict, the ego must maintain a perilous, vital balance by using the energy won over from and ultimately owed back to the Death Instinct.

In the Shavian dispensation the superego is not set up to punish a weak, guilt-ridden ego for real or imaginary crimes. Rather, the ego takes over the aggressive drives for extensive uses against the environment—especially against those social, political, and religious institutions that are experienced as hostile to life—and for preserving the organism for its natural dénouement. Considering his record of good health and his near-centenarian triumph, one is inclined to acknowledge the strength of Shaw's ego-instincts. (Not surprisingly, psychological studies have found that outwardly aggressive people live longer than the socially controlled.) But for the very reason that he externalized so much of his aggression, Shaw had little conscious awareness or appreciation of the prominent and problematic function of aggression in life, of which we are so aware today. He was pointedly aware of the flaws in society, politics, religion, and the theater, but he was not painfully aware of the form his own aggressive wishes took in striving to remove Capitalism, replace Christianity, and reform the stage. This deficiency, if it can be so called, affected his works by simplifying them and robbing them of a more profound dualism and modernity, although it may have made them possible in the first place.

The Devil in *Man and Superman* speaks for the destructive side of the instincts that Mendoza and Octavius exemplify, but their plight, indeed their damnation, arises from the repetition-compulsions and fixations of the sexual instincts. Their pleasures are ritualized into the fixed pattern of convention that Shaw viewed as antagonistic to life. But the more fitting and formidable adversary to Shaw's Vitalism would have to be the aggression of the Death Instinct, which was as inaccessible for him to dramatize as it was for him to perceive the appeal made by "Mister Hitler" to human aggression. He viewed the destructive energies of the modern dictator with the same benignity as he regarded his own reforming-by-destroying drives. That he was taken in well beyond the limits of lesser minds is undeniable, nor can it be dismissed as dotage. The point is worth lingering on, because aggression—whether it is viewed technologically as nuclear power, or politically as power struggles within democratic systems and the limited or guerilla wars in the Third World, or in its more genteel forms of racism, bigotry, and intolerance—has become the central public issue for modern man, just as the sense of alienation and purposelessness is his principal private problem. And the more important these facts become, the less Shaw has to say to us and the more difficult it is to grant him his hypotheses—stupidity, hypocrisy, ignorance, the Life Force, and longevity do not suffice—and the stronger the conviction grows that the "Man of the Century" has not confronted the twentieth century. Perhaps he will fare better in the next.

When Shaw championed the ego, he did not see (granting Freud's hypothesis) that it had entered into an alliance with the Death Instinct. "Life cannot will its own extinction either in its blind amorphous stage or in any of the forms into which it has organized itself" (MS, p. 636). And if one doubts that Don Juan is Shaw's spokesman, we have it from the prophet's mouth : "We must believe in the will to good—it is impossible to regard man as willing his own destruction" (RS, pp. 34–35). Even Andrew Undershaft's seemingly destructive power was found by Major Barbara to be adaptable to constructive aims because all power derives ultimately from the Life Force. Left to themselves, the sex instincts can choose romance over life, or their "artificial system" over Vitalism, making enough dualism for dramatic conflict; but Shaw never reckoned on man's savage nature as being equal to the Life Force. Quite out of hand would he reject Freud's bitter insight that man is wolf to man.

Nor did he reckon the tyranny of a civilization that demands from its members more and more desexualized energies. He was blind to the role of the sex instincts as release from this domination. "Society can conceive of no more powerful menace to its culture than would arise from the liberation of the sexual impulses and a return to their original goal."[3] Freud should not be misunderstood; he was no more a sexual revolutionist than Shaw was a violent political one. But Freud recognized the power of the raw sex instincts, whereas Shaw never seemed able to unscramble the egg of his transformed instincts to get at their fertile yolk. Or to put it in a less sticky way, Freud listened to the instincts, Shaw browbeat them.

Shaw knew he was different from the lot of mankind. He tried to overcome this by bringing reality over to his side, making it conform to his model rather than he to its. Although at a certain level the demiurgic task of the artist at all times is to forge a vision of reality that will be accepted as more real than reality, Shaw's enterprise burned with an evangelical urgency. The chaotic conditions of his early life along with the Rationalist and Darwinian references of his cultural milieu forced him to choose between being a biological sport and product of random

[3] "First Lecture" in *A General Introduction to Psychoanalysis* (New York, 1949). To put this distinction in contemporary parallels: Shaw would not distinguish between the Playboy type of Establishment promiscuity and recent experiments among students and hippies in communal sex. Society readily condones the former as a beneficial lubricant in the machinery, but it is threatened by the latter because it is primitive and anarchistic, a defiant refusal to transform sexual energy into socially approved and economically productive areas; whereas the rampant materialism of the Playboy ethos fattens the economy, promotes the status quo, and makes its founding genius a highly respected Capitalist.

selection or an advanced experiment of the Life Force. He chose the latter and adapted Darwin's natural selection to Creative Evolution. Freud's insight into the nature of the instincts compels him to say, along with Shakespeare in his tragic phase, that "the aim of all life is death." But even this existential fact Shaw turns inside out. "Death is for many of us the gate of hell; but we are inside on the way out, not outside on the way in" (PMI, p. 4). How can this be? we ask our catechism: simply because Creative Evolution enables us "to be born again and born better" (p. 5).

As a vital genius Shaw was most at home with other vital geniuses now among the "mighty dead." The struggle that had most meaning for him was not between Eros and Death or between reason and absurdity, those being decided in favor of the Life Force, but one between reformed and regressive instincts, between vital genius and a laggard, inhospitable society. Conversions and new combinations prevail in his works until the outbreak of World War I. With *Heartbreak House* the outlook darkens, and the conflict itself is either not always clearly drawn, or it often gets crowded out by minor issues. *Saint Joan* stands out as an instance of this struggle between stabilization in civilization and evolution through vital genius at its most lucid and completely realized.

There are three major types of vital genius in his plays. Marchbanks, Bluntschli, and Dick Dudgeon are young intruders who acquire, or are distinguished by, special gifts that enable them to master their situations. Ann Whitefield, Major Barbara, and Joan stand out as gifted, independent women chosen by the Life Force to advance civilization biologically, socially, politically. Caesar, Undershaft, and Higgins are vital geniuses in full maturity: guiding, assembling, creating the forces of life toward new stages.

The psychological sources of the three types are the Diabolonian son, the symbiotically accessible mother, and later on the accomplished artist as creative father. Although there were other varieties and interrelationships, these types stand out as rooted in Shaw's development and nearest his creative center. From these sources not only did the vital genius evolve, but Shaw's conception of the role of artist as well. In the Brieux Preface, which is virtually a Shavian poetics, he defines the artist's "supreme function" as "interpreter of Life," which for Brieux meant "to pick out the significant incidents from the chaos of daily happenings and arrange them so that their relation to one another becomes significant, thus changing us from bewildered spectators of a monstrous confusion to men intelligently conscious of the world and its destinies" (BX, p. 205); but while this may equally apply to Shaw's Unpleasant phase, for him to interpret life meant to interpret the Life Force and influence its direction. This "identification of the artist's purpose with the purpose of the universe . . . alone makes the artist great" (pp. 201–2).

The distinction between the Shelleyan-Joycean view of the artist as rival with God the Creator and the Shavian is that in Shaw's conception of life as continually evolving there is no Prime Mover or Promised End, no stasis, but rather a process in which the artist immerses himself and advances by allowing himself to be used by it. "We are all experiments in the direction of making God" (RS, p. 35). Outside of Victorian capitalism and ethics, he can implicate his audiences in that society's wrongs; in touch with the Life Force, he can proceed to involve audiences in Creative Evolution. As he said, the difference between Hell and Heaven is the difference between drifting and steering.

Divinity is the perfection of Life at some unknown point in the future, and hence god is immanent, not transcendent. He is in his handiwork not sacramentally or pantheistically but potentially, as Shaw is in his plays through his energy, ideas, and structure. The belief in Divine immanence brings Shaw's drive toward usefulness to its most highly developed stage.

But the artist is also hastening his own annihilation, and the greater his skill and vision the sooner it will come. For as his purpose is to create forms for the Life Force to advance toward in the future, then the more closely life comes to realize itself as pure thought, the less is the need for the image-making occupation of the artist. The evolutionary appetite devours art as it is nourished by it, and it may be in this manner that Shaw has transformed the Death Instinct to serve the Life Force, just as the ultimate aim of Life as being the contemplation of itself (MS, p. 617) may be the crowning transformation and apotheosis of narcissism.

COMEDY AND ENERGY

If the question were raised as to whether Shavian comedy belonged in the Roman-Renaissance tradition of Terentian plots and Plautine farce or in the Greek-Modern tradition of Aristophanic mingling of intellectual wit and buffoonery of the body, the answer would be that he belonged to both; and, insofar as Shavian comedy is *sui generis,* that he belonged to neither. That his situations and characters frequently mirror the conventions of the comic masters from Terence to Boucicault has been demonstrated, and that his political extravaganzas have an Aristophanic quality is also true. Comedy itself is as unchanging as the human condition and as conservative as the need to laugh; it is as liberal as its sympathy for the victory of new life over old and as innovative as progressive ideas can make it. Therefore, somewhere within the range of continuity and change resides Shavian comedy.

One of the technical innovations of Roman Comedy was to base the recognition scene on wish fulfillment. It gracefully dissolved the obstacles, taboos, and realistic odds against libidinal gratification (marriage). Typically, the members of two families, divided as their two stage houses indicate, are united in the son of one family and the daughter of the other through the ingenious enterprises of wily servants, sly parasites, and ancient nurses with long memories. These minor functionaries are the instruments of the author's imagination, joining on stage what is separated off stage, and fulfilling in art what is so often frustrated in life.

Shakespearean comedy is a crossing of the lines from varieties of narcissism to the socially required and individually more mature level of genital sexuality. In *Twelfth Night* Malvolio is "sick of self-love"; Olivia, indulging in the emotion of mourning, gives away her portrait when she falls in love with a girl parading as a page; Antonio bears a manly love for his friend Sebastian, who is later confused by Olivia with his sister; and the Duke finds himself attracted to his page before "he" is revealed as Viola. Narcissism, represented by doubling and disguise, must be surmounted before sexual lines can be crossed and sexual roles and identities clarified.

Much of the energy in the comedies of Jonson and Molière aims as discrediting through ridicule, exposure, and expulsion those male imposters who block the flow of libido among the young.

In Restoration Comedy we accompany Etherege's rake as he moves from window-breaking rampages, carousing, railing, whoring, and cuckolding to the concentration of his energies on a single sex object, and eventually consents to dwindle into marriage. The development here is from polymorphous perverse (infantile) sexuality to genital, monogamous sexuality.

Eighteenth-century comedy (both sentimental and laughing)

neutralizes the explosive forces of the preceding period by entangling the characters in plot complications (*méprises* and *quid pro quos*) which, once removed, lead to the libidinal satisfaction of "good nature."

Nothing more happens in stage comedy until the modern period. Boucicault kept the conventions alive. Gilbert's topsy-turvydom has been mentioned. Oscar Wilde, too, inverted Victorian values of duty and high seriousness, except that he operated through the principle of play. "He plays with everything : with wit, with philosophy, with drama, with actors and audience, with the whole theatre," Shaw once observed. But this universal playfulness asserted that sex is only sex play, love is only love play. In inverting the value system of the patriarchal majority, Wilde was also undermining one of its key tenets : genital sexuality. The initial impulse may be defiance, the trend regressive, and the outcome nothing, but at the same time the effect is peculiarly modern :

ALGERNON : What shall we do after dinner? Go to a theatre?
JACK : Oh, no! I loathe listening.
ALGERNON : Well, let us go to a Club?
JACK : Oh, no! I hate talking.
ALGERNON : Well, we might trot round to the Empire at ten?
JACK : Oh, no! I can't bear looking at things. It is so silly.
ALGERNON : Well, what shall we do?
JACK : Nothing!
ALGERNON : It is awfully hard work doing nothing. However, I don't mind hard work where there is no definite object of any kind.

For a society too busy with externals and too devoted to definite objects, "nothing" is an impertinent and disarming alternative; but it is the cleverness of the child turned into dandy, and the audience applauded accordingly. When Wilde's own deviation became public, audiences were stunned into silence perhaps by their own former collusion, and the plays were quickly removed along with their author. (By comparison Shaw's more radical, Socialist deviations were treated remarkably well.)

Revolting against the blocking force of authority or disarming it, separating from members of one's own sex to encounter the other, organizing one's energies in a genital direction, these processes of growth—or what we now prefer to call psychosexual development—are the very stuff of life, and their successful deployment is what makes for comedy. And although Shaw used the conventions that conveyed these forces, he had little real use for them. The happy ending came down to a question of how much coating was needed to sugar the unpleasant pill; it was not modeled after organic processes of ripening and decay (even though the sugar was an organic substance and the pill a concoction). Not only was modern life basically open-ended and ongoing, but the Life Force was continually moving, hopefully upward. It was better known through its process than by its product, and at bottom it was more akin to will than to nature.

Paradoxically, for all its soaring thought, the world of Shavian drama is a limited and altogether human one; it is bounded by despair at one end and aspiration at the other, and not by the great ocean of life or the immensity of the natural world. The idea of nature during Shaw's formative years as "red in tooth and claw" was rejected for a nature in which the giraffe with his evolutionary appetite can strain for ever-higher berries and manage to grow a superneck. The mode of Shavian drama is rational, its medium is verbal and rhetorical, its rhythms dialectic and operatic. The myths, images, and symbols that reverberate deep in the psyche and reconnect man with nature and fate are replaced by the safer and firmer substantives linked by the clear verbs that involve man in society. The continual hum of discourse and the rapping clamor of debate prevail over the silence and the soliloquy of alienation. The extent of control by means of language can be measured by the exclusion of sexuality and death, which entail either a temporary "ego-loss" or a permanent letting go. The pull of the irrational is transformed into the striving for the suprarational, where "all life is human and all humanity divine." But this vision is purely verbal. Whereas Shakespeare expressed an ideal social order through romance, and the great satirists, from Jonson through Congreve and Gay to Sheridan, always had a clear humanistic mirror for reflecting the distortions and failings of their society, Shaw's mirror differed in being tinted by his economics and framed by his biology.

The libidinal energies surging through traditional comedy, rendering it "intensely Freudian in shape,"[4] are desexualized by Shaw into mental energies with social combinations and economic aplications, cemented together by libidinal leftovers. It is in this sense that Shavian comedy is revolutionary and his instinctual adaptations relevant to Erikson's "history of changing ideas." Psychic energy has been lifted from the sexual sphere and instinctual aims forgone, in order to serve goals beyond the sexual and the aesthetic, and even beyond society itself as it is presently constituted. Aggression serves the processes of growth and the removal of obstacles along the path of evolutionary development; sexuality conceives the Superman. Man is challenged to make further instinctual renunciations and better uses of his energies, to use agression to destroy his collusion in society's artificial system and to dissolve his romantic fixations. He is denied the pleasure of handy scapegoats for his failings; his nostalgic return to familiar pleasures and his ideal of a golden past are equally discouraged. The energy in Shavian drama demands his ascent ever higher into the evolutionary unknown. It stirs and at the same time disturbs.

We are no longer sure it can happen; worse, we doubt

[4] Northrop Frye, *A Natural Perspective* (New York, 1965), p. 75.

its necessity. The Iceman cometh, but the Superman, like M. Godot, does not come. Perhaps he will come tomorrow. Perhaps further conversions to make new combinations are called for. Perhaps the conditions of existence are inescapable. Beckett is Shaw's *bête-noir*.

The two Irishmen could hardly be more antithetical. Yet, at some absolute point they are one. They recognize human instincts as centripetal forces pulling man into the swing of his mortality along with the diurnal and seasonal cycles of nature. For Beckett the pull is ineluctable; consciousness constructs elaborate games of delay and resistance to no avail; and man finally feels his striving reduced to the twitching of the repetition-compulsion.

The instincts threaten to pull Shaw into a cycle of repetition and in fact succeed to a degree in his life as his continual attachments to actresses and his addiction to speech tend to indicate, but his creative work illustrates the extent that his instincts have been transformed by the ego into great dynamos of energy intended to lift mankind off from his earthbound origins and their gravitational pull into the natural cycle upward toward some greater destiny. It is as if his life and work, when placed back to back and seen as a whole, reproduce only then nature's pendulum. But it should be mentioned parenthetically that his work also reveals the extent to which his instincts have not relinquished their original claims. For even the psychic resources summoned against the instincts were still to some degree instinctual. The Shavian ego does not always emerge the decisive champion it may appear to Shaw to be. In other words, what Shavian drama advocates should be distinguished from the paradoxical means it employs. Creative activity has been described as "highly libidinized" and "highly aggressive" (PA, p. 67), but the creative product may be pacifist and puritanist—as Shaw and his work often were and still are called.

The things that Shaw was advocating in his plays—pragmatic reason over sensuality and sentiment, evolutionary will over fatalism, thought over matter—all have their psychological analogue in sublimation, but they are not to be confused with the creative energies at his disposal that went into making his plays. The implications of the *advocacy* of Shavian drama are what is being explored here.

Without questioning the need for Shaw's instinctual conversions, the fact of his gravitational rise, or the value of his faith in evolutionary advance, we may agree that no matter how this irrepressible ascent may be reflected, it does not bring man around to face himself and grapple with his own nature. His characters may represent abstractions such as Capitalism, the middle class, and the Life Force; they may embody unregenerate instincts and reformed instincts; or they may stand for the national traits of England and Ireland; but none of them is a complex creature of inner will with antagonistic drives and aspirations. Insofar as Tanner is an exception he also proves the rule. There is operative throughout Shaw's plays a kind of simplification of character and separation of function that undoubtedly makes for an effective, dramatic vision, but at the same time imparts a sense that something is missing from the vision as a whole. And this frequently expressed feeling (Spender's "two-dimensional giant moving in his two-dimensional world"[5]) is reinforced when one takes into account his personal passions and fails to find an equivalent amount of mental or emotional conflict in his plays. The conflict may be behind them, but apart from *Man and Superman* it is not deeply felt in them. It is as if Shaw, instead of wrestling with his angel like Jacob, talked it into submission. Shaw might want to add that it was the more civilized thing to do, and he may be right.

But the trouble was, Shaw had to keep on talking, which

[5] "The Riddle of Shaw," p. 237.

meant writing more disquisitory plays. It may be unfair to raise the point that had he been able to come to terms with himself differently, he might have found the means to fuse his vision into a final synthesis. As it is, a most curious sort of synthesis takes shape in his last years.

An article, entitled "Bernard Shaw, Mathematical Mystic,"[6] traces Shaw's increasing interest in mathematics as he advanced in years. Apparently it took Einstein to draw him beyond Darwin, Lamarck, Nietzsche, Bergson, and around Freud. In *Back to Methuselah*, the banalities of sexuality have long since been supplanted by "oviparous" reproduction, and the only awakening a poor girl of the future can have is a mathematical one.

> THE MAIDEN. . . . Have you ever thought about the properties of numbers?
>
> THE YOUTH. *(sitting up, markedly disenchanted)* Numbers ! ! ! I cannot imagine anything drier or more repulsive.
>
> THE MAIDEN. They are fascinating, just fascinating. I want to get away from our eternal dancing and music, and just sit down by myself and think about numbers . . . I have not slept at all for weeks past. I have stolen out at night . . . wandered about the woods, thinking, thinking, thinking; grasping the world; taking it to pieces; building it up again; devising methods; planning experiments to test the methods; and having a glorious time. (BM, pp. 209–10)

We have traced the progress of Shaw's instincts from a "mob of appetites" into moral passion and thence to further conversions; Nethercot suggests that the final phase of Shaw's "mystical journey" is, in Shaw's words, "intellectual passion, mathematical passion, passion for discovery and exploration, the mightiest of all the passions" (FF, p. 520).

And indeed, numbers do seem to acquire magical properties. They become as fixed and eternal as the heavens to a medieval

6 Arthur H. Nethercot, *The Shaw Review* 12, no. 1 (1969): 2–26.

astrologist and every bit as much a sign of immutable order. Should one counter that mathematics leads to physics and eventually on to Hiroshima, Shaw would only reply with Major Barbara that power for destruction can be used for good. Well, yes, but—

The Adventures of the Black Girl in Her Search for God (1932) is a fable of religious quest as an evolutionary process. The black girl, having been put on the track of God by an English missionary, encounters a series of figures representative of historical stages of religion. There are Old Testament patriarchal gods of creation and wrath, the argumentative god of Job, the disillusioned god of Ecclesiastes, and a Pavlovian scientist for comic relief. Then the girl encounters Christ, the conjurer who tells her God is within herself.

> "But what is He?"
> "Our father," said the conjurer. . . ."
> "Why not our mother?"

Love, even Christian love, is not enough, and the girl thereafter encounters some modern agnostics in the "Caravan of the Curious." A woman tells her that the universe is mathematical and its key, the "square root of minus X." Puzzling over this, the girl comes to the conclusion that "through numbers you find eternity," and only their truth "is eternal."

> Every other truth passes away or becomes error, like the fancies of our childhood; but one and one are two and one and ten eleven and always will be. Therefore I feel that there is something godlike about numbers. (p. 49)

Her new faith does not lead to her mastering Einstein's relativity but to cultivating Voltaire's garden, where she eventually marries a red-haired and rather uncouth Irish Socialist. But more to the point is the devious means by which her faith develops. After hearing of the mathematical key, she wants to know where the "square root of Myna's sex" grows. The black girl's quest is for the goddess Myna and the "root of her womanhood" which is "bodiless like a number" (p. 48). If Christ can pun His Church into being with the rock of Peter, Shaw can certainly pun mathematics into the latest visitation of the Life Force with his Myna's sex. "In the beginning was the pun," as Beckett noted.

Shaw's pun, regardless of its scientific fallacy, is a brilliant leap of wit. It links numbers not only to sex but to the omnipotence of the Primordial Mother. Myna is the name given to that prehistoric moment of matriarchal parthenogenesis discussed by Don Juan and later in Lilith. "Something like" Myna's sex multiplied by itself "must have been the beginning."

> Since I was a child I have meditated on numbers and wondered how the number one came; for all the other numbers are only ones added to ones; but what I could not find out was what one is. But now I know through Myna that one is that which is multiplied by itself and not by a married pair. (p. 48)

While we may be awed at the adaptive facility, consistency, and sublimating power of the Shavian ego, we should also be reminded that it is this tendency toward abstraction that compels a writer like Norman O. Brown to indict civilization (a number being only the shadow of the image of the woman). But in this instance, Shaw is redeemed by his wit; for once, his leap is backwards when it connects an abstraction with a sexual source. In this respect, "all genuinely intellectual work is humorous." And it does not seem to matter that his new-found faith in mathematics, like so many connections, commitments, and cathexes in his life, is overdetermined.

SHAW'S GENIUS AND HIS CREATIVITY

Whatever the value so far of this study, I have not intended it to penetrate the core of Shaw's genius. That particular fish swims through the best of critical and Freudian nets. Excursions into the mysteries of creativity and participation in the creative process have become distinctively modern enterprises. Whether this amounts to an unwholesome democratization of art with everyman his own analyst and artist, a shortcut to the hard-won riches of an inner life that society fails to furnish, or a great frontier of experience, I cannot say. So far I have attempted through an energy-and-structure method to bring formalist criticism and psychoanalytic insights into a closer alignment and working relationship. The practical use of this method has been to uncover correlations between Shavian drives and defenses and their resultant content and structure in dramatic form. But hidden in mists behind all these considerations is creativity. And whether finally it is to be defined as a derivative (like love?), as an adaptation, or to remain irreducible, we must attempt to understand what it may have meant for Shaw.

We recall Kohut's assertion that one of the adaptive values of narcissism is creativity. The narcissistic self by means of its grandiose fantasy exhibits its perfection either to the ego or the external world. In order to avoid painful failure resulting in the sense of shame, the ego-ideal controls and directs the narcissistic urges. It would be interesting to transpose the creative process onto this intrapsychic process. The original creative impulse to exhibit dramatic characters is conceivably taken over by Shaw's exacting ego-ideal when it reforms and redirects them to serve its own realistic ends. In so doing, Shavian drama introduces at once a reform of popular theater—which sentimentalizes life to suit wish fulfillment—and a reform of society—which is complacently in love with its own self-image.

If you must be exhibited, says Shaw's ego-ideal to his narcissistic self, I will exhibit you as my writing machine and its productions. And if you would be admired, you must work. For a machine (until recently) is not intrinsically an object of admiration; it can be admired only so long as it is productive. And this may be the reason his writing machine never rested, for then it would cease to be, would "die for want of something to do."

It is necessary to push the sources of Shaw's creativity back to the origins of personality because he maintained that he could not recall any time when he could not read and write, nor any time when he did not exercise his imagination in dreams of the Uranian Venus (SS, p. 176). He unofficially endorsed Freud's theory of infantile sexuality when he remarked that "between Oscar Wilde who gave 16 as the age at which sex begins, and Rousseau who declared that his blood boiled with it from his birth, my personal experience confirms Rousseau and confutes Wilde" (*ibid*). "I have only had to shut my eyes to be and do whatever I please" (SS, p. 86). He also stated, "I never felt inclined to write, any more than to breathe" ((SS, p. 82), and, "I write plays because I like it, and because I cannot remember any period in my life when I could help inventing people and scenes" (LS, pp. 461–62). Reading and writing, day dreaming and creativity, are coextensive with consciousness, almost with life itself.

We recall that Shaw initially found in Art the religious power to redeem him from the "abomination of desolation" of his early years. And when he remarked that the religious people are not empty, he had in mind the religious power of Beethoven as well as orthodox religions. "The presence of a permanent and usually severe injury to infantile narcissism" has been recently offered as a possible prerequisite to creativity.[7] This injury may

---

[7] William G. Niederland, "Clinical Aspects of Creativity," *American Imago* 23 (1967): 6–34.

be induced by physical defects from birth or childhood illness, or from "object loss." Creativity then assumes a restitutive or restorative role.

We may also recall Owen Jacks' creative response to abandonment; and once when Shaw felt "detestably deserted" during his courtship of Charlotte, he refused to admit that he was truly alone. Years earlier he wrote similarly to a London love, whose failure to keep an engagement had left him "catching my death in unutterably lonely railway waiting rooms" (LS, p. 98). And again he did not feel alone, for he adds, "At least they would be lonely did not my imagination people them." Narcissism is called upon to heal its own wounds through the family romance. And his response to this situation is analogous to the earlier time when he countered his mother's "almost total neglect" by idolizing her to the "utmost peak" of his "imagination." Thus his creativity may well have dual origins related to the dual role his mother performed in his life. It may be grandiose in its original omnipotence as well as restorative in its response to loss. When the tendency to escape into flights of ideas is joined with an attempt to fuse disparate aspects of the mother, the result may well turn into the conception of the Life Force.

Freud has remarked on the artist's "special gifts," his "flexibility of repression," and his power to transform the unconscious and to bring his fantasy into accord with reality. This latter ability seems sufficiently evident in Shaw, even though the fantasies may be buried deep in the prose. "Special gifts" is an unanalyzable component that makes all the difference and also serves as a handy escape clause for the more limited gifts of the psychoanalytically-minded student of art. "Flexibility of repression" requires some elaboration.

Repression "proceeds from the ego" (IV, p. 50) under the auspices of the ego-ideal, or, as Freud added, from the "self-respect of ego." Two closely related processes that reduce repression come into play here. Sublimation, primarily concerned with object-libido, induces a "deflection from the sexual aim" (IV, p. 51), "so that what was originally a sexual instinct finds satisfaction in some achievement that is no longer sexual but has a higher social or ethical valuation" (V, pp.122–23). By means of idealization the sexual object, without changing its nature, is "aggrandized and exalted in the mind" (IV, p. 51). Deflection of instinctual aim in effect meant that the original object could in some other manner be retained, and its idealization meant that while it could not be shaped by normal development and reexternalized as a genital love-object, it could be a source of energy and inspiration. In the plays we find on the one hand that the omnipotence of woman is transformed, like Mrs. George, Nina, and Lilith, into the Life Force; or on the other, exalted and idealized like Candida, Ann Whitefield, Major Barbara, Saint Joan, and others into vital geniuses. The undifferentiated idealization of the mother is subjected to the controlling and reforming processes of the Shavian ego, so that the final result is not an object of worship or an aesthetic ideal, and especially not a love-object, but a peculiarly Shavian force or figure of "higher social or ethical valuation," which now figures in the creative romance with the world. For just as the mother was once the whole world to the infant Shaw, the world is invested through the creative romance with some of the same concerns and values as the mother once had for him.

Since Shaw was a vital genius in his own eyes, and many of his characters share Vitalist qualities, we are led to reconsider the importance of Shaw's earliest steps toward self-object differentiation. Because our reconstructions suggest that Shaw incorporated his mother in a magical or global fashion instead of gradually, he continued to idealize her through a succession of actresses, or rather several generations of actresses, since he was still going strong with Greer Garson, Vivian Leigh, and Ingrid Bergman in his nineties. And because writing and play-making may be conceived as sublimations of the primal dialogue between mother and infant, we may be prepared to inquire further into Shaw's identification with his mother.

Shaw was creatively productive but not biologically repro-ductive, and one wonders how his creativity relates to pro-creativity. In the plays the Diabolonian and Vitalist sons give way to the creative and pragmatic fathers. I earlier suggested that behind the rescue fantasy of Higgins and the poor flower girl is the self-rescue of the superfluous child from neglect or abandonment. When this creature is molded into a woman, she is freed from her creator to lead her own life. This externaliza-tion marks both a release of the internalized feminine image and the opportunity for a masculine self to be asserted, but one, how-ever, which is identified as the creative artist, whose reliance on primitive oral omnipotence is shown by the power of his word made flesh.

The issues are further complicated by an obsession with reproduction in the plays, which really gets started shortly after Shaw's celibate marriage. Up until 1898 most of his writings were Fabian pamphlets and critical essays, and his plays were mostly criticisms of society. Then with *Man and Superman* (1901–3), *Back to Methuselah* (1920), and up to *Farfetched Fables* (1948), there is a concentration on, and an evolution of, the forms of reproduction.

The earliest form is matriarchal parthenogenesis, presented by Don Juan as the original method of life reproducing itself. It is followed by varieties of sexual reproduction historically practiced by the military man and the romantic man, "tedious failures," who are to be replaced by the combination of the Vitalist philosopher ("who seeks in contemplation to discover the inner will of the world" [MS, p. 628]), and the vital genius of woman (directed to "the great central purpose of breeding the race; ay, breeding it to heights now deemed super-human" [MS, p. 637]). This combination rises from Shaw's project to convert the instincts to the task of Creative Evolution, but they are so far not separated from sexuality. The result is a brilliant synthesis of life and civilization, which would have been a safe stopping point. But Shaw plunges on; he will provide the will to evolve that his fellowmen apparently lack. And the real and virtually only evolution in the plays that follow concerns reproduction. Even mathematics is bound up with human multiplication.

Perhaps our dismissal of these plays has been premature and injudicious. After all, we are familiar with only one kind of sexual reproduction ourselves; and because it is merely part of the status quo, we may take for granted, as being in the nature of things and divinely ordained, what is in fact altogether arbitrary and conventional. It is quite possible that even the most emancipated, modern intelligence among us would harbor some secret prejudices against other methods, such as oviparity. But Shaw has broken free from such archaic inhibitions. In "As Far As Thought Can Reach," for the first time in the history of the theater, the act of birth is presented on-stage in full view of the audience.

> The She-Ancient takes her two saws, and with a couple of strokes rips the egg open. The Newly Born, a pretty girl who would have been guessed as seventeen in our day, sits up in the broken shell, exquisitely fresh and rosy, but with filaments of spare albumen clinging to her here and there. (BM, p. 215)

It is quite possibly the *only* time an act of birth of this kind will be presented on-stage. It is one of the experiments—apparently the latest and socially accepted one—of the Life Force still at it in the year of Our Lord (or is it of Shaw?) 31,920.

The Newly Born is getting along famously with her sylvan friends when the Pavlovian Dr. Frankenstein, here called Pygmalion, enters. He has created in the laboratory a man and a woman who must resort to the disgusting sexual practices persisting as late as the twentieth century in order to reproduce their own kind. "They have no self-control, and are merely shuddering through a series of reflexes" (BM, p. 243).

> THE NEWLY BORN. Can they make love?
> PYGMALION. Yes : they can respond to every stimulus. They have all the reflexes. Put your arm around the man's neck, and he will put his arm around your body. He can not help it. (p. 236)

Evolutionary throwbacks, they are also an inversion of Keegan's vision of a "godhead in which all life is human and all humanity divine : three in one and one in three" (JB, p. 611). The Male Figure, trapped in his vanity and mortality, calls himself Ozymandias; the Female Figure, in her sensuality and thralldom, is Cleopatra-Semiramis.

> The actions of the king are caused, and therefore determined, from the beginning of the world to the end; the actions of the queen are likewise. The king logical and predetermined and inevitable, and the queen logical and predetermined and inevitable. And yet they are not two logical and predetermined and inevitable, but one logical and predetermined and inevitable. Therefore confound not the persons, nor divide the substance; but worship us twain as one throne, two in one and one in two lest by error ye fall into irretrievable damnation. (p. 238)

They speak for the Pavlovian determinism of the unreformed instincts and, to call it by its rightful name, viviparity. Before long they fatally bite the hand of their maker; and when they demonstrate their inability to evolve feelings of compassion, they grow discouraged and die. Once again the history of the instincts turns into the cycle of futility, and the real enemy of life is now flesh itself.

The Ancients have advanced beyond the oviparous mode and come closer to Keegan's ideal : "One moment of the ecstasy of life as we live it would strike you dead" (p. 208), an oviparous youth is told. But they have not totally mastered life :

> THE HE-ANCIENT. Look at us. Look at me. This is my body my blood, my brain; but it is not me. I am the eternal life, the perpetual resurrection; but (striking his body) this structure, this organism, this makeshift, can be made by a boy in a laboratory, and is held back from dissolution only by my use of it. Worse still, it can be broken by a slip of the foot, drowned by a cramp in the stomach, destroyed by a flash from the clouds. Sooner or later, its destruction is certain.
>
> THE SHE-ANCIENT. Yes : This body is the last doll to be discarded. (p. 250)

On that day they will achieve their immortal destiny. In the year 31,920 A.D., they can only predict "the day will come when there will be no people, only thought" (p. 253). They have mastered their bodies; they have distilled their instincts into the essence of thought; but tomorrow a tree limb may fall on one of them and shatter the body's hull. The key seems to be in reproduction. Sexuality has been abandoned, oviparity is being tried; but what must be called for is a purely mental process to reproduce thought vortexes; perhaps a mathematical formula will be found on the scale of $E = MC^2$ that will convert body into mind as matter into energy.

Some sort of miracle as this seems to have occurred in *Farfetched Fables*. Seminal fluids are made in the laboratory for chemical reproduction, which is an advance over that atavistic practice of "personal contacts which I had rather not describe," one of the artificial inseminates remarks (FF, pp. 508–9). Once again a middle phase of a future period, enabling a backward and a forward perspective, is dramatized. One of the speakers mentions that some of mankind evolved into the "superman who evolved into the disembodied" (p. 516).

> The theory is that the Disembodied Races still exist as Thought Vortexes, and are penetrating our thick skulls in their continual pursuits of knowledge and power, since they need our hands and brains as tools in that pursuit. (p. 517)

That this was accomplished through improved reproductive processes is not stated; apparently with their will they have found a way. I would be quite willing to view these projections as a colossal joke by Shaw at our expense if I had any indication that he so intended them. But he seems to be in dead earnest; and worse, these late developments are consistent with earlier tendencies. It is as if his ego in the flush of its mastery over instinct could not restrain itself and became obsessed with the process of mastering as a panacea for every problem, or, more likely, that the instincts are so powerful and felt to be so pervasive, the ego cannot refrain from grinding up all of reality in its mechanism of mastery.

In addition, it is precisely this body-mind dualism that is held by Norman O. Brown as the crime perpetrated by modern man from overinvesting in sublimation. Naturally, one need not agree with Brown in order to disagree with Shaw. Nor is that exactly the point. What is objectionable is Shaw's failure to confront the problem of dualism heart-whole; instead he locates life in the mind, which he champions discursively without exploring dialectically. The flesh becomes the enemy of spirit every bit as much as in the "Crosstianity" of St. Paul and St. Augustine, which Shaw once had brilliantly attacked. Nor is there in the teachings of Shaw any resurrection of the body; rather there is a "redemption from the flesh" (BM, pp. 260–61) through an evolution of life in which man is "born again and born better" (PMI, p. 5).

"Dialectics means that a proposition elicits a counter-proposition; and dramatists are people with a keen sense of this to-and-fro," Eric Bentley wrote about another committed theater (*NY Times,* Oct. 20, 1968). Shaw exercised his dialectic structure in various ways, but most often his plays were antitheses to assumed theses of his audience. Is the proposition that life is in thought (antithesis) meant to jar the audience loose from their complacent assumption that life is in the body or the reproductive organs (thesis)? Are the ideas of these late plays based on some colossal miscalculation? Let the question be phrased differently. Did Shaw conceive of his mind as so fertile and so omnipotent that thought processes could take over the task of reproduction? Is Creative Evolution a substitution for those disgusting practices Freud had the "vulgar indelicacy" to expose?

Mental processes in the Freudian view are a derivative through fantasy of instinctual processes, which makes the body either more real than mind or at the very least indispensable to it. And since fantasy retains what is relinquished in reality, "the original fantasies are negations; sublimations are negations of negations . . . symbols of symbols" (*Life against Death,* p. 169). Was the evolutionary appetite pursuing an illusion? In plain words, are we witnessing in Shaw's substitution of mental processes for sexual ones an endeavor through sublimation to achieve woman's procreative power? Is this grandiose fantasy behind his creative transformation of narcissistic libido?

Or there may be explanations other than overworked sublimations and overdetermined mental processes to account for these obsessive themes and the plays' failure to seize the reader's imagination and stir his evolutionary will. Perhaps the varieties of reproduction are attempts to remove the male from his established, but relatively minor, procreative function because Shaw needed to deny as well as undo his father's sexual role, and preferred to think of himself as exclusively and symbiotically the mother's offspring? Could this be closer to what the black girl means when she says, "One is that which is multiplied by itself and not by a married pair"? Was Shaw compelled to remove his father from any sexual role as he was driven to remove Jehovah and Paul from Christianity, bankers and businessmen from economics, actor-managers and archaic bards from the theater: because he feared their intrusion and wanted to believe they were all imposters? And where does that leave him? His capacities for mastering instinctual energies have been duly stressed, but can sexual activity be desexualized without being demolished? And when you come right down to it, was not this what Shaw was trying to do in these plays—abolish the sexual equation?—the real secret to sustaining the Life Force and producing the Superman being "minus sex." And thus in speaking about this period of his work, one cannot escape noticing that the line between creative adaptation and unresolved psychic conflict is far from clear. I will raise only one further disturbing aspect of this tendency in Shaw's late plays. Did Shaw have difficulty transforming early conflicts into art because they were clearly pathological? "I postulate that the creation of great art," K. R. Eissler has written in his study of Goethe, "may involve the transformation of psychotic-like structures by means of mechanisms that resemble sublimation" (p. 1097).[8] And therefore do the bizarre sexual schemes in these plays represent not the extremes of sublimation but its failure, and if not the "transformation of psychotic-like structures," then at least the intrusion of primary process, which in actual life would be severely pathological?

These questions can be posed differently. As a child, did Shaw solve the riddle of his own existence?—did he associate himself with the sexual intercourse of his parents? He speaks

---

[8] "This line of speculation has been continued in Eissler's *Discourse on Hamlet and "Hamlet"* (New York, 1971), pp. 519–53.

about his disillusioned perception of the woman visitor (in chapter 1), about his freedom to roam through the house with an adult's prerogatives, and about his rich fantasy life; but about any investigations initiated by sexual curiosity he is silent. It is the sphinx's riddle, for the figure of the sphinx, with its woman's head and shoulders, bird's wings, and lion's body, has been interpreted psychoanalytically as the image of intercourse;[9] and the answer to the riddle of the sphinx, which is man, is the same as the answer to the riddle of parental intercourse, which is the child: "three in one and one in three." This may be the original trinity that Shaw found unacceptable since it stemmed from the "twain as one throne, two in one and one in two," of Pavlovian coupling, and that he exhausted his talents in trying to replace by returning to "one multiplied by itself." Practically speaking, he knew that the "real George Bernard Shaw was born into the world not by parthenogenesis but in the vulgar way"; yet his very disclaimer in this 1905 letter means that he had at least considered the matter and did not find the truth necessarily to his liking (PP, p. 31).

Traces of primal-scene witnessings in Shaw's writing have eluded me. An intruder does witness a flirtation scene in *Misalliance*. But it appears that if Shaw saw, he did not tell. One is led to ask whether there was anything to see anyway; and if so, who would it be—Mr. Shaw or Mr. Lee? Nor should one be surprised to find an asexuality in Mrs. Shaw not unlike her son's. Anyway, Shaw did not seem to tell, but he did reveal in a flight of fancy what sort of fantasies he harbored on the subject in general.

9 "For, the Sphinx is the combined symbol of man and woman joined in the natural act of our animal heritage, the one method by which we know how to create life in our own image, the act which brings man the infant-animal out of his mother into manhood's youth, maturity and old age. To confront this riddle of the creative forces of life, the sexual act of our parents, and to solve it, is for the infant to *see* that which is forbidden to watch." Daniel E. Schneider, *The Psychoanalyst and the Artist* (New York, 1952), p. 33.

They came out on a June night in 1897 aboard a joggling train in a letter of "jogged scrawls" to Ellen Terry.

> I *must* talk to you : nowhere else, no time else, can we be so perfectly alone. Yes, as you guess, Ellen, I am having a bad attack of you just at present. I am restless; and a man's restlessness always means a woman; and my restlessness means Ellen. And your conduct is often shocking. Today I was wandering somewhere, thinking busily about what I supposed to be high human concerns when I glanced at a shop window; and there you were—oh disgraceful and abandoned—in your 3rd Act Sans Gene dress—a mere waist band—laughing wickedly. (LS, pp. 774–76)

Both alarmed and aroused by her seductive image, he tells her, "you are worse than Lilith," but quickly adds, "these silly longings stir great waves of tenderness . . . ." He refers to his exhaustion from overwork. "I'm tired in all my bones," he had written her a few days earlier and had begged her to sustain him in his work : ". . . love me hard, love me soft, and deep, and sweet, and for ever and ever and ever" (LS, p. 774). But on this night his restlessness wants to break out of the confines of their writing relationship :

> I must say something : I can't in pen and ink rest these bruised brains in your lap and unburden my heart with inarticulate cries. When I can think, when I can write, then my ideas fly like stones : you can never be sure that one of them will not hurt you—my very love gets knit into an infernal intellectual fabric that wounds when I mean it to caress; and when I am tired and foolish I am flat and apparently bored.

His customary defenses for keeping distance are frayed; the late hour and the jogging rhythm of the train have apparently further lulled him out of his habitual control.

> I am particularly tedious at present in this midnight solitary journey, wanting to sleep, and yet to sleep with you. Only, do you know what the consequences would be? Well, about tomor-

row at noon when the sun would be warm and the birds in full
song, you would feel an irrestible impulse to fly into the woods.
And there to your great astonishment and scandal, you would
be *confined* of a baby that would immediately spread a pair of
wings and fly, and before you could rise to catch it it would be
followed by another and another and another—hundreds of
them, and they would finally catch you up and fly away with
you to some heavenly country where they would grow into
strong sweetheart sons with whom, in defiance of the prayerbook, you would found a divine race. Wonld you not like to be
the mother of your own grandchildren? If you were my mother,
I am sure I should carry you away to the tribe in
Central America where—but I have a lot of things to say and
we are at Redhill already.

A double consciousness emerges from this passage. The
seductive image of Ellen Terry has gotten through to him as a
man, and their sacred relationship is temporarily disrupted. The
feelings of tenderness and empathy of the child for the mother
are overtaken by the sensuality of the man for the woman. His
manic defense of keeping the woman, but keeping her at a
distance by writing (wounding and caressing), is breaking down
and revealing the passive needs beneath it. His wish for union
with her may be a child's wish; but he is aware that he can only
sleep with her as a man, so that incest becomes an imminent
reality with real consequences. "In defiance of the prayerbook"
would be in violation of taboo. "If you were my mother," their
union would partake of the timelessness and omnipotence of
the mother and child : a whole "divine race" of "strong sweetheart sons" would ensue, and not in nine months but overnight.

It is as though when his "infernal intellectual fabric" has
come unraveled, his distance-keeping ideas are returned to their
instinctual sources. The "ideas that fly like stones" dissolve in
that troublesome seminal fluid so fertile that it can propagate
overnight as many winged offspring as there are spermatozoa
swimming in it, possibly because for Shaw the male's potency

and the woman's nurturing powers are part of the same symbiotic substance.

In one variant of the rescue fantasy Freud detects a complex of gratified instincts. These are "the loving, the grateful, the sensual, the defiant, the self-assertive and independent" (OC, pp.200–201), and they all converge in the child's "wish to be father of himself." The child seeks to liquidate the debt of paternity and to "save" the mother by returning to her a life as much like the one that she bore as possible: "rescuing the mother acquires the significance of giving her a child or making one for her—one like himself, of course." So much does Shaw reveal to Ellen Terry in his proposing that she become the mother of her own grandchildren. But that is not all. The omnipotent images of flying and of bearing a divine race suggest the intrusion of much earlier material. Specifically, the "illusion of flying or floating" may be stimulated by "infantile experiences of nursing" (PB, p. 54). In just this way may the "grandiose fantasy" of primary narcissism interfuse the rescue fantasy of the family romance. For indeed, it appears to descend from the "heavenly country" of symbiosis, which, in disregarding the father and in usurping the prerogatives of the gods and a mythical tribe in Central America, produces the Titan sons who are going to be further transformed by the ego and projected from the past onto the future as the Superman. Are Shaw's works transformations and elaborations of just such a powerful wish forbidden in reality—spin-offs from the grandiose fantasy of omnipotent flight and infinite fertility that compelled his sense of gravitational rise, underlaid his spritelike behavior as well as his belief in the ascent of man through Creative Evolution? The correspondences are too close to be ignored. It is conceivable if not certain that the "divine race" of "strong sweetheart sons" serving the Great Mother is behind the vision of all life human and "all humanity divine." (When Shaw once defined this ideal as the "just man made perfect" [PMI, p. 71], could he have been punning on "made"?) Keegan's "three in one and one in three" may have originated from the Shavian trinity of the Great Mother, the prolific son, and the Superman offspring; and the obsession in his work with reproduction may spring from attempts to produce in the real world viable alternatives to the child's wish and to reify his mystical vision. "Every dream is a prophecy" of "realities as yet unexperienced" (PMI, p. 105). And incidentally, if what Keegan allows to be the "dream of a madman" is based on a fantasy in turn derived from an earlier wish, then the universality of incest set forth in *Totem and Taboo,* linking the conduct of the savage, the life of the child, and the unconscious of the adult, is surprisingly affirmed in Shaw's flight of fancy.

But what may have been more immediately relevant to Shaw psychologically is that Evolution as a creative process, with the Superman as its product, breaks—or at least bends— the narcissistic bond of mother and son by forming a third corner, a transformation of narcissism of the kind that Kohut refers to. "After all, what man is capable of the insane self-conceit of believing that an eternity of himself would be tolerable even to himself?" (PMI, p. 4). And the way out then is to be "born again and born better." While this ostensibly means the necessity of evolutionary advance and finding in the Superman ideal an immortality ordinarily sought by the parent in the mortal child, it also, perhaps at an unconscious level, means finding an alternative to the phallic male, thus rendering the Superman something like a colossal erection of the mind.

The greater implications of this line of inquiry will have to be examined after a look at subsequent events in Shaw's life. At the time of the 1897 letter, he had already begun having a series of minor accidents—twisted knee-caps and sprained ankles—that were to keep him on crutches for eighteen months.

He grew thin. He attributed his diminished appetite to lack of exercise, although he was working harder than ever—reviewing, preparing his first two volumes of plays for publication, writing new ones, speaking. By the spring of 1898, he was "in an almost superhuman condition—fleshless, bloodless, vaporous, ethereal, and stupendous in literary efficiency" (AH, p. 419). Because in his words he was actually suffering from "exhaustion and starvation" (p. 419), his weakened condition and a too-tightly laced boot caused an abscess that turned into necrosis of the bone. An operation became necessary, and shortly before it someone "suggested the possibility of my dying under the anaesthetic, and I then found that the prospect was not in the least disagreeable to me—rather too tempting to be dwelt on, if anything" (ibid.). His Irish millionairess, Charlotte Payne-Townshend, whom he had met two years before through the Fabian Society and attached to himself as his secretary, and whom he had been entertaining the idea of marrying, heard of his condition of uncertain convalescence and rushed to his apartment to rescue him. In order to avoid scandal among the Fabians (an outrageous motive in view of the way some Fabians carried on), and because he claimed that "my objection to my own marriage had ceased with my objection to my own death" (ibid.), Shaw permitted their marriage on June 1, 1898. The wedding has been described in a celebrated passage without which no account of Shaw's life is complete:

I was very ill when I was married, altogether a wreck on crutches and in an old jacket which the crutches had worn to rags. I had asked my friends, Mr. Graham Wallas, of the London School Board, and Mr. Henry Salt, the biographer of Shelley and De Quincey, to act as witnesses, and, of course, in honour of the occasion they were dressed in their best clothes. The registrar never imagined I could possibly be the bridegroom; he took me for the inevitable beggar who completes all wedding processions. Wallas, who is considerably over six feet

high, seemed to him to be the hero of the occasion, and he
was proceeding to marry him calmly to my betrothed, when
Wallas, thinking the formula rather strong for a mere
witness, hesitated at the last moment and left the prize to me.
(AH, p. 418)

Beggared and disabled ("castrated," WA, p. 159), the superfluous child re-creates the image of his deprivation and brings
about a corrected revision of it. And then several days later a
fall down a flight of stairs breaks an arm and lands him in a
wheelchair.[10] Back on his feet, he sprains his ailing foot and an
ankle three times each (HP, p. 207). Though I hesitate to call
all of this one of his better melodramas, I cannot forbear asking
whether anyone had gone to greater extremes in denying any
sexual aspirations in marriage. (It may be coincidence and
nothing more that Shaw's crippled condition resembled Lee's
lameness when he invaded the Shaw family, but it does not
require a club-footed actor to play the part of Oedipus.) Shaw
believed that a "childless partnership" and hence a sexless one
"between two middle-aged people who have passed the age at
which it is safe to bear a first child" (HP, p. 205) was only
sensible. (Why he included himself [43] along with his wife
[42] as being beyond child-bearing is not explained.) One biographer hastens to assert in Shaw's behalf that he was a "man
who delighted in women and enjoyed carnal concurrence with
them" (JE, p. 315), and that it is "almost certain that the
delay in their marriage was due to Charlotte's condition that

---

10 After the death of Charlotte in 1943 Shaw remained in Ayot St.
Lawrence with his housekeeper, Mrs. Laden, to whom he was strongly attached. Shortly before he died, she informed him of her plans for a holiday.
The news left him dejected, but he insisted that she go. Two days later,
while trimming a plum tree, he fell and broke his leg. She returned immediately and found him in the hospital: ". . . he looked at me with
sad eyes and said in a very soft, pathetic voice, 'take me home' " (RM,
p. 182).
    It will hardly go unnoticed that in creating real conditions for the rescue
fantasy to be enacted, Shaw not only disavows phallic ambitions, but reveals
the more buried wish of being the one rescued.

there should not be consummation" (p. 316). But without any evidence, it is most uncertain. Another biographer rushes to Charlotte's defense. If Shaw was "perfectly normal as a man," Charlotte was perfectly normal, too. "It is probable" that "they enjoyed as normal an intimate life as other married couples do; but they were not young" (JD, p. 153). Not young? Well, it is true that Shaw had little more than a half-century of life left in him, and his wife somewhat less. But they were not teenagers either.

Obviously, many factors contributed to Shaw's marriage, but among them I believe the pressure of those incestuously tinged impulses he had begun to feel for Ellen Terry to be paramount. His diminishing diet, his literally crippling workload, and his series of incapacitating accidents, all had some function as defensive measures of control and efforts at undoing. But apparently they were not enough. Finally he had to regress to the sexless, impoverished infant and reproduce the bountiful nursing mother in order to be free of those impulses. "The situation was changed" between Charlotte and himself "by a change in my own consciousness" (AH, p. 419). He is referring here to the imminent prospect of his death in the operation preceding his marriage. His fear of the doctor's power to invade the integrity of his body was apparently only exceeded by his fear of woman's invasion of his privacy, and both had to be mastered. The change of consciousness also involved letting go of his public life (it was around this time that G.B.S. resigned as drama critic), and becoming an invalid who was, like an infant, innocent of the forbidden nature of incestuous desires. His falls and accidents may have also signified the fall from omnipotence of the self-sufficient sprite in order to share again in the woman's omnipotence.

In Charlotte he may have sought the "nurturing mother" (WA, p. 161), and she may have been a loyal and devoted homemaker, but she was a complicated person; as a wife she made her share of unpleasant demands on her husband, especially when it involved her addiction to travel. And if Shaw's maneuvering served to reproduce the anaclitic object for the child to lean on, there were interesting parallels between them as well. Her rigid upbringing by a "managing and domineering mother" somewhat resembled Mrs. Shaw's, and Charlotte's father had some of the remoteness and appeal for Charlotte that Shaw's mother had for Shaw. She wrote to T. E. Lawrence (whom the Shaws somewhat adopted), "I had a perfectly hellish childhood and youth"; and "my own home life made me firmly resolve never to be the mother of a child who might suffer as I had suffered. The idea was physically repulsive to me in the highest degree."[11] Along with her husband she had developed a "fearful streak of conscience, and sense of duty"; and along with Shaw's mother, Charlotte was interested in spiritualism and the occult. Shortly before meeting Shaw, she was rebounding from a hapless Continental romance, which could have served as a precondition for Shaw's rescue fantasies.

It would be fairly accurate to say that they both sought qualities of the beloved parent in each other, and insofar as such an expectation was normal, theirs was a normal marriage. The aversion to the conjugal bed, which was more peculiar to them, must have been mutual for the marriage to survive as long and as relatively happily as it did.

But the conclusions that Shaw did not seek a mother for his children-to-be so much as one for himself, and that he did not seek an object for sex so much as an ally for repression, are hard to escape. That he sought to align himself with the maternal woman in an alliance against the sexual male and

11 B. C. Rosset, "Peagasus and Rozinante," *The Shaw Review* 6, no. 3 : 111–19, in a review of *Mrs. G.B.S.* by Janet Dunbar, in which the original letter may be found. Miss Dunbar chose to replace the last-quoted sentence with ellipses (JD, pp. 251–53).

in an attempt to use himself as the penis-child who will restore the early mother's phallic integrity are conclusions no less difficult to avoid. It is not long after his marriage that the foot heals, and not much longer after that when he begins to write the play that will reflect his new integration of sexual and mental energies. And from *Man and Superman* on, the alternatives to sexual reproduction are introduced.

SHAW'S CORNER

We may now return to the content of the Ellen Terry letter. If I have begun to describe a grandiose fantasy coursing through the complex currents of Shaw's life, it has not been to yield to the tempting whirlpool of reductionism, nor to pluck out of it the secret of his creative genius. My aim has rather been to locate a nucleus of psychic energy and to trace its myriad vicissitudes in order to find some kind of organic unity within one of the most elusive, most unbelievably expansive, contradictory, and achieved lives of recent times. And I trust the grandiosity has not been unduly contagious when I suggest that we have found testimony to the existence of this unity.

The flying fancies scribbled aboard that joggling (rocking?) train are the most inclusive representation of this grandiose fantasy. The binding together in it of a primordial wish for union with the mother, omnipotent flight, and prolific offspring equally encompasses the emphasis assigned earlier to narcissism and the family romance as well as to other divergent spheres of Shaw's life. We have noted the ascensive hallmark of his manic disposition, the association of nursing with the illusion of free flight. We have observed the flight of the soaring comet, and have heard of ecstasies on the "plains of heaven with a deathless, ageless creature of coral and ivory" (MS, p. 632). We have seen the gravitational rise from the Uranium dreams and magical faculties of the Dublin child; the London sprite materializing in families and vanishing without warning, descending on women and being pursued actually or fancifully by them; his Icaruslike fall into crippled flesh before marriage, and his later rise to "fullest stature" to "wear my head nearest the skies" and join Mrs. Pat, the "mother of Angels," on their heavenly throne (PC, p. 173). He has stepped figuratively from the bosom of more than one actress onto the heavenly heights and founded the rock of his religion on the eternally feminine star of Stella. Always woman, always flight. And the flight into reality, that is, into external reality, soars into the airless spheres of Creative Evolution.

I have noted the mercurial, spritelike descriptions of his wit in its quest for truth, and marked its power to leap from mathematics to the root of womanhood. We may recall how "with the utmost good-humor he clasps us affectionately round the waist and jumps overboard with us, and that too, not into a majestic Atlantic where we might perish tragically, but into a sea of ridicule amid shrieks of derisive laughter" (SS, p. 187) as an apt description of his acrobatic wit.

He has given us the image of the little army of "bouncing" Fabians conquering the country. Throughout every endeavor he emerges invulnerable, indeed invincible—was he ever bested? Even death had to wait until he had had his say, and then it came as a mild anticlimax to his nonagenarian life. And beyond all, there is the Superman, the "executive organ of godlike knowledge and power" (HP, p. 280), which would master symbiosis by turning the mother into energy, the energy into mind, and then use it along the path of Creative Evolution to free man from nature. And when this process becomes a means of reproduction by which man can be "born again and born better," I have suggested certain obvious failings, which can be attributed to an overload on the original, energizing, grandiose fantasy. For it is only at this point that we begin to speak of the fantasy and the drives it stirred up as grandiose. In the sense that Oedipus did not have an Oedipus complex, Napoleon a Napoleonic delusion, or that Christ to a Christian did not have a Messianic complex, a genius cannot be accused of grandiosity. Grandiosity in another is realism in himself. Frank Lloyd Wright apparently recognized this when he said that as a young man having to choose between honest arrogance and hypocritical humility, he chose the former and chose rightly.

Shaw's many accomplishments attest to his ability to transform the grandiosity of his narcissism. It is even used against man to attack the complacency and inertia of his self-love.

> The power that produced Man when the monkey was not up to the mark, can produce a higher creature than Man if Man does not come up to the mark. What it means is that if Man is to be saved, Man must save himself. There seems no compelling reason why he should be saved. He is by no means an ideal creature. At his present best many of his ways are so unpleasant that they are unmentionable in polite society, and so painful that he is compelled to pretend that pain is often a good. Nature holds no brief for the human experiment: it must stand or fall by its results. If man will not serve, Nature will try another experiment. (PBM, p. xvii)

Here too is expressed in the harshness of Nature's method the damaged narcissism, the edge of despair looming up, the threat of abandonment, and the insistence on utility. (In a subsequent play the Angel of Death must decide who is a "social nuisance" and who is a "social asset.")

Shaw's Vitalist heroes, like Dick Dudgeon, could appropriate maternal functions by acting irrationally against the logical dictates of patriarchy in order to save life. In a sense they were acting the mother, who often may be thought of as behaving irrationally when it comes to saving her own flesh and blood.

And such a view could be dramatically projected. But as hard as Shaw put his narcissism to work for himself and mankind, there were some things it could not do. In particular, it could not control life and death. Out of his fears of separation and abandonment grow his aims to control the processes of life. But that alone is not enough. He must appropriate the powers of creating life; he must remake sexuality and eliminate death. He must found a new religion. And instead of performing miracles, he exposes the limits of his grandiosity. To be a genius for Shaw meant fulfilling the conditions of the family romance, a heroic and hallucinatory task. To be a genius meant he had to become Zeus, the fertile father, and inescapably "the concept of fatherhood," Freud warns, marks the "beginning of idealistic thinking." In the end Shaw could not father himself any more than he could mother himself.

But if he was failing in his "wishful thinking," as he referred to his imagination late in life, and growing strident in his public capacities, as a private man he ripened into serene old age that enabled him to view mortality with stark and poignant honesty. Shortly before he died, the smoke from a bonfire in his garden brought a phone call from a neighbour. Shaw immediately penned a reply:

> I thought of you very sympathetically on Saturday when the west wind was smoking you out. You will have your revenge on me when the wind goes south and smokes me out. I know of no remedy for the autumn bonfires, which have smoked for all my 94 years and thousands of centuries before that . . . I shall be burnt up myself presently; but the fumes will get no further than Golders Green. (RM, p. 166)

After the crematorium of Golders Green, his ashes were returned to Ayot St. Lawrence as he had requested, and scattered along with his wife's in the garden of their home, referred to by their neighbors as Shaw's Corner.

Wisdom and man's "capacity to contemplate his own impermanence" are included by Kohut among the transformations of narcissism. Shaw had more humanity than he put in his plays, and greater complexity than I have put on paper. For when it is asked why the urge behind his particular grandiose fantasy somehow should have either enabled him to become the original genius he was, or at least guided him along the course of his achievements, the question and our partial answers only draw us into the mists of deeper mysteries.

BIBLIOGRAPHY

A *Works by Shaw*

The Adventures of the Black Girl in Her Search for God. New York : Dodd, Mead and Co., 1933.

Bernard Shaw and Mrs. Patrick Campbell: Their Correspondence. New York : Alfred A. Knopf, 1952.

Complete Plays with Prefaces. 6 vols. New York : Dodd, Mead & Co., 1963.

The Complete Prefaces of Bernard Shaw (containing prefaces to *Three Plays by Brieux, London Music, The Irrational Knot, Immaturity,* and *Widowers' Houses*). London : Paul Hamlyn Ltd., 1965.

Ellen Terry and Bernard Shaw: A Correspondence. New York : G. P. Putnam's Sons, 1932.

Everybody's Political What's What? New York : Dodd, Mead & Co., 1944.

The Intelligent Woman's Guide to Socialism and Capitalism. New York : Brentano's, 1928.

Love Among the Artists. New York : Viking Press, 1962.

My Dear Dorothea: A Practical System of Moral Education for Females Embodied in a Letter to a Young Person of That Sex. New York : Vanguard Press, 1956.

Our Theatres in the Nineties. 3 vols. London : Constable and Co., 1932.

Platform and Pulpit. New York : Hill and Wang, 1961.

The Quintessence of Ibsenism. New York : Hill and Wang, 1957.

The Rationalization of Russia. Bloomington, Ind : Indiana University Press, 1964.

Sixteen Self Sketches. New York : Dodd, Mead & Co., 1949.

B *Biography*

Du Cann, C. G. L. *The Loves of George Bernard Shaw.* New York : Funk & Wagnalls Co., Inc., 1963.

Ervine, St. John. *Bernard Shaw: His Life, Work and Friends.* New York : William Morrow, 1956.

Farmer, Henry George. *Bernard Shaw's Sister and Her Friends.* Leiden : E. J. Brill, 1959.

Fremantle, Anne. *This Little Band of Prophets.* New York : New American Library, 1960.

Harris, Frank. *Bernard Shaw.* New York : Simon and Schuster, 1931.

Henderson, Archibald. *Bernard Shaw: Playboy and Prophet.* New York : Appleton, 1932.

———. *George Bernard Shaw: Man of the Century.* New York : Appleton-Century-Crofts, 1956.

———. *Table Talk of G.B.S.* New York : Harper Bros., 1925.

Lawrence, Dan H., ed. *Bernard Shaw: Collected Letters 1874– 1879.* New York : Dodd, Mead & Co., 1965.

McNulty, Edward. "George Bernard Shaw as a Boy." *The Shaw Bulletin* 2 no 3 (Sept. 1957).

Minney, R. J. *Recollections of George Bernard Shaw.* Englewood Cliffs, N.J. : Prentice-Hall, 1969.

O'Bolger, T. D. Their unpublished correspondence dating from 1913, Harvard University Library.

O'Donovan, John. *Shaw and the Charlatan Genius.* Dublin : Doleman Press Ltd., Dufour Eds., 1966.

Pearson, Hesketh. *G.B.S.: A Full Length Portrait.* New York : Harper, 1942, 1950.

Rook, Clarence. "George Bernard Shaw," *The Chap-Book*. 5 no. 12 (Nov. 1896) : 529–40.

Rosset, B. C. *Shaw of Dublin, the Formative Years*. State College, Pa. : Penn State University Press, 1964.

Smith, Warren. *The Religious Speeches of George Bernard Shaw*. State College, Pa. : Penn State University Press, 1963.

Tauber, Abraham, ed. *George Bernard Shaw on Language*. New York : Philosophical Library, 1963.

Weintraub, Stanley, ed. *Shaw: An Autobiography, 1856 to 1898*. New York : Weybright & Talley, 1969. Vol. 1.

———. *Shaw: An Autobiography, 1898–1950, The Playwright Years*. New York : Weybright & Talley, 1970. Vol. 2.

C   *Literary, Critical, Other*

Bentley, Eric. *Bernard Shaw*. New York : New Directions, 1957.

———. *The Playwright as Thinker*. New York : Meridian Books, 1957.

———. "The Making of a Dramatist" (1892–1903), in *Twentieth Century Views*. Edited by K. J. Kaufmann. Englewood Cliffs, N.J. : Prentice-Hall, Inc. : 1965, pp. 57–75.

Barber, C. L. *Shakespeare's Festive Comedy*. New York : World Publishing Co., 1963.

Brustein, Robert. *The Theatre of Revolt*. Boston : Little, Brown & Co., 1962.

Buechner, George. *Complete Plays and Prose*. Translated by Carl Richard Mueller. New York : Hill and Wang, 1963.

Carpenter, Charles. *Bernard Shaw and the Art of Destroying Ideals*. Madison, Wis. : University of Wisconsin Press, 1969.

Chesterton, G. K. *George Bernard Shaw*. New York : Hill and Wang, 1956.

Cole, Margaret, ed. *Beatrice Webb's Diaries*. 2 vols. London : Longman's Green, 1952, 1956.

Crompton, Louis. *Shaw the Dramatist*. Lincoln, Neb. : University of Nebraska Press, 1969.

Fergusson, Francis. *The Idea of a Theatre*. Princton, N.J. : Princeton University Press, 1949.

Frye, Northrop. *A Natural Perspective*. New York : Columbia University Press, 1965.

———. "The Argument of Comedy." *English Institute Essays*. New York : Columbia University Press, 1948, 1949.

———. *The Modern Century*. Toronto : Oxford University Press, 1967.

Gassner, John. "Shaw on Ibsen and the Drama of Ideas." *English Institute Essays*. New York : Columbia University Press, 1964, pp. 71–100.

Gatch, Katherine Haynes. "The Last Plays of Bernard Shaw : Dialectic and Despair." *English Institute Essays*. New York : Columbia University Press, 1954, pp. 126–47.

Holland, Norman. *The Dynamics of Literary Response*. New York : Oxford University Press, 1968.

Ibsen, Henrik. *Letters and Speeches*. Evert Sprinchorn, ed. New York : Hill and Wang, 1964.

———. *Ghosts*. Translated by Peter Watts. Baltimore, Md. : Penguin Books, 1963.

Johnston, Brian. "The Mythic Foundation of Ibsen's Realism." *Comparative Drama* 3, no. 1 (Spring 1969).

Kaufmann, R. J., ed. *G. B. Shaw, A Collection of Critical Essays, Twentieth Century Views*. Englewood Cliffs., N.J. : Prentice-Hall, 1965.

Kaye, Julian B. *Bernard Shaw and the Nineteenth-Century Tradition*. Norman, Okla. : University of Oklahama Press, 1958.

Kronenberger, Louis, ed. *George Bernard Shaw: A Critical Survey*. New York : World Publishing Co., 1953.

Leary, Daniel J. "The Evolutionary Dialectic of Shaw and Teilhard : A Perennial Philosophy." *The Shaw Review* 9, no. 1 (1 Jan., 1966) : 15–33.

Meisel, Martin. *Shaw and the Nineteenth Century Theatre*. Princeton, N.J. : Princeton University Press, 1963.

Meyer, Michael. *Henrik Ibsen: The Making of a Dramatist (1828–1864)*. London : Rupert Hart-Davis, 1967.

———. Translation of Ibsen's *Brand*. New York : Doubleday Anchor, 1960.

Nethercot, Arthur H. "Bernard Shaw, Mathematical Mystic." *The Shaw Review* 12, no 1 (Jan. 1969) : 2–26.

———. "Shaw and Psychoanalysis." *Modern Drama* 11, no. 4 (Feb. 1969) : 356–75.

———. *Men and Supermen, The Shavian Portrait Gallery*. Cambridge, Mass. : Harvard University Press, 1954.

Ohmann, Richard M. *Shaw: The Style and the Man*. Middletown, Conn. : Wesleyan University Press, 1962.

Rosset, B. C. "Pegasus and Rozinante." *The Shaw Review* 6, no. 3 (Sept. 1963) : 111–19.

Smith, Warren S. "An Early GBS Love Poem." *The Shaw Review* 10, no. 2 (May 1967) : 70–72.

Spender, Stephen. *The Struggle of the Modern*. Berkeley and Los Angeles, Calif. : University of California Press, 1965.

Stanton, Stephen, ed. *Camille and other Plays*. New York : Hill and Wang, 1957.

Taylor, John Russell. *The Rise and Fall of the Well-Made Play*. New York : Hill and Wang, 1967.

Valency, Maurice, *The Flower and the Castle*. New York : Grosset and Dunlap, 1966.

———. *In Praise of Love*. New York : Macmillan, 1958.

Webb, Beatrice and Sidney. *Our Partnership*. New York : Longman's, Green, 1948.

West, Alick. *George Bernard Shaw: A Good Man Fallen Among Fabians*. New York : International Publishers, 1950.

Woolf, Leonard. *Beginning Again, An Autobiography of the Years 1911–1918*. New York. Harcourt, Brace, ,World, 1963.

Yeats, William Butler. *The Autobiography*. New York : Macmillan, 1965.

D *Psychological*

Aichhorn, August. *Wayward Youth.* New York : Viking Press, 1935.

Arlow, Jacob, and Brenner, Charles. *Psychoanalytic Concepts and the Structural Theory.* New York : International University Press, 1964.

Bergler, Edmund. *The Writer and Psychoanalysis.* 2d ed. New York : Robert Bruner, 1954.

Blanchard, William H. "Psychodynamic Aspects of the Peak Experience." *The Psychoanalytic Review* 56, no. 1 (1969) : 87–112.

Brill, A. A. *Lectures on Psychoanalytic Psychiatry.* New York : Alfred A. Knopf, 1955.

Brown, Norman O. *Life Against Death.* New York : Random House, 1959.

———. *Love's Body.* New York : Random House, 1966.

Eidelberg, Ludwig, ed. *The Encyclopedia of Psychoanalysis.* New York : Macmillan, 1968.

Eissler, K. R. *Goethe, A Psychoanalytic Study, 1775–1786.* 2 vols. Detroit, Mich. : Wayne State University Press, 1963.

Erikson, Erik H. *Childhood and Society.* New York : W. W. Norton, 1963.

———. *Identity: Youth and Crisis.* New York : W. W. Norton, 1968.

———. *Young Man Luther.* New York : W. W. Norton & Co., 1958.

Freud, Anna. *The Ego and the Mechanisms of Defense.* New York : International University Press, Inc., 1946.

Freud, Sigmund. *Civilization and Its Discontents.* New York : W. W. Norton & Co., Inc., 1962; London : Hogarth Press, 1930.

———. *Collected Papers.* 5 vols. New York : Basic Books, 1959.

———. *The Ego and the Id.* New York : W. W. Norton & Co., 1962.

———. *A General Introduction to Psychoanalysis.* New York : Doubleday, 1949.

————. *Jokes and Their Relation to the Unconscious*. New York : W. W. Norton & Co., 1963.

————. *Moses and Monotheism*. New York : Vintage Books, 1939.

————. *New Introductory Lectures*. New York : W. W. Norton & Co., 1964.

————. *Totem and Taboo*. New York; Vintage Books, 1960.

Greenacre, Phyllis. "The Childhood of the Artist." *The Psychoanalytic Study of the Child*. vol. 12. New York : International University Press, 1957.

————. "The Family Romance of the Artist." In *The Psychoanalytic Study of the Child*. vol. 13. New York : International University Press, 1958.

Hartmann, Heinz. *Ego Psychology and the Problem of Adaptation*. New York : International University Press, 1958.

Jacobson, Edith. "Depersonalization." *Journal of the American Psychoanalytic Association* 7 (1959) : 581–610.

Jones, Ernest. "The Phantasy of the Reversal of Generations." *Papers on Psychoanalysis*. Boston : Beacon Press, 1967.

————. "The God Complex." *Essays in Applied Psychoanalysis*. London : Hogarth Press, 1951.

Kaplan, Donald M. "Theatre Architecture : A Derivation of the Primal Cavity." *The Drama Review* 12, no. 3 (Spring 1968) : 105–16.

————. "On Shyness." *International Journal of Psychoanalysis* 53 (1972) : 439–53.

Kaplan, Linda Joan. "The Family Romance : Theoretical and Clinical Implications," publication pending. *The Psychoanalytic Review*.

Kohut, Heinz. "Forms and Transformations of Narcissism." *Journal of American Psychoanalytic Association* 14, no 2 (1966) : 243–72.

Kris, Ernest. *Psychoanalytic Explorations in Art*. London : George Allen & Unwin Ltd., 1953.

Lewin, Bertram D. *The Psychoanalysis of Elation*. London : The Hogarth Press, Ltd., 1951.

Meyer, Bernard C. *Joseph Conrad, A Psychoanalytic Biography.* Princeton, N.J.: Princeton University Press, 1967.

Niederland, William G. "Clinical Aspects of Creativity." *American Imago* 24, nos. 1, 2 (Spring, Summer 1967): 6–34.

Rank, Otto. *The Myth of the Birth of the Hero and Other Writings.* Translated by Philip Freund. New York: Vintage Books, 1959.

Sachs, Lisbeth J. and Stern, Bernard H. "Bernard Shaw and His Women." *British Journal of Medical Psychology* 37, (1964): 343–50.

Schafer, Roy. *Internalization.* New York: International University Press, 1968.

Schneider, Daniel. *The Psychoanalyst and the Artist.* New York: New American Library, 1962.

Stamm, Julian. "Shaw's Man and Superman: His Struggle for Sublimation." *American Imago* 22, no. 4 Winter 1965): 250–54.

Thornburn, John M. *Art and the Unconscious.* London: Kegan Paul, Trench, Trubner & Co., Ltd., 1925.

Vredenburgh, Joseph. "The Character of the Incest Object: A Study of Alternation between Narcissism and Object Choice." *American Imago* 14, no. 1 (Spring 1957): 45–52.

Weissman, Philip. *Creativity in the Theatre.* New York: Dell, 1965.

———. "Theoretical Considerations of Ego Regression and Ego Functions in Creativity," *Psychoanalytic Quarterly* 36 (1967): 37–50.

Winnicott, D. W. *Collected Papers.* New York: Basic Books, 1958.

INDEX

Achurch, Janet, 59, 100, 102, 132, 178, 224
Archer, William, 64, 82, 140n, 178, 186, 190, 209–10

Bentley, Eric, 16, 120, 130, 188n, 194n, 274, 286, 322
Bergler, Edmund, 59n, 87n, 131n
Brecht, Bertolt, 175, 280–82
Brown, Norman O., 131, 167, 312, 320, 322
Brustein, Robert, 70n, 186, 187, 188, 194, 200n, 288n, 290–91

Campbell, Mrs. Pat, 54n, 59, 62, 63n, 98–99, 102, 110, 132, 173, 224, 245n, 247, 272n, 333–34
Chesterton, G. K., 15, 157n, 174
Creative Evolution, 70, 76–77, 101, 110, 132, 134–35, 149, 151, 192, 193, 202, 207, 226–27, 267, 273, 292, 294, 301–2, 318, 322, 327, 334

Eissler, K. R., 22, 24, 224n, 245n, 323
Erikson, Erik, 17, 112, 114, 123n, 172–73

Fabian Society, 70, 74, 86, 121, 153, 163–64, 169, 175, 177–78, 190, 334
Freud, Anna, 91, 94, 173
Freud, Sigmund, 17–18, 21, 35, 42, 54, 59n, 62–63, 69n, 70, 75–76, 84, 99n, 100, 118, 121–22, 128, 131, 144, 193, 219n, 254, 275, 293–301, 336
Frye, Northrop, 184n, 216n, 307n

Greenacre, Phyllis, 19n, 54–55, 63–65, 106, 131n, 142, 175, 308, 327

Holland, Norman, 59n, 87n, 123n, 252n

Ibsen, Hendrick, 136n, 139, 167n, 178–79, 180–205, 220, 233n, 278; *Love's Comedy*, 182–84, 200; *A Doll's House*, 178; *Ghosts*, 178, 181, 187, 193, 194–200, 233n; *When We Dead Awaken*, 181, 189; *The Master Builder*, 181; *Brand*, 187–89; *Peer Gynt*, 189; *Emperor and Galilean*, 189, 203; *The Wild Duck*, 193

347

Irving, Henry, 95n, 108n, 126, 133, 136–43

Jones, Ernest, 79n, 95n

Kaplan, Donald M., 55n, 176n. *See also* Shyness
Klein, Melanie, 46–47n, 79n
Kohut, Heinz, 68n, 79n, 98–99n, 313, 328, 337
Kris, Ernst, 19n, 54n, 118, 122n

Lee, Vandeleur, 33–34, 37–38, 53–55, 86, 110, 114, 124–27, 129, 154, 157–59, 330
Lewis, B. D., 102n, 266n
Life Force, 55, 57, 59–61, 70, 73, 76–77, 86, 89, 100–101, 103–4, 106, 109, 121, 131–32, 147–48, 151, 164, 170, 192–93, 203, 207, 219–20, 226, 230, 235, 254, 262, 266, 268, 273, 286, 297, 300–303, 316; affinity with Bergson's *élan vital,* 77, 275; mother as model for, 86, 104–6

McNulty, Edward, 59n, 83–84n, 128n
Meisel, Martin, 208n, 209n, 211, 225n, 227, 268n
Morris, May, 62
Nethercot, Arthur C., 167n, 293n, 310

Patterson, Jenny, 62, 166, 174, 218

Shakespeare, William, 64, 95n, 108n, 136–43, 183, 220, 280–81, 285
Shavian Drama: its achievement, 174; attempt at grouping, 207; its components 59–61, 101; as compression of personal history 169–70, 218, 232–34, 248–51,

258n, and theatre history, 212; dialectical structure, 122, 202, 207–10, 247n, 274–78, 322; differing from novels, 160–61; distinctive treatment of energy, 184–85, 275–78; early stages of, 209–12; its ideal audience, 175–78; link between self-image and popular stage, 227–30; not all talk, 88; opposition to conventional morality, 149–51, 230; personal sources for character types, 227–30, 242, 247–48n, 258n, 217; phases, 220, 285–92; its raw components, 60–61, 266n; relationship patterns of characters in, 301; relation to early development, 82, 97, 220–24, 229–30; relation to fantasy and family romance, 54n, 234–36; relation to Ibsen, 136n, 139, 178–79, 180–205, 233n, 278; relation to language, 49n, 86–91; relation to Shakespeare, 136–42, 174, 242n, 304; relation to traditional comedy, 191–92, 208–9, 220, 252n, 303–7; relation to well-made play, 190–91, 211–12; Shavian element in, 60, 230, 275, 307–11; Shavian poetics, 206, 302, 306–7; synthesis, 290–92, 310–12; universality of, 89–90; visionary features of, 101, 109–10, 202–5, 310–12
Shaw, Bernard
Life: earliest years, 33–34, 38, 65–66; developmental stages, 57–58, 71–72, 170–74, 245n; education, 41, 43, 66; family background, 30–39; relationship with mother, 39–53, 73, 94–95, 103–6, 155–56; with father, 65–66,

111–21, 184n; with wife, 50n, 258n, 329–33; youth and adolescence, 83–84n, 129, 145–49, 170–71, 228–30, 251n; young manhood, 155–79

Personality: adaptation (*also* reality mastery, transformation of instinct), 20–21, 51–53, 56, 121, 152, 157–59, 205, 223–30, 247n, 299–301, 328, 337; in plays, 277–78, 316, *see also* creativity; anality, 73–74, 85n, 133, 218; castration, 81–85, 127, 134, 153; conversions, 161–66, 168–71; in plays, 220–26, 230, 263–66, 309; creativity, 87n, 105, 157–59, 161, 291–92, 308, 313–37; defenses: denial, 49, 81, 91–96, 97–98, 103, 127, 289, *see also* manic phase; externalization (*also* purified ego), 67, 70, 74, 133, 165, 218, 235, 316; identification, 49n, 63n, 85n, 86, 87n, 97, 127, 147–49, 162, 170, 335; with phallic mother, 86; with father, 112–19, 134, 146; with uncles and Lee, 124–27, 129, 157–59; reaction formation, 91–96, 147, 289, *see also* vegetarianism; sublimation, 99n, 126–27, 131, 312, 316, 322; depersonalization, 49n, 76, 90–91; in plays, 217–19; depression, *see* denial, manic defense; family romance, 19n, 53–58, 67, 73, 87, 91, 96–97, 106, 128, 333–34; fantasy, 52, 79n, 91–93, 97, 274n, 327, 333–36, *see* family romance; flight into reality, flight of ideas, *see* denial; grandiosity, *see* narcissism; guilt, 128, 144–46, 151; in plays, 208, 217, *see also* castration and oedipal conflicts;

hypomania, 7n, 51, 82, 131, 144–45, 243; identity: as imposter, 78, 96, as artist and playwright, 63–65, 69, 78, 87, as genius, 75, 172–74, 204, 301, 313, 333–37, as intruder, 125–27, 154, 169–70, 242; manic phase, 46–51, 71, 79n, 102n, 118; narcissism, 65–82, 92, 98–99n, 102, 121, 130, 134, 170, 185–86, 219, 290–92, 304, 314, 328, 333–36; oedipal conflicts, 17, 58, 61–63, 130, 141, 144–45, 326–33; negative, 85n; phallic mother, 47n, 84–85, *see also* Mrs. George, 286–87 *and* Myna's Sex, 311–12; pre-genital sexual posture, 82, 99n, 107, 127, 133, 193, 317–37; screen memory 45, 112–14; sense of humor, 75, 114–21; shame, 153, father's, 115, 191; shyness, 55, 74, 76, 153, 155, 160, 191; symbiosis and ecstasy, 96–103, 109–10, 121, 260, 327–28; vegetarianism, 44n, 51, 71, 86, 92, 97, 142, 147

Works (dramatic): *Androcles and the Lion*, 92n, 207, 225, 275; *The Apple Cart*, 75, 110, 290; *Arms and the Man*, 54, 60, 119–20, 154, 169–70; *Back to Methuselah*, 6, 68, 203, 207, 253, 279, 288–89, 310, 317–20; *Caesar and Cleopatra*, 103, 207; *Candida*, 60, 100, 102, 123, 127, 130, 150, 181–82, 187, 207, 220–21, 238–44; *Captain Brassbound's Conversion*, 54, 191, 207, 221–24, 239; *The Devil's Disciple*, 54, 89, 181–82, 207, 224, 225n, 230; *Farfetched Fables*, 110, 204, 317, 320; *Geneva*, 290; *Getting Married*, 54,

207, 268–74; *Heartbreak House,*
89, 124, 181, 207, 232, 286–87,
289, 301; *John Bull's Other
Island,* 203, 275; *Major Barbara,*
151, 170, 192, 207, 275–78; *Man
and Superman,* 44n, 54, 63n, 87n,
88, 110, 135, 153, 171, 176,
207, 236, 237–66, 267–68, 273n,
289, 298, 309, 317; *Man of
Destiny,* 137; *Misalliance,* 54,
180, 181, 207, 268, 274, 324;
Mrs. Warren's Profession, 60,
151, 181–82, 200, 207, 217–18,
275; *The Philanderer,* 149, 218–
19, 243n; *Pygmalion,* 54, 86–88,
93, 181, 232; *Saint Joan,* 207,
290–91, 301; *The Showing-up of
Blanco Posnet,* 54, 207, 225–26;
*The Simpleton of the Unex-
pected Isles,* 290; *Too True to
be Good,* 290; *Why She Would
Not,* 108–9; *Widowers' Houses,*
151, 178, 182, 207, 209–16;
You Never Can Tell, 192
Works (nondramatic): *The Adventures of the Black Girl in
Search for God,* 44n, 311–12;
Cashel Byron's Profession, 156;
Collected Letters, 94; *Immaturity,* 122, 156, 161; *The Irrational Knot,* 156; *Love Among
the Artists,* 157–59; *My Dear
Dorothea,* 96; *The Quintessence
of Ibsenism,* 150, 184, 205; *Sixteen Self-Sketches,* 30n
Shaw, Charlotte-Townshend (wife),
54n, 58, 106, 258n, 315, 329–
33

Shaw, George Carr (father), 32–34,
38, 65–66, 94, 112–19, 166,
184n
Shaw, Lucinda Elizabeth Gurly
(mother), 30–58, 63n, 93; as
model for Life Force 104–6
Socialism. *See* Fabian Society
Spender, Stephen, 45n, 75, 288n,
309
Spitz, René A., 48; his "primal
dialogue," 176–78
Stamm, Julian, 17n, 20n, 51, 131n
Strindberg, August, 244, 247, 251–
52n, 259, 280–82, 285
Superman, 55, 58, 94, 104, 149,
166–68, 307, 327–28, 334

Terry, Ellen, 39, 54n, 55, 59, 62,
63n, 79, 96, 98–99, 125–26, 132,
136–43, 223, 224n, 238, 245n,
325–27, 331, 333

Valency, Maurice, 58, 59n, 188n,
189n, 195, 211n, 251–52n
Vitalism. *See* Creative Evolution;
Life Force

Webb, Beatrice, 15, 108
Webb, Sidney, 163
Weiss, Edoardo, 144, 145n. *See also*
Shaw, Bernard (Personality), ex-
ternalization
Weissman, Philip, 17, 19n, 52n, 70,
87, 93, 107n, 126n, 172n, 233
Williams, Tennessee, 235, 283–85
Winnicott, D. W., 47–51, 52n, 79n,
177